HALIFAX
AT WAR

'B-Beer', a Mk 5 srs 1 (Special)
of No 434 'Bluenose' Squadron,
RCAF, was based at Tholthorpe.
Called *Pubwash*, its operations
were recorded not in bombs, but
in pint tankards on the nose.
This photograph was taken on
21 October 1943.
Public Archives of Canada

Below:
This No 76 Squadron B Mk 5, DK205, *Johnny the Wolf*, lost an engine and landed safely on three on 25 July 1943, only to be written off in a minor accident a few months later. *IWM*

HALIFAX
AT WAR

Brian J. Rapier

Edited by
Alan Hollingsworth

OM
358.4

Acknowledgements

The author would like to thank all concerned with the production of this book, especially the following: L. R. Howard, Air Historical Branch, MoD; G. Appleyard of Leeds; F. A. Brinton; K. Burchett; P. Callan of 'The Bombers', Seaton Ross; Mrs B. Carter; Mrs A. Chapman; The City of York; B. Collis, NSAM; Connery; S. R. Cook; Miss Lettice Curtis; J. Davies; Gp Capt M. E. H. Dawson DFC, DFM; H. H. Drummond; Sqn Ldr R. N. Elsworth; J. R. Falconer, cameos; P. Finch; P. A. Fletcher, HAPS; F. Ford; G. French; E. B. Goodall and R. M. 'Dolly' Gray of 'Shiny' 10; D. Green; L. Greenham; R. Gunst; E. G. Hill; R. Hines, RAAF; J. Hochkins; Mrs D. Hogg; A. Hollingsworth; Imperial War Museum; J. E. Johnson; M. Jordan; W. Kay; A. Kopp; T. O. Kraul; Flt Lt Ling; R. Lyne; N. McKay; W. E. Miller; Big 'D' Moss; J. Muirhead; Den Murray; R. Nash, No 614 Squadron; F. Nicholson; *Northern Echo*; D. Petty; Maj C. I. Phipps; Public Archive of Canada; Public Record Office; D. Pullan; J. Rabbets, illustrator; Mrs K. Rapier; Mrs M. Rapier; Royal Air Force Museum; Royal Australian Air Force; J. D. R. Rawlings; Royal Canadian Air Force; D. Reed, Pickerings Bookshop, York; R. Riding; Jack Ropero and comrades of the Free French Air Force; C. Shingles; W. Shingles; T. Staniforth; N. Stannard; Sqn Ldr F. Stuart, RAAF (ret); R. C. Sturtivant; J. Taylor; J. S. Tickel, researcher; P. Thorkildsen; S. C. Thorne; T. Todd; K. J. Trelfer; B. Webb; C. J. Wicks BEM; Mrs N. Willis; J. Wilson; P. Wilson; G. Wolf; H. D. Wood DFM; the Mike Wright Collection; Yorkshire Air Museum; G. J. Zwanenburg.

Further reading by the same author: *White Rose Base, Melbourne Ten*.

Prints of photographs credited to the Imperial War Museum are for sale on application to its Dept of Photographs, Lambeth Road, London SE1 6HZ.

To Margaret

This title first published by Ian Allan as 2 separate volumes
Halifax at War © Brian J. Rapier 1987
Wellington at War © Chaz Bowyer 1982

This edition published 1994 by The Promotional Reprint Company Ltd, exclusively for Bookmart Limited, Desford Road, Enderby, Leicester LE9 5AD, Coles in Canada, Treasure Press in Australia and Best Books in New Zealand.

ISBN 1 85648 173 5

Printed in China

CONTENTS

L9495:B of No 35 Squadron, Linton-on-Ouse, was often flown by Wg Cdr Collings. This was one of the first HP57 photographs to be released to the public. 'B-Beer' was written off in a belly landing at Linton during July 1941. *RAF*

CHAPTER I

INTO BATTLE

Faces peered into the sky from the high Georgian and Victorian buildings of the white-walled medieval city of York, eyes strained to glimpse the source of noise as a large seemingly all-black aircraft appeared for an instant and then was lost behind vibrating rooftops. Its growling engine note was replaced by shouting from a crowd in the street — 'Is it one of ours?' said one voice; another declared 'The sirens haven't gone' — but one or two knew the mysterious four-engined bomber was one of a squadron based just up the road at Linton-on-Ouse. For over a year, Whitley aircraft from the many bomber squadrons stationed around the city had droned their slow solitary ways across the county, over the North Sea and on into Germany, their crews sometimes spending more than 10 hours in the air before appearing back over Yorkshire. Later — released between sorties — they had favoured haunts like the 'Punch Bowl' in Stonegate, 'Betty's Cafe' just up the street near the Mansion House and the 'Half Moon' a few yards further down. For months there had been talk

among them of a new aircraft to replace the elderly Whitley and now here it was — the Halifax had arrived. But it had been touch and go.

In 1937 the Air Ministry had accepted the new Rolls-Royce Vulture engine, believed to be ideal for a new generation of twin-engined bombers. One of them was the Handley Page Design No 56 which had almost reached building stage when the Vulture ran into technical trouble. Handley Page's Chief Designer, G. R. Volkert, looked quickly for a suitable alternative. The Avro Manchester was also built to the same specification, AM P13/36, and eventually became operational despite insufficient development of the Vulture engine. The grave shortcomings of the Manchester caused mainly by its unreliable Vultures, resulted in its rebirth in the form of the Lancaster, powered by four Rolls-Royce Merlin engines. The HP56 was also redesigned to take four Merlins, and became the Handley Page HP57, which was ordered straight from the drawing board exactly two years before the outbreak of war in Europe.

Below:
Work on the new four-engined heavy bomber began in January 1938 at Handley Page's Cricklewood factory. HP57 'L7244' was flown for the first time by chief test pilot Maj J. L. Cordes from Boscombe Down on 25 October 1939. *RAF Museum*

Right:
In August 1940, the second prototype HP57 flew for the first time as a fully armed heavy bomber. Its yellow underside shone in the August sunshine identifying it as an experimental aircraft. *Aeroplane*

The first prototype (L7244) of Handley Page's Design No 57 was taken by road from Cricklewood in London, to Bicester, Oxfordshire, where it was re-assembled and flown from the grass airfield by Handley Page's Chief test pilot, Maj J. L. Cordes, on 25 October 1939. The flight was a success despite the fact that the all-up weight had reached nearly 23 tons instead of the designed 18. The second prototype (L7245), equipped with nose and tail turrets, flew on 17 August 1940 from Handley Page's own airfield at Radlett in Hertfordshire, and was passed on to the Aeroplane & Armament Experimental Establishment (A&AEE) at Boscombe Down where test flying and acceptance checks were made during October. The aircraft had now reached an all-up weight of 24½ tons. More ominously, the A&AEE found the twin rudders somewhat inadequate in keeping the aircraft straight on take-off. There was also a tendency for them to overbalance at low airspeeds, when making tight turns and also when power was asymmetric as when a propeller was feathered. To

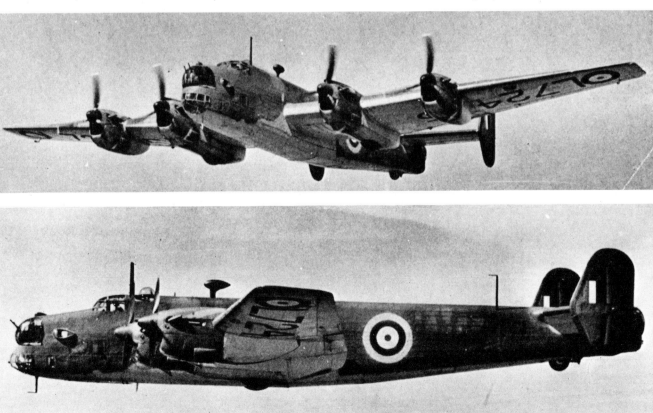

compound these problems, the rudders were unresponsive at speeds below 120mph. It was a serious shortcoming in an operational aircraft which was to dog the early marks of Halifax and cause a plethora of costly aircraft and aircrew losses, despite various palliative remedies.

The first Mk 1 production aircraft (L9485) flew on 11 October 1940 and joined the other prototypes at Boscombe Down. The following month, No 35 Squadron, under the command of Wg Cdr R. W. P. Collings DFC, assembled to take charge of the new aircraft and introduce it

into service. On 20 November the squadron flew north to Leeming, a No 4 Group bomber airfield situated next to the Great North Road in North Yorkshire. No 35 Squadron began its conversion training with just L9486 and the first prototype L7244, both of which were fitted with dual controls. By December 1940 runway construction at Linton-on-Ouse had been completed and No 35 moved in, another one or two aircraft arriving to join the first prototype and some production versions. Just after Christmas 1940, the squadron lost its first Halifax when L9487 caught fire in the air and crashed near Dishforth killing Flg Off M. T. G. Henry DFC and his crew. Like many of the crews joining the squadron at that time, Flg Off Henry's had completed their first tour on Whitleys.

When he joined No 35 Squadron, Sgt D. P. Hogg, tour-expired from No 58 Squadron, had completed 28 operations on Whitleys mostly as a wireless operator but sometimes filling the position of tail gunner. His new captain was Flg Off 'Bunny' Warren DFC, who flew ninth production HP57 aircraft coded 'G-George'. The wireless operator sat in a small compartment below the pilot, whilst towards the nose the observer/navigator was seated facing sideways at his table with the bomb-sight further forward in the nose under the front turret. With the growing

LUFTPOST

Von der Royal Air Force abgeworfen

No. 5
23. Juni 1941

Keine Luftherrschaft ohne Seemacht

über den Weltmeeren

BEI Beginn des Krieges waren die deutschen Führer der Ansicht, dass sie mit ihrer zahlenmässig überlegenen Luftwaffe ein Gegengewicht gegen die überwältigende Seemacht Englands geschaffen hätten.

Jetzt wissen sie, dass das ein Irrtum war. Das Bombenflugzeug hat keineswegs über das Kriegsschiff gesiegt. Im Gegenteil, gerade seine überlegene Seemacht hat England ebenso zur Luftherrschaft über den Weltmeeren verholfen.

Gerade so wie die deutsche Armee sich ihrer Stukas als einer Fernkampfartillerie bedient, so macht auch die Royal Navy denselben Gebrauch von den Torpedobombern der „Fleet Air Arm" (Luftwaffe der britischen Flotte). Diese Maschinen und ihre schwimmenden Flugplätze, die grossen Flugzeugträger, haben die Strategie dieses Krieges tiefgehend beeinflusst.

Italien besitzt nicht ein einziges Flugzeugmutterschiff. Deutschland hat eines — aber es hat bisher keine Rolle in diesem Krieg gespielt. England besitzt viele. Verloren hat es zwei (die „Ark Royal" — dies sei eigens bemerkt — ist nicht darunter!) Aber seine Werften sind nicht müssig gewesen; und so oft es zu einem grösseren Seetreffen kam, hörte die Welt überrascht den Namen eines neuen britischen Flugzeugmutterschiffs — *Formidable* bei Cap Matapan, *Victorious* gegen die *Bismarck*.

Taten der Torpedobomber

Im November 1940 griffen britische Torpedobomber die italienische Schlachtflotte in ihrer Basis in Tarent an. Von den sechs italienischen Schlachtschiffen wurden drei, unter ihnen das neueste, schwer beschädigt, und auch mehrere Kreuzer wurden schlimm mitgenommen.

In der Schlacht von Cap Matapan im letzten März setzten die Flugzeuge der *Formidable* in erfolgreichen Angriffen auf die fliehenden italienischen Schiffe das Schlachtschiff *Vittorio Veneto* ausser Gefecht und verringerten die Geschwindigkeit der Italiener so wesentlich, dass die britische Flotte den Feind abfangen und drei Kreuzer sowie mehrere Zerstörer versenken konnte.

Im vorigen Mai erzielten Torpedobomber von der *Victorious* und der *Ark Royal* an zwei Tagen mehrere Treffer gegen die *Bismarck* und reduzierten deren Geschwindigkeit so sehr, dass ihre letzte Hoffnung, der britischen Flotte zu entkommen und im Hafen von Brest unterzuschlüpfen, zunichte wurde.

Schon ein Jahr vorher, im April 1940,

FORTSETZUNG S. 4

Der deutsche Kreuzer „Königsberg" lief in den Hafen von Bergen am 10. April 1940 ein. Kurz bevor dieses Bild aufgenommen wurde, hatte ein britisches Bombenflugzeug der Fleet Air Arm einen Treffer mittschiffs erzielt. Der Mast der „Königsberg" legt sich auf die Seite. Das Schiff ging innerhalb von zehn Minuten unter.

30 000 FLIEGER
jährlich aus Kanada

KANADA hat 67 Schulungslager errichtet, in denen Flieger aus allen Teilen des britischen Weltreichs ausgebildet werden. Gegenwärtig befinden sich viele Tausende in diesen Lagern in Ausbildung, die dann als hervorragend geschulte Flieger auf den östlichen und westlichen Kriegsschauplätzen eingesetzt werden sollen. Wie der kanadische Minister für Munitionserzeugung, Howe, im Januar 1941 erklärt hat, werden programmgemäss jährlich über 30.000 solche Flieger aus den Schulungslagern von Kanada hervorgehen.

Schneller als vorgesehen

In den letzten 3 Monaten sind 3 amerikanische Schlachtschiffe vom Stapel gelaufen: die „North Carolina" am 9. April — 6 Monate vor der plangemässen Fertigstellung; die „Washington" am 15. Mai — 6 Monate vor der plangemässen Fertigstellung und die „South Dakota" am 7. Juni — 5 Monate vor der plangemässen Fertigstellung.

Wer ist Bormann?

DER NACHFOLGER VON RUDOLF HESS

HITLER hat seinen entflogenen Stellvertreter durch keinen andern ersetzt. Aber die NSDAP musste einen neuen Reichsleiter bekommen: den Hess-Ersatz gab Herr Martin Bormann ab. Wer ist das?

Er liebte es stets, im Hintergrund zu stehn; im Schatten eines andern liess es sich besser an den Drähten ziehn. Nur einmal fiel das volle Licht der Öffentlichkeit auf ihn, als er 1924 in einem Mordprozess vor dem Leipziger Staatsgerichtshof stand.

Damals schon war er „Geschäftsführer," und das Geschäft, das er führte, war eine Abteilung des illegalen Freikorps Rossbach. Die Gesellschaft, alles gute Nationalsozialisten, trieb sich auf mecklenburgischen Rittergütern herum, abwechselnd mit Streik- und mit Friedensbruch beschäftigt. Wenn einer auszubrechen drohte, machte man kurzen Prozess, um ihn endgültig am Ausplaudern zu verhindern. Bormann übernahm damals die Exekution des jungen Lehrers Kadow, der ihm nicht ganz zuverlässig erschien.

Wie er das Geschäft führte

Er besorgte das Geschäft natürlich nicht selber, er führte es bloss. Den Auftrag gab er seinen Freunden Hoess und Pfeiffer und

FORTSETZUNG S. 4

510/va

mechanical complexities of multi-engined aircraft, the need arose for an additional specialist crew-member, the flight engineer who was located, in the Halifax, above and directly to the rear of the pilot. Aft of him could be seen an astrodome used for sextant shots by the observer/navigator, and further aft on the two pillars in the port and starboard beam position were mounted twin Vickers machine guns. At the rear of the fuselage between the two fins and rudders sat the rear gunner in his turret. He had a wonderful view of where the aircraft had just been.

At that time seven or eight aircraft were available for operations and more of them were joining daily. Handley Page and Rolls-Royce representatives busied themselves ironing out various snags and a high state of readiness was achieved by the end of February 1941. On 10 March the squadron was briefed for its first operational sortie — an attack on the French port of Le Havre. Seven aircraft were serviceable, but as Wg Cdr Collings took off in 'B-Beer', a hydraulic problem in Plt Off J. W. Murray's aircraft forced him to abort. 'G-George', with Doug Hogg in the wireless operator's seat, climbed out from Linton to make up the six aircraft in all heading for the French coast. Handley Page's HP57 was finally operational — but not for long.

Wg Cdr Collings had little difficulty in finding Le Havre, not least by its searchlights and flak. Through a gap in the cloud the dock area became visible and the wing commander, flying straight and level, dropped a stick of 500lb semi-armour-piercing bombs. There was just time to see these explode along the dock edge before cloud closed in. Flt Lt Bradley, flying the second aircraft, 'N-Nuts', found the target obscured by cloud so he flew on to the secondary Boulogne, which also turned out to be cloud-covered. Finally, the load was dropped on Dieppe from 12,000ft, but the bombs were not seen to explode. Meanwhile, back at the primary target, Sqn Ldr Gilchrist in 'F-Freddie' bombed through slight cloud from 11,800ft in heavy flak. 'G-George', with Flg Off Warren at the controls and Doug Hogg in the wireless operator's position, had just arrived.

Warren had to circle until the cloud cleared, before the aircraft ran up to bomb from 11,000ft where 'G-George' collected quite a bit of accurate light flak. Then a shell exploded very close by, causing holes to appear all over the aircraft and wounding the observer, Sgt Wilson; but this did not stop him from releasing a second stick of bombs. The starboard inner engine radiator was punctured, the engine overheated and Flg Off Warren had to feather it. At the same time the hydraulics failed and the undercarriage leg on the same side dropped as they turned for home.

Plt Off Hillary flying 'L-Love' bombed Le Havre from 10,000ft through obscuring cloud and could see a medium-sized fire in the docks, but conditions worsened as he headed for the coast. By the time Flt Lt Lane in 'M-Mother' reached the target area, cloud-cover was complete, so he jettisoned his bombs over the Channel and turned for base.

'F-Freddie', L9489, crossed the English coast and Sqn Ldr Gilchrist set course for Linton, but a mile or so south-southwest of London he was attacked by an RAF night-fighter. 'F-Freddie' caught fire very quickly and as it fell flaming the squadron leader and his flight engineer, Sgt Aedy, baled out successfully to see 'F-Freddie' crash near Normandy, Surrey. The rest of the crew were killed. At the same time 'G-George' was growling on over England on three engines and with its starboard undercarriage leg hanging limply down,

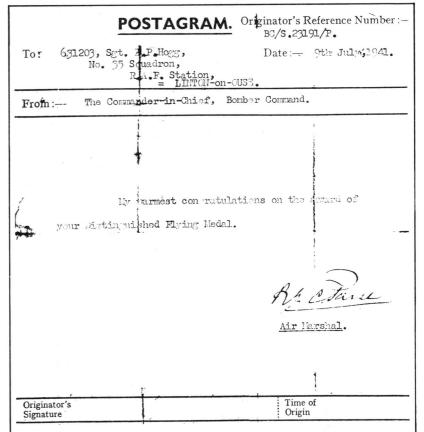

eventually to land safely at Linton-on-Ouse five hours after take-off, complete with a wounded observer and a tired Doug Hogg. A debriefing showed that the attack had been scattered, mostly due to the weather, but aircraft serviceability was seriously questioned — not a good operational beginning to the Halifax story.

Just after 21.00hrs on 12 March, three aircraft took off for Hamburg and the Blohm und Voss works. Doug Hogg flew with Flg Off Warren in 'L-Love', L9490, Flt Lt Bradley was in 'N-Nuts', L9496, and 'M-Mother', L9488, was flown by Flt Lt

Right:
L9530:L of No 76 Squadron was flown by Plt Off Chris Cheshire (brother of Leonard who was later awarded the Victoria Cross). 'L-London' crashed near Bremen in August 1941, but its pilot survived. *IWM*

Below:
HP59 B Mk 2 aircraft began to arrive on the squadrons by October 1941. Here a No 35 Squadron crew await the signal for take-off. It was waiting to go that was so hard to take; crews would often sit in the aircraft for an hour before start up of engines. *Fox Photos*

Lane. Hydraulic failure in both turrets caused Bradley to turn back, but Flt Lt Lane bombed the target from 13,000ft. Flg Off Warren approached the target at 15,000ft, switched off his engines and glided into the bombing run over Hamburg — it was thought at the time that enemy sound locators would be deceived by this tactic; it rarely worked, and it certainly did not on this occasion as the aircraft was surrounded by intense flak. At the end of the bombing run and 2,000ft lower, one stick of Warren's bombs had hit the Hamburg-Harburg railway line and the other had straddled the main target.

On the way back, Flt Lt Lane in 'M-Mother' was attacked by a Messerschmitt Bf110 night-fighter north of the island of Norderney, his gunners engaging four attack passes before 'M-Mother' made its escape to land safely at Linton — it had become the first RAF four-engined aircraft to bomb Germany.

Another operation was carried out on Hamburg during the night of the 13th, but repeated hydraulic problems caused the squadron to be grounded for several days until modifications could be completed. Meanwhile more aircraft were delivered and further crews joined the squadron for conversion training. Despite its technical problems, the new bomber force was growing steadily. During April and May 1941, No 76 Squadron commanded by Wg Cdr S. O. Bufton DFC was formed from 'C' Flight of No 35 Squadron at Linton, and extra airmen went into training on the flight line apace with crews in the air. But hydraulic failures were still prevalent; Plt Off E. G. Franklin flying L9486 back from air-fighting development trials at Duxford could not get the undercarriage down and had to belly-land at Linton on his return.

Operations were resumed on 15 April when five aircraft (one flown by Flt Lt Leonard Cheshire, later awarded the Victoria Cross) were despatched to Kiel; Doug Hogg flew with his new skipper, Plt Off Owen, in L9501. They took off at 22.30hrs to the accompaniment of bombs bursting to the north of the airfield. (It was in fact a Heinkel He111 of KG53 with an engine out, dumping its load before crashing.) The weather was good on the out bound leg but the aircraft went in to bomb Kiel through intense anti-aircraft fire and German night-fighter attacks. 'G-George', L9493, Doug Hogg's old aircraft which had been repaired after the Le Havre operation, suffered from the same hydraulic problem as before, the starboard undercarriage leg falling down.

13

Above:
L9608 was the last Handley Page HP57 Halifax Mk 1 srs 3 produced. The name Halifax was bestowed upon it by Lady Halifax at Radlett on 12 September 1941. This aircraft served with No 35 Squadron at Linton and No 1652 Heavy Conversion Unit, Marston Moor, until written-off when at the end of November 1942 a swing on take-off caused the undercarriage to collapse.
Fox Photos

Sgt Lashbrook, its new captain, nursed it back to Linton only to find German aircraft were still flying across the north of the field after bombing Belfast. Whilst he was orbiting, both the port engines failed and he was unable to hold the aircraft on the rudders. 'G-George' side-slipped into the ground, coming to rest at Tollerton near Linton after hitting a tree. Luckily all the crew survived, although two were slightly injured.

During the month of May 1941 the Luftwaffe made many night raids over the United Kingdom, attacking London, Manchester and Hull. Attacks were also made on Bomber Command airfields; Linton-on-Ouse was heavily bombed and several aircraft were damaged, the Station Commander, Gp Capt Garraway, plus a number of airmen being killed. 'B-Beer', L9495, was flown to Abingdon to enable the King and Queen to see the new type — still known as the HP57 — whilst Doug Hogg went with Plt Off Owen in L9491 on a three-hour cross country exercise to make sure the Royal Observer Corps knew what the aircraft looked like — to the gratification of Sqn Ldr Gilchrist, who had been shot down once by his own side. At Abingdon L9495 was allowed to be photographed by the Press, for the arrival in service of a new bomber was a welcome tonic to public morale after a winter of sustained enemy bombing.

On the night of 11 June, No 35 Squadron was on operations again. The target this time was Duisburg in the Ruhr, and Doug Hogg was in L9496 with Plt Off Owen at the controls. The following night he went to Huls in the same aircraft but with the newly promoted Sqn Ldr Bradley as captain. The next operation was to

Hanover in L9491 with his own Skipper; this time they had to land at Dishforth, several miles north of Linton, on their return. Next day the crew went down to Northolt to pick up their own aircraft 'Y-Yolk', L9501, which they used on the 20th and 23rd against Kiel and once again on 26 June. No 35 Squadron was now firmly back in business and more was to come. Formation flying was practised on 29 June in preparation for a daylight raid, and next morning two vee formations of three aircraft each were in the air and heading for Kiel. The first was led by Sqn Ldr J. B. Tait and the second by Flt Lt Robinson, flying 'Q-Queenie'. After an uneventful flight over the North Sea the formation ran into a heavy anti-aircraft barrage at 17,000-18,000ft over the target. 'Y-Yolk' had dropped its bombs when it was attacked by three Messerschmitt Bf110 fighters which caused considerable damage. Doug Hogg moved from his position in the radio compartment to take charge of the beam guns in place of Sgt Simpson who had been mortally wounded in the attack, and then maintained a steady rate of fire from the twin Vickers until Flg Off Owen could reach the cover of cloud. 'Y-Yolk' had been holed in the fuselage and starboard wing, and the WT set seemed to have been damaged — Doug Hogg was forced to replace 20 leads from spare wire before it would work again. Whilst leading the second formation, 'Q-Queenie's' gunners had just shot down a fighter when they themselves were hit and were last seen descending in a shallow dive. The aircraft did not return to Linton. Subsequent awards were announced for the crews taking part in the Kiel daylight raid. Sqn Ldr Tait was awarded a bar to his DSO, Flg Off Owen of 'Y-Yolk' received the DFC, and Sgt Doug Hogg the DFM.

The squadron continued to operate at night over the next few weeks, Hanover, Frankfurt and Leuna the targets. Flg Off Owen's crew got their old aircraft back after it was repaired and 'Y-Yolk' set out for Hanover on 19 July only to return and land at Bircham Newton in a damaged condition. After several attempts at collecting the aircraft, including a trip in the first prototype used as a communications hack for the squadron, 'Y-Yolk' arrived back at Linton in the afternoon of 23 July. The same evening the crew took off again for Stanton Harcourt near Oxford, and another daylight operation against a very tough target.

In March 1941 the two German battle-cruisers, *Scharnhorst* and *Gneisenau*, had slipped into Brest after wreaking havoc amongst Allied shipping in the North Atlantic. The *Scharnhorst* later went into dock for engine repairs at La Pallice near La Rochelle on the Bay of Biscay. In the course of two months they had sunk or captured 22 ships amounting to 115,000 tons and it was imperative that they should not be allowed to leave Brest again. The task fell primarily to the RAF, and to Bomber Command in particular. Night attacks had met with limited success, but with the arrival of the new heavy bomber with its longer range, greater bomb load and stronger armament, it was decided to mount an attack in daylight. Thus two large formations assembled over Stanton Harcourt and set course for Lizard Point at

Above:
Wg Cdr Tuck was CO of No 10 Squadron at Leeming; the nose of this aircraft appropriately carried a 'Friar Tuck' motif.
IWM

Left:
Two from a section of three Halifax aircraft during their bombing run over Brest. Their target, the battleships *Scharnhorst* and *Gneisenau*, can be seen on the left of the picture beneath the smoke screen. The *Prinz Eugen* is on the far right.
IWM

Far right:
Halifax B Mk 1 srs 1, L9501:Y of No 35 Squadron flown by Flg Off Owen with Sgt Doug Hogg as WOp/AG during a daylight raid on Kiel, 30 June 1941.

Below:
'E-Edward' was delivered in time for No 10 Squadron's first daylight bombing raid, and in fact stayed with it until early 1942 when the crew abandoned 'Edward' after becoming lost and low on fuel near Keld, Yorkshire. *IWM*

around 10.30hrs on the morning of 24 July 1941.

Nine of the 15 aircraft were from No 35 Squadron and the remainder belonged to No 76. Both formations, with 'Y-Yolk' in the van, flew as low as they could to avoid radar detection until approaching Ushant. They then climbed steeply to 15,000ft. As the force began its run in to La Pallice it was attacked by over a dozen Bf109s. Sgt Godwin's 'M-Mother', L9527, went into a slow spiral dive, hit in two of its engines, and only two parachutes were seen to deploy. 'U-Uncle' flown by FS Greaves hit the *Scharnhorst* with five bombs, only to be pounced upon by fighters which set the aircraft on fire, and the crew baled out. (Some were wounded but they all survived to return to Linton-on-Ouse 40 years later in an aircraft piloted by FS Stan Greaves DFM — not however in a Halifax.) 'U-Uncle's' navigator, Wilf Walters, wrote to Doug Hogg some time after the attack to ask whether the 'Punch Bowl' in York was still frequented by the squadron, but it was to be a long time before he saw that hostelry again, as he was a prisoner of war in Germany.

'Monty' Dawson, now Group Captain Dawson DFC and Bar, DFM, was a sergeant observer in Sgt Drummond's crew on the daylight raid on La Pallice:

'The Pallice raid is an event etched in my memory for ever. It happened on a peerless summer day. Our bombs landed alongside the battleship, one may have hit but the stick was a little short. There was a great deal of flak and constant fighter attacks. As we flew over the battleship there was a yellowish explosion — whether from our bombs or not, I just don't know. We were extensively damaged with the windscreen and some of the instruments shot away and the rear gunner wounded, but we also got two Me109s and George Fraser was awarded an immediate DFM.

'As I recall, of the 13 Halifaxes that set out from Abingdon that morning, only five returned. We saw our No 2 shot down and landed ourselves with only two engines and zero fuel. Harry Drummond's flying was magnificent and he was awarded the DFM afterwards, as I was.'

Life expectancy on the squadron at that time was reckoned to be about three weeks, but Doug Hogg and his crew survived a trip to 'Big City' (Berlin) and finished their second tour. Their aircraft, 'Y-Yolk', L9501, was lost in other hands over Duisburg the same month. During

Entry into Service Nov 1940-Dec 1941

No Built	Type	Serial Block	Constructed
50	Halifax Mk 1 srs 1	L9485-L9534	Oct 1940-Jun 1941
25	Halifax Mk 1 srs 2	L9560-L9584	Jun 1941-Sept 1941
19	English Electric (EE)-built Halifax B Mk 2 srs 1	V9976-V9994	Sept 1941-Dec 1941
9	Halifax B Mk 1 srs 3	L9600-L9608	Oct 1941
16	Halifax B Mk 2 srs 1	L9609-L9624	Oct 1941-Dec 1941
30	Halifax B Mk 2 srs 1	R9363-R9392	Oct 1941-Jan 1942

Unit	Representative Aircraft	Base
No 4 Group, Bomber Command		
35 Squadron	L9486, L9566, V9979, L9603, L9610, R9364	Leeming
76 Squadaron	L9531, L9578, L9601, L9617, R9379	Linton-on-Ouse
138 Squadron	V9976, L9613	Newmarket
10 Squadron	L9622, R9369	Leeming
102 Squadron	R9378	Dalton

Note: Aircraft constructed by Handley Page are referred to simply as Halifax.

HP57 Halifax B Mk 1
1940 to December 1941

Type
Heavy bomber

Power Plant
Four 1,130hp Rolls-Royce Merlin X engines (srs 3) 1,220hp

Performance
Maximum speed: 255mph at 7,000ft
Cruising speed: 195mph at 15,000ft
Service ceiling: 18,000ft
Range: 1,860 miles

Armament
Six .303in Browning machine guns in nose and tail turrets; four Vickers K gas-operated guns in beam positions
Bomb load: 13,000lb

Weights
Empty: B Mk 1 srs 1, 34,000lb; srs 2/3, 35,000lb
Loaded: B Mk 1 srs 1, 55,000lb; srs 2/3, 60,000lb

Dimensions
Span: 98ft 8in
Length: 70ft 1in
Height: 20ft 9in

September 1941, aircraft of Nos 35 and 76 Squadrons bombed Hamburg, Brest and Berlin followed by a trip over the Alps to Turin. In October both squadrons began to receive modified Halifaxes — the name now official after a formal naming ceremony by Viscountess Halifax at Radlett in September. In November bad weather interfered with operations and only four sorties were flown. By December, however, two more squadrons had converted to the Halifax — Nos 10 and 102. On the 18th, 'Shiny' 10 Squadron was ready to join the others on operations, sending five aircraft on a daylight raid to Brest. On this occasion Stirlings led the attack followed by No 10 Squadron at 15,000ft; No 35 Squadron flew two sections of three each and No 76 Squadron placed six more aircraft at the rear of the formation. Wg Cdr Collings, No 35's CO, was shot up and had to ditch 60 miles off the English coast. He and his crew were rescued later in the day.

The newer Handley Page HP59 Halifax B Mk 2 aircraft had extra range, more powerful engines and better defensive armament in the form of a Boulton Paul dorsal turret. But once again, the all-up weight had risen, this time to nearly 27 tons, and the rudders were still unchanged. Already, however, there were doubts about using the aircraft in daylight and the operation against Brest was to be the last daylight sortie over Europe with Halifaxes until just before D-Day in 1944. On 30 December 1941, formations similar to those used on 18 November made timed runs from Ushant as thick yellow smoke, from German generators, rolled across the target area. Bf109s again attacked and Sqn Ldr Middleton's aircraft from No 35 Squadron went down. No 10 Squadron's Plt Off Hacking was also attacked on the run in to the target, tail gunner W. J. Porritt shooting one Bf109 down and a Polish Spitfire pilot claiming another. With the smoke and the strength of the defences the bombing results were unobservable and inconclusive. The Air Staff decided the Halifax would in future be used as a night-bomber.

CHAPTER 2

NIGHT OPERATIO

At the beginning of 1942, the War Cabinet's deep concern over the threat posed by the German surface fleet to Allied shipping was made more acute by the discovery at the end of January that the battleship *Tirpitz* had arrived in Aasen Fjord near Trondheim. Moreover, she was believed to be the most powerful battleship in the world — and this at a time when Britain's surface fleet was desperately stretched by the outbreak of the war in the Pacific.

On 25 January in a directive to the Chiefs of Staff, Winston Churchill, the Prime Minister, pointed out that there could be no more important target than *Tirpitz*. He went on to direct that: 'A plan should be made to attack both with carrier-borne torpedo aircraft and with heavy bombers by daylight or at dawn . . .

I regard this matter as of the highest urgency and importance.' The direct result was that two Halifax squadrons, Nos 10 and 76, were sent secretly to Lossiemouth on the Moray Firth in Scotland. Lossiemouth was closer to Trondheim than Linton but it was still over 600nm away and required a round trip perilously close to the Halifax's maximum range if a worthwhile bomb load was to be carried. Furthermore, there was an almost total absence of navigational aids — endless miles of trackless empty winter sea ending in a landfall on a desolate mountainous coastline where in winter it was often impossible to tell where the snow ended and the cloud began. Nor was it unusual for the fjords to be filled with fog. Indeed there was 10/10ths cover over Norway when the first sortie was flown and only

Below:
This Handley Page-built Halifax B Mk 2, R9376, flew with No 10 Squadron on the Norwegian raids and had a long career for the time, going to No 138 (Special Duties) Squadron, then to No 10 Conversion Unit, then back to first line service at Melbourne with 'Shiny Ten' until it sheared a prop and crashed in November 1942. *IWM*

Right:
When No 35 Squadron needed a 'Gee'-equipped aircraft for a raid on Norway, this older aircraft, R9441, was exchanged for one from No 102 Squadron which carried the advanced aid. *RAF Museum*

one aircraft out of nine was able to bomb — and then only blind at the site of flak seen coming up through the cloud. On the return, one Halifax ran out of fuel and had to ditch off Aberdeen.

The importance of finding and hitting these major German naval units increased still further when on 11 February, *Scharnhorst* and *Gneisenau* accompanied by the cruiser *Prinz Eugen* escaped from Brest in foggy weather and ran through the Channel virtually unscathed. Halifaxes from Nos 35 and 10 Squadrons were part of a Bomber Command force sent out to locate and bomb the enemy warships. In the poor weather conditions they caught only a fleeting glimpse and only one aircraft was able to drop its bombs blindly into the murk. When he visited No 35 Squadron at Linton later that month, the Prime Minister again stressed the vital importance of *Tirpitz* as a target. As it happened, the Fleet Air Arm had the first chance. On 6 March *Tirpitz* came out of Aasen Fjord intent on attacking a major convoy on its way to Murmansk — PQ12 — but headed for Narvik when she discovered that there were three British battleships and the carrier *Victorious* supporting the convoy. Albercores from

Left:
Nose art on Australian Wg Cdr D. C. T. Bennett's aircraft, W1041, which was shot down attacking the *Tirpitz* on 27 April 1942. He managed to return to England within a month and resume command of No 10 Squadron. *IWM*

19

Victorious carrying torpedoes attacked the German battleship but scored no hits. *Tirpitz* later slipped back to Trondheim. Three Halifax squadrons were again deployed to Lossiemouth and on the night of 30 March, 34 aircraft set out to attack *Tirpitz* but could not find her because of low cloud and fog in the fjords. The time spent searching took a heavy toll — six Halifaxes failed to return, all believed to have run out of fuel. The weather was better when the next attack was mounted on 27 April 1942 and 32 Halifaxes took part. No 76 was armed with SAP bombs to keep the defences quiet whilst Nos 10 and 35 carried spherical mines which had to be dropped from 200ft close to the warship. The attack was led by Wg Cdr D. C. T. Bennett, CO of No 10 Squadron and an acknowledged navigation expert. He made a timed run in from an island off the mouth of Aasen Fjord but was hit by flak from the ships as he descended and an engine was set on fire. At the same time, the Germans set up a smokescreen which made an accurate mine drop impossible. By now the starboard wing of Bennett's aircraft was burning and the undercarriage leg had dropped making control difficult. As he struggled to keep the Halifax level, Bennett ordered his crew to bale out

21

before jumping himself. He successfully evaded capture and returned to No 10 Squadron within a month. Most of the rest of his crew escaped into neutral Sweden.

Another Halifax hit by flak was 'S-Sugar', W1048, of No 35 Squadron. The starboard outer was set on fire and fearing the wing would be burned through, her captain, Plt Off Donald McIntyre, made a crash landing on a frozen lake. The crew climbed out, some escaped to Sweden and others were captured, but when spring and the thaw came 'S-Sugar' sank into the waters of the lake. There she stayed for the next 31 years until raised by a team of enthusiasts in June 1973. She was remarkably well-preserved. Her squadron markings and airframe number were still clearly visible, and it is said, when a battery was plugged into her electrical system, the instrument panel lit up. As the only 'surviving' Halifax, 'S-Sugar' is now on display at the Bomber Command Museum at Hendon.

Although it was later to prove to have been a blessing in disguise for the Royal Navy, the escape of *Scharnhorst*, *Gneisenau* and *Prinz Eugen* through the English Channel was seen at the time as something of a national disaster. Particular criticism was directed at Bomber Command and there were vociferous demands from the naval lobby that the Command should be disbanded and its aircraft used in the maritime role. Happily, Churchill did not agree. Leadership of the Command had been taken over by ACM Sir Arthur Harris on 23 February and he set about putting things to rights in his characteristically energetic way.

The main problems facing the bomber force at the time were a shortage of front line aircraft and the inability to locate its targets by night. Only about 600 serviceable aircraft could be called upon, many of them obsolete types with only 100 or so of the new four-engined heavy bombers. Navigation was based entirely on dead-reckoning (DR) whose accuracy was dependent upon frequent 'pin-points' — positions obtained by map-reading and other ground observations. When the ground was obscured, as it so frequently was in winter, DR became a matter of relying upon winds forecast by the Met Office back at base in England and on the ground. Astronavigation was of limited value even if the sky was clearly visible. At best it told a navigator where he had been to an accuracy of about 10 miles, but some 20min previously. The aircraft problem could only be solved by higher aircraft production at the factories and better

Far left:
Here incendiary canisters are being loaded into a Halifax bomb bay in readiness for a night attack on Hamburg, 3/4 March 1943. *Associated Press*

Above:
The first RCAF squadron to use the Halifax was No 405 at Pocklington. Here, Merlin 20 engines are seen having their tappets adjusted on a summer's day in 1942.
Public Archives of Canada

Left:
A typical area bomb-load of high explosive and incendiaries are about to be loaded aboard 'Q-Queenie', of No 405 Squadron RCAF, Pocklington.
IWM

serviceability on the squadrons. Both of these would come as experience was gained in building and servicing the new types. There was also help with the navigation problem in a new fixing aid called 'Gee'. High frequency radio ground stations transmitted a pattern of coded signals which could be translated by a special receiver in the aircraft into numerical data which, when plotted on a latticed 'Gee' chart, gave a 'fix' within about one minute and accurate to between one and five miles depending on the distance the aircraft was from the ground station. The first 'Gee' chain set up was directed towards Germany and its useable cover extended about as far as the Ruhr.

Halifaxes equipped with TR1335, the 'Gee' receiver, began arriving on squadrons at the end of February and Nos 35 and 102 — the latter a new squadron — were screened from operations for the purpose of training their navigators in its use.

The bomber force also began to improve its tactics. Until the end of 1941, crews tended to operate individually, frequently finding their own way to the target and bombing on arrival at whatever time that happened to be, depending upon the route chosen and the height and speed they had chosen to fly it at. The result was that attacks often spread over several hours and though this may have kept German workers out of their beds all night, it also meant that the defences were able to concentrate upon a succession of individual targets. One of the main objections to a greater concentration of aircraft over the target in time and space was the very apparent risk of collision. At the end of 1941 Bomber Command's new Operational Research Branch, staffed by scientists, was asked to examine the collision problem on a probability basis. Specifically the question was: if 1,000 bombers were to be required to concen-

trate their attacks on a single target during one hour, how many collisions would be likely to occur? Assuming some simple rules about the routes into and out of the target, the astonishing answer was — one! Bomber Command put the theory to the test with a highly concentrated raid on the Renault works at Billancourt in Paris with 235 aircraft — with great success. They then repeated it with similar numbers against Cologne and further afield against the Baltic ports of Lübeck and Rostock. Results had been spectacular and with the defences swamped, losses had been low.

But to quieten its critics and demonstrate its immense destructive potential against the Nazi war machine, Bomber Command needed something more spectacular. 'Bomber' Harris decided to launch three concentrated raids on selected German cities and they were to be undertaken by a force of 1,000 bombers —

a figure almost unheard of at the time and intended not only to strike the maximum fear into German hearts but also to evoke maximum publicity and public support at home.

The first target chosen was Cologne. It was within the range of the Gee coverage and its location on the Rhine meant that even crews without Gee should be able to locate it on a clear moonlit night. To achieve the 1,000-bomber target meant not only a maximum effort from the front-line squadrons, but full use of aircraft from the Operational Training Units manned by instructors as well. In the event, 1,046 bombers took off for Cologne on the night of 30/31 May 1942.

For the first time the target was marked — there was a 'pathfinder force' of Wellingtons and Stirlings equipped with Gee and carrying loads of incendiaries and flares to mark the aiming points. Behind

them came the main force — more Wellingtons and Stirlings and Hampdens, Whitleys and Manchesters. Halifaxes — about 100 were operational at the time — and a handful of the new Lancasters made up the third wave. The Halifaxes all came from Yorkshire — No 78 Squadron from Croft, No 10 Squadron from Leeming, No 35 from Linton-on-Ouse, No 102 from Dalton, No 405 RCAF Squadron from Pocklington and No 76 Squadron from Middleton-St George all took part, including their conversion flights.

When the Halifaxes crossed the coast, intruders from No 2 Group's Blenheim force had already been operating against the nightfighter airfields to good effect. Flak was encountered over the usual defensive belt, but Cologne's defences had been overwhelmed. The searchlights simply pointed straight up, ringing a city that was already burning fiercely, thick smoke rising out of the older parts to a height of 10,000ft. On the ground, the destruction was immense: 36 major factories destroyed, 300 damaged, 2,000 other commercial or industrial premises wrecked, 469 people killed, 5,000 injured and 21,000 homes wiped out. In under two hours Bomber Command had inflicted almost as much damage on the enemy as it had during the previous year. Next day the German press admitted that a great deal of damage had been done in a 'terror' raid on Cologne. But the size of the attack was concealed from the German people. Only 70 bombers were said to have taken part and half of them had been shot down. In

Top:
A Halifax Mk 2 srs 1 (Special) of No 102 Squadron reaches the point of no return as the end of the runway looms closer at Pocklington. *Crown Copyright*

Above:
With the throttles banged through the gate and the tail right up, No 77 Squadron's 'W-William' is poised to take off from Elvington. *IWM*

Right:
As the last streaks of daylight stain the western sky, B Mk 2 srs 1 (Specials) of No 102 Squadron stand with their engines idling, awaiting the green light from the flarepath caravan that will send them hurtling down the runway and off into the gathering gloom. *IWM*

fact the raid had cost Bomber Command 43 aircraft including two from the intruder force. Of the Halifax force, three were lost — one of them as the result of a collision with a Hampden.

The second '1,000-bomber' raid took place two nights later and the chosen target was Essen, home of the Krupp works and the heart of German heavy industry in the Ruhr Valley. It was not as easy a target to find as Cologne — there was no river to help the crews without Gee and the weather was poor, with thick mist obscuring the target. A total of 127 Halifaxes took part and eight of them were lost. The third '1,000-bomber' raid was on Bremen on the night of 25/26 June 1942 and proved to be the least successful of the series because heavy cloud covered the area. Of the 124 Halifaxes involved, nine were lost.

Although their success in terms of damage inflicted was less than had been anticipated — and less than claimed — the three great raids of May and June 1942 had served their broader purpose. Doubting voices about Bomber Command's value were stilled. Despite propaganda to the contrary, the Germans had been shaken by the weight of the attacks and had to divert resources into home defence. German civilian morale was also affected and with it the morale of soldiers serving in Russia and North Africa. The attacks marked the real beginning of the bomber offensive that was to continue until the German surrender. They marked too, the beginning of a new technique — specially

equipped 'pathfinding' aircraft locating and marking the target ahead of the main attacking force which delivered its bombs in a devastating concentration in time and space. Two Halifax squadrons, Nos 76 and 35, had already had experience of marking when the latter became one of the four squadrons selected in August 1942 to join the new 'Path Finder Force' formed at Graveley under the control of No 8 Group and commanded by Don Bennett — the

Top:
**Doug Petty, a flight engineer
with No 429 Squadron, RCAF,
was based at Leeming.** *D. Petty*

Inset right:
**In No 6 Group (RCAF) in North
Yorkshire, 'Target Tokens' were
awarded. Doug Petty figures in
the crew list; a mine with its
small parachute deployed is
entering the water in the centre
although the Halifax drawings
leave a lot to be desired.**

Above right:
**The briefing room for No 78
Squadron at Breighton on 1 May
1945.** *P. Finch*

Right:
**The aiming point on the airfield
of Mulheim photographed by
'D-Donald' of No 102 Squadron,
Pocklington, as a 2,000lb HC,
two 1,000lb MC and eight 250lb
bombs explode at 14.37hrs on
24 December 1944, an early and
unwelcome Christmas present.**
S. Cook

Entry into Service Jan-Jul 1942

No Built	Type	Serial Block	Constructed
70	Halifax B Mk 2 srs 1	R9418-R9540	Jan-Apr
96	Halifax B Mk 2 srs 1	W7650-W7784	Mar-Jul
174	English Electric-built B Mk 2, srs 1	W1002-W1253	Jan-Jul
35	London Aircraft Production Group (LAPG)-built Halifax B Mk 2 srs 1	BB189-BB223	Jan-Jul
12	Rootes-built Halifax B Mk 2 srs 1	DG219-DG230	Apr-Jul

Unit	Representative Aircraft	Base
No 1 Group, Bomber Command		
103 Squadron	DG229	Elsham Wolds
No 4 Group, Bomber Command		
35 Squadron	R9422, W1015, BB203, W7656, DG226	Linton-on-Ouse
76 Squadron	R9456, W1017, BB195, W7660, W7666	Middleton St George
10 Squadron	R9492, W1037, BB201, W7673, DG222	Leeming
102 Squadron	R9532, W1066, BB197, W7708	Dalton/Topcliffe
78 Squadron	R9437, W1061, BB199, W7702, DG220	Croft/ Middleton St George
405 Squadron	W1096, BB216, W7769, DG228	Pocklington
158 Squadron	W1164, BB209, W7777, DG225	East Moor
138 Squadron	W7773	Stradishall

HP59 Halifax B Mk 2 srs 1
January to July 1942

Type
Heavy bomber

Power Plant
Four 1,220hp Rolls-Royce Merlin XX engines

Performance
Maximum speed: 254mph at 12,750ft
Cruising speed: 190mph at 15,000ft
Service ceiling: 22,000ft
Range: 1,900 miles

Armament
Eight .303in Browning machine guns in nose, mid-upper and tail turrets
Bomb load: 13,000lb

Weights
Empty: 35,800lb
Loaded: 60,000lb

Dimensions
Span: 98ft 8in
Length: 70ft 1in
Height: 20ft 9in

Halifax pilot and squadron commander who had escaped from Norway earlier in the year.

The launching of the three '1,000-bomber' raids also had considerable impact upon civilian morale in Britain. After what had been the worst winter of the war — the terrible defeats in the Far East, disappointments in North Africa, losses at sea, steadily growing austerity and shortening rations, all accompanied by repeated enemy air raids — in May 1942, 399 British civilians had been killed and 425 injured in air raids — there was a desperate need for a success of British arms. That it came in the form of handing out to the Germans a double measure and more of what they had been giving to

Britain's cities was welcomed with open delight everywhere. In war, revenge is always sweet and nowhere was this felt more strongly than in the historic city of York — the capital of what was now becoming 'Halifax Country'. In the spring of 1942, York had been heavily bombed by the Luftwaffe in an attack upon Clifton airfield and on the LNER Carriage and Wagons Works. Many lives had been lost, homes destroyed and ancient buildings burned, including the Guildhall and the Exhibition Hall. Off-duty bomber crews always enjoyed a warm welcome in the hostelries of York — 'Betty's' still boasts a mirror bearing hundreds of their names — but never warmer than after the '1,000-bomber' raids in the summer of 1942.

Above:
Halifax B Mk 2 srs 1, W1041:U of No 10 Squadron, was flown by Wg Cdr D. C. T. Bennett but coded B when shot down during a raid on the *Tirpitz* in Aasen Fjord, 27 April 1942.

CHAPTER 3

'MORE DANGERO

Until the end of 1941, the training of crews coming into the Halifax force took place in the conversion flights of operational squadrons. Although this system was adequate for crews coming from other front line units — Whitley, Hampden and Wellington squadrons — it could not cope with the increasing flow of novice crews coming out of the Empire Air Training Scheme. Special conversion units were therefore set up early in 1942 on the basis of one Heavy Conversion Unit (HCU) to each Group. The first for No 4 Group was No 1652 HCU which was based at Marston Moor, that for No 6 Group was No 1659 which formed at Leeming. Others were formed during late 1942 and 1943; until the end of 1944 all were equipped with Mk 1, Mk 2 or Mk 5 Halifaxes — battleworn heroes from front-line squadrons for the most part. Not only did they still have in good measure the shortcomings of all the early Halifaxes, but their serviceability was also low and their performance even when serviceable was both sub-standard and unpredictable — a sure recipe for a high accident rate among novice crews. (There was nothing peculiar to the Halifax in this respect — it happened with all operational training units regardless of type.)

The experience of one new Halifax crew at No 1652 HCU in 1942 is recalled here by Bill Webb:

'The servicing at Marston Moor was so deadly that it was generally accepted that conversion training was far more dangerous than operations over Germany. This was not so much the fault of the ground crews as all the Halifax aircraft had done several tours of operations and were really "clapped out". In order to do a training cross-country it was necessary to start at one end of a long line of Halifax aircraft and begin the pre-flight checks on quite a few before one was found to be "acceptable". None was ever totally "serviceable" as anyone who wanted to go by the book would never have flown at all.

'Among the many tips and instructions we received, two stand out from our Heavy Conversion Unit flight training. One was a system of help in the air, ranging from distress to just plain lost. It was called "Darkie". Each aircraft had a transmitter fitted which had a range of some 10 miles and every Observer Corps Post and airfield had a special D/F receiver so that when an aircraft crew in trouble transmitted, the nearest post would reply and would know the aircraft's position to the nearest 10 miles whilst alerting the nearest airfield for emergency measures to be taken. There was a special training gramophone record on "Darkie" transmissions as it was important to be very precise in speech and to repeat everything three times so a bearing could be taken. The correct method was demonstrated by a very English voice repeating the callsign three times and so on, but the other, "how not to do it" side, was a broad Australian voice saying "'Ello Darkie, 'ello Darkie, where are you, you black bastard?"

'A much more frightening side to the Merlin-powered Halifax was its proneness to engine failure and was the second thing learnt by the crew at Marston Moor. An engine would suddenly heat up to boiling point and the trouble seemed to spread from one engine to another very rapidly at high altitude. This overheating was the dread of all Halifax crews and probably caused more casualties than enemy action.

Right:
Sqn Ldr P. Dobson flying R9430 on test from No 1658 HCU at Riccall. Only the starboard inner is operating and in this state it was considered safer to bale out rather than attempt a landing. Sqn Ldr Dobson is here assessing the rate of height loss.
H. H. Drummond (via Mick Wright)

Below right:
'R-Roger', a Mk 5 srs 1 (Special), arriving at No 1663 Heavy Conversion Unit, Rufforth. Some of the HCU aircraft were new, delivered straight from the factory, while others first saw squadron service. *IWM*

JS THAN OPS...'

(On the other hand the Lancaster had its peculiarities as had every other type of aircraft, I wouldn't want you to think that the "Halibag" was not a marvellous aircraft.) We were returning north one night from a cross-country when an engine had to be switched off and feathered through overheating and, as per standing orders, "Darkie" was called upon. We received an immediate reply from what sounded like a delightful WAAF: "Hello Mongoose Queen, hello Mongoose Queen, hello Mongoose Queen, this is Nuneaton. How can I help you?" After the Skipper had told her about our problem and said we had to land immediately we were offered runway 27 with lights, airfield level pressure for our altimeter, windspeed and what have you until our Skipper said, "Mongoose Queen undercarriage down and locked, coming straight in". Just as we turned finals for landing and were descending rapidly, we were asked how many engines we had and after four were mentioned, the controller said in a panicky voice, "Runway 27 is too short! Change to runway 18, runway 18!" and the silly girl switched off the lights on 27 and switched on 18. It was much too late to overshoot even with four good engines, so Bill Steel had to go ahead and do a marvellous landing on our landing lights alone. There was such a crunch! It amazed me how we got away with it especially as Bill was only under training on the Halifax. On our arrival in the control we found the WAAF was also under training and also very beautiful so everything was left unsaid. Bill actually thanked her for help received. A little joke was played by us by saying she was lucky not to have a big hole in the middle of her airfield as we still had our bomb load on board. She immediately tannoyed for the duty armourers who appeared with their heavy lifting gear, but after finding eight 11lb practice bombs, both Bill and the WAAF caught the rough edge of their tongues. After this we headed for Jim Carter's house in Coventry by taxi.'

An excerpt from a poem written by Barbara Carter, wife of the rear gunner, and about the crew covers this period:

> They made a forced landing at Nuneaton one night
> But no one explained what had caused their sad plight
> And there's a question unanswered to this very day,
> Why did Fletcher bring his night wear if he didn't mean to stay?
> The Carter's, always glad of a chance to make merry,
> Took the boys to the 'Phantom' to toast thumbs down to 'jerry',
> Soon filled with beer they became slightly boozy,
> Joe making love to a Yank's grim-looking floozey.
> He was only put off with persuasion and tact
> As the rest of the company thought he was cracked.
> Bill Webb caused a panic just for a while
> By selling his boots to a charmer 'cos he liked her smile.
> Bill's price was three quid plus the key of the door
> Which was smartly snapped up by this cold footed girl.
> When finally kicked out they roared all the way home
> With Joe hopping about like a well plastered gnome,
> Poor lad he had his Bing (Crosby) on the brain
> But after a while had a date with a drain.
> In spite of having to sleep four in a bed
> Nobody complained next day of a head.
> So back to Yorkshire they went feeling gay
> And remembered the 'Phantom' for many a day.

Right:
A Halifax Mk 5 undergoing a major service at No 1669 HCU, Topcliffe.
Public Archives of Canada

Right:
During operations over the new front in France, Halifax aircraft were called upon to fly more hours than the norm, so creating a greater strain on air and ground crews alike. In order to facilitate a faster turnaround, repairs were carried out on the airfield instead of in the hangars, as this No 51 Squadron Halifax shows. *Both IWM*

Left:
'S-Sugar' of No 102 Squadron, Pocklington after a major inspection and repairs to the port wing necessitated by bombs falling from other aircraft over Germany. A large fern is painted on the nose since its original 33 ops were flown by a New Zealand crew. Later the aircraft was repaired again and re-issued as 'S-Sugar'. *R. Lyne (via Mick Wright)*

'Next day we found that Nuneaton was a Wellington training station. They had not seen a four-engined aircraft, so large crowds came round to look at it. We were all very scruffy. Only Jim Fletcher our flight engineer, thought to bring his overnight kit. We all used his towel and razor, but after that experience we all carried the essentials on every trip and many times they came in handy.

'Due to the manner of our landing the undercarriage had been somewhat bent and as the weather was too bad for us to be picked up by air we found ourselves on Birmingham station on a two-hour wait for a train, flying gear and all. We actually got fed up with the number of passengers who wanted to know the facts; I suppose the lionisation was nice at first especially as they all wanted to shake hands with a crew that was carrying the war to Germany. We dare not tell them it was only a training flight, but we all felt those flights from Marston Moor, Yorkshire, were far more "dicey" than bombing Germany with first-line aircraft serviced by the finest ground crew anywhere.

'During another cross-country, we had to test and move our gear in and out of five different aircraft before we found one that was acceptable, and we were feeling weary before we started. We got off OK with our load of eight 11lb flash practice bombs and had reached Reading when the Gee packed up. The Skipper decided to continue the cross-country using D/F bearings and visual map reading when the main fuel tank started to leak. All engines were switched in turn to feed off the offending tank and we set course for base.

By the time we had arrived there we were fairly short of fuel and when we began the landing run the air speed indicator was found to be out of action, and only one leg of the undercarriage had gone down. Neither leg would go up nor down so the Skipper began heading for the crash strip at Carnaby near Bridlington which was three times the size of a normal runway. He ordered the signaller to radio Marston Moor but both sets were out of action as well. He told me to flash a quick signal on the Aldis lamp whilst we passed low near the tower. That didn't work either so we set course for Carnaby. We dropped the bomb load and I photographed the place against any claim by farmers (needless to say the camera didn't work either). We then landed safely, making a grab for the Perspex from the busted H2S scanner. It made lovely rings for the girls.'

CHAPTER 4

MIDDLE EAST BO

Public elation in Britain at the success of the first two '1,000-bomber' raids during early June 1942 was soon abated by the steady stream of bad news from the Middle East. In the Western Desert the British 8th Army, in retreat before Rommel's Afrika Korps, had left behind it a powerful garrison at Tobruk, the only sizeable port on the North African coast between Benghazi and Alexandria. Without Tobruk, Rommel could not hope to have enough petrol and ammunition to sustain his forward thrust into Egypt and must soon come to a halt. The 8th Army, on the other hand, with Tobruk as a strongpoint in Rommel's rear and its own supply lines secure with fresh troops and new tanks arriving almost daily from around the Cape, could regroup and counter-attack whenever it chose. With Tobruk in his hands, however, Rommel's supply problems would be considerably eased. His bombers could be moved to forward airfields to threaten all Egypt and his armour would be poised to sweep through to Cairo and the Suez Canal. But with its strong battle-hardened garrison standing behind deep defences and under RAF air cover, Tobruk was a tough nut for Rommel to crack . . . or so everyone from Churchill downwards firmly believed.

Tobruk fell on 21 June and 25,000 men surrendered — to an enemy force of less than half their number. As Churchill said afterwards: '. . . it was one of the heaviest blows I recall during the war'. And it had immediate repercussions all over the world. The Royal Navy's Eastern Fleet in Alexandria had to be moved south of the Suez Canal to avoid air attack and its role in hampering Rommel's supplies across the Mediterranean and in preventing a seaborne invasion of Egypt had to be taken over by the air forces. In response to an appeal from Churchill to President Roosevelt, a force of USAAC B-24 Liberators was transferred to Egypt from assignment in India. In England, two detachments of 16 aircraft each from Nos 10 and 76 Squadrons were ordered on 22 June to fly out to Aqir in Palestine.

MBER FORCE

Below:
Another operational bomb is painted on the nose of a Desert Air Force Halifax during maintenance. *RAAF*

Right:
Armourers from No 10/227 Squadron with Sgt Brinton on the extreme right preparing to move up to Landing Ground (LG) 224 from Aqir in Palestine. *F. Brinton*

Centre right:
Cpl Jones, smoking his pipe, poses for the camera next to a wounded armourer outside a desert-style barracks of No 10/227 Squadron.

Far right:
No 10/227 Squadron's armourers sweat and toil to hoist high explosive and cases of incendiaries into the bomb bay of Halifax 'F-Freddie'.

Below right:
No 10/227 Squadron armourer's lorry called 'Kathleen', during the summer of 1942.

Far right bottom:
Arming a heavy bomber was a tough job even in the cooler climes of England, but in North Africa the task was made far more arduous by the extreme heat.

Wg Cdr Bennett was to have led the No 10 Squadron detachment but at the last minute he was posted and promoted to take over the new No 8 Group. His place was taken by Wg Cdr Seymour-Price and he led the advance party of Halifaxes to Hurn airfield on 4 July 1942. The route to Palestine was by way of Gibraltar and Kasfareet in the Canal Zone, and although it lost several of its aircraft on the way out, the detachment was able to mount its first operational sortie on the night of 11/12 July. Not surprisingly, the first target was Tobruk.

Tobruk continued to be an almost nightly target for the Halifax detachment — now called No 249 Wing and operating under No 205 Group — for the next three months. Inevitably it became known as a 'milk-run' as all such monotonously regular sorties became known. Nonetheless, it was not always easy. There were no night fighters but the flak was heavy and accurate and both squadrons suffered losses on that account. But the main cause of loss was engine failure largely brought about by overheating in the high ambient temperatures encountered on the ground. Hydraulic failures were frequent and keeping the Halifaxes serviceable, hard as it had been in the UK, was made infinitely more difficult in the Middle East with spares almost non-existent and specialist equipment totally lacking. At first the task of keeping the Halifaxes in the air fell to the faithful ground crews of Nos 10 and 76

but when the detachment moved to airfields in Egypt — LG40 and Shallufa — help came from the ground crews of two Beaufighter squadrons, Nos 227 and 459, whose aircraft had been detached to Malta. The regular night attacks on Tobruk continued until September when the Halifax became a day bomber again. For some time the Germans had been using the airfield at Heraklion on the island of Crete as a base for their Ju52 transport aircraft, flying men and supplies by night into Rommel's forward airstrips. The airfield was heavily congested with both supplies and aircraft, and in the continuing battle against Rommel's supply lines it was a target that could not be ignored. No 249 Wing was ordered to

Above right:
The other end of the winch: an armaments officer checks loading. The bomb-release mechanisms are attached to the bombs before they are winched up into the bomb bay. *RAAF*

Above:
Fuel is pumped into the tanks of 'F-Freddie', W7659, at LG 224 in August 1942.

Right:
Like huge crouching vultures, a group of Halifaxes taxi out through the swirling sand and another trip to Tobruk begins.

Far right top and centre:
'Z-Zebra', W1176, of No 10/227 Squadron made a successful crash-landing near Fayid on 29 September 1942 after suffering engine failure.

Far right bottom:
On the same day 'E-Edward', W7672, also crashed; once again the crew survived.

mount a maximum effort attack in daylight
on 5 September 1942. Meanwhile in the
Western Desert, Rommel's final thrust
towards Egypt had been halted by the 8th
Army at Alam Halfa, three enemy tankers
had been sunk in the Mediterranean by
British submarines and Rommel was in
dire straits over supplies of petrol. For the
attack on Heraklion both squadrons put up
six aircraft, but hydraulic and engine
failure took their toll before and after
take-off, and only eight Halifaxes made up
the final formation. Numerous parked
aircraft were destroyed and Heraklion's
runways were badly cratered but two
Halifaxes were shot down — W1114 flown
by Flt Lt Bryana and W7679 flown by Sqn
Ldr Hacking, one of the most experienced
crews in the Wing. No 10's CO, Wg Cdr
Seymour-Price in W1174 was badly damaged by defending Bf109s, but managed to
get back to Fayid.

Next day the two squadron detachments
were amalgamated to form a new squadron, No 462 RAAF, under Wg Cdr Young
DSO, DFC, AFC. At that time the

Far right:
Venice, Trieste, Udine all show up on the ever-changing flak battery maps in the area of operation for No 614 (Pathfinder) Squadron and its Mk 2 Halifaxes.

Right:
A modified 'special' of the Desert Air Force is seen here at Gardabia being manoeuvred by a highly magnetic tractor on a compass swing. *RAAF*

Below right:
No 614 (Pathfinder) Squadron was still using No 462's old B Mk 2 srs 1 (Specials) out in Italy, but eventually new aircraft were to come. *Neil McKay*

Below:
As part of their survival kit, bomber crews carried papers in several languages as an aid to identification. As No 614 Squadron operated over Eastern Europe, this one is in Russian.

detachment had flown 154 sorties since its arrival two months earlier and had not received a single replacement aircraft. It was a great achievement for a detachment originally intended to last only 16 days.

The attack on the Afrika Korps supply lines continued unabated throughout September and October 1942; the procedure whereby the RAF Wellingtons and Halifaxes kept Tobruk under nightly attack while the USAAC Liberators dealt with Benghazi was now an established routine. Tobruk received over 183 Halifax sorties during the two months before the battle of El Alamein but there were other targets. In an attack on Crete again on 10 October, Halifax W1183 flown by Sqn Ldr Warner was hit by flak and badly damaged, the navigator receiving serious wounds. At one point the aircraft lost height to 1,000ft but struggled on to make a crash-landing in the desert near Dikirnes. The navigator had continued his duties despite his wounds and was given an immediate DSO.

Halifaxes were now to remain in the Mediterranean until the end of the war. Night bombing of a variety of targets was their primary role until 1944, but the series of battles that preceded the final defeat of the Afrika Korps in Tunisia in May 1943 gave them a variety of unusual roles and a succession of home bases. One of the most spectacular roles was that of what is now called 'close air-support' — bombing and strafing retreating enemy transport from levels as low as 1,200ft — and at night. For

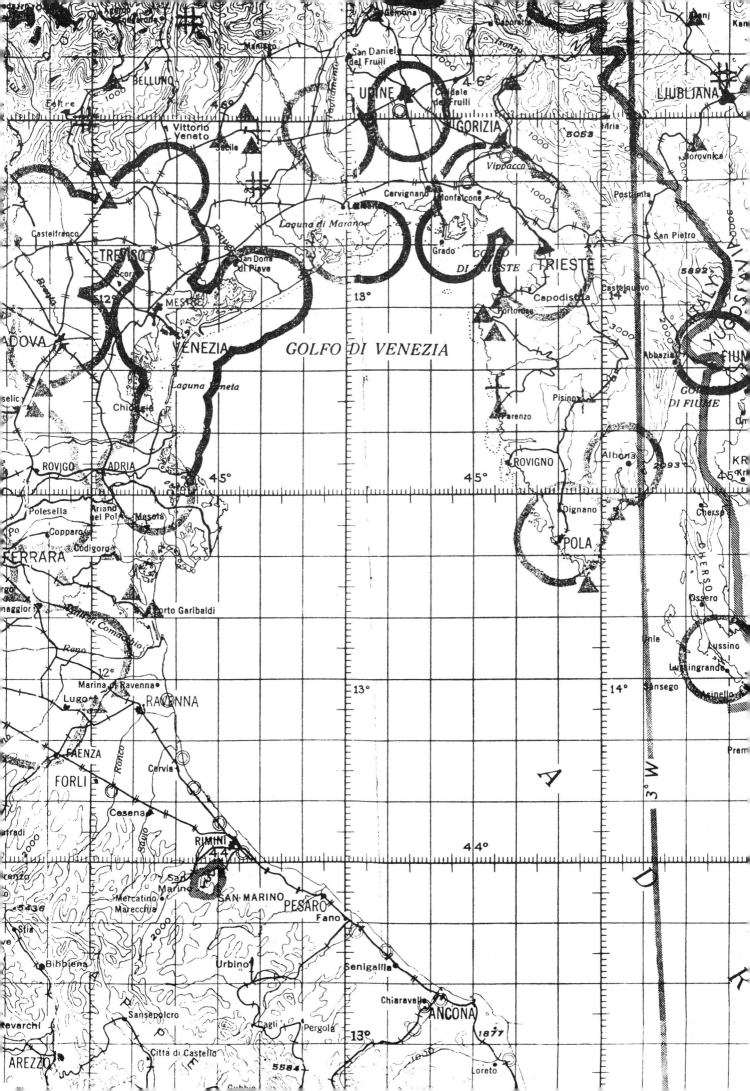

Right and bottom:
Roy Nash dropped his green target indicator with great precision on Verona marshalling yards from a height of 7,000ft on 11/12 October 1944. The bottom photograph is a daylight view of the wrecked marshalling yards after the raid.
Crown Copyright

Below:
Christmas Day in Italy, 1944: No 614 Squadron's menu for what was to become the last wartime Christmas.

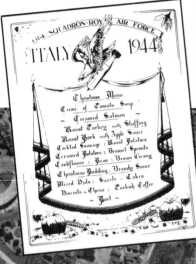

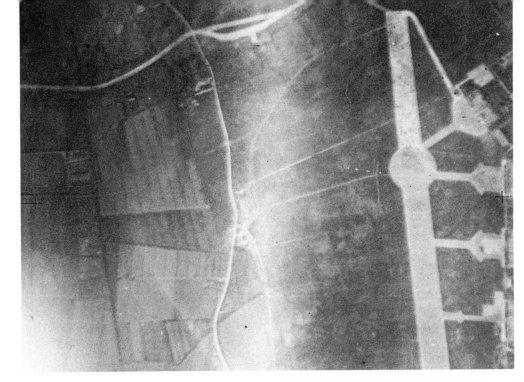

No 462 Squadron, there was a regular change of base — from Fayid in the Canal Zone where it was formed, to forward landing grounds, first in Egypt then behind the advance, in Libya where it eventually settled for some time at El Adem. Early in January 1944 it moved to Italy and in one of those strange squadron number juggling acts for which the Royal Air Force is renowned, ceased to be No 462 (RAAF) Squadron and became No 614 (RAF) Squadron — the aircraft and crews being largely unchanged — the latter, ironically, mainly Australian. But with the new number came a new and exacting role — pathfinding and target marking for the entire No 205 Group night bomber force — Wellingtons and Liberators — in the manner of Don Bennett's No 8 Group PFF squadrons in Bomber Command at home.

Although finding targets in the Mediterranean was largely dependent upon the same fallible system of DR and astronavigation that had been used in the early Bomber Command attacks on Germany, the generally better weather conditions for much of the year coupled with a prevalence of targets on or not far from coastlines has meant a reasonable measure of success in most, but not all, of the earlier Halifax missions. With the ending of the North African campaign, the invasion first of Sicily and then of the Italian mainland had brought about an extension of No 205 Group target area to include the industrial north of Italy, Austria and all the Balkans where many important and potential targets were deep inland and well clear of easily identified landmarks. From the summer of 1943, the squadron had been operating a somewhat primitive form of 'pathfinding' by using its

No. 205 Group
Royal Air Force

Flight Sergeant R. E. Nash, is qualified in Pathfinder technique and is authorised under the provisions of Air Ministry Order A.1244/42 (as amended) to wear *THE PATHFINDER BADGE*

Air Officer Commanding, No. 205 Group, ROYAL AIR FORCE Mediterranean Allied Air Force

Dated 26th OCTOBER 1944

HP59 Halifax B Mk 2 srs 1 (Special)
August 1942 to February 1943

Type
Heavy bomber and general reconnaissance aircraft

Power Plant
Four 1,220hp Rolls-Royce Merlin XX engines

Performance
Maximum speed: 254mph at 12,750ft
Cruising speed: 190mph at 19,000ft
Service ceiling: 22,000ft
Range: 1,900 miles

Armament
Four .303in Browning machine guns in the tail, later in a mid-upper turret

Weights
Empty: 35,000lb
Loaded: 60,000lb

Dimensions
Span: 98ft 8in
Length: 70ft 1in
Height: 20ft 9in

Above:
Halifax B Mk 2 srs 1 (Special), DT579:P of No 77 Squadron based at Elvington.

Entry into Service Aug 1942-Feb 1943

No Built	Type	Serial Block	Constructed
255	EE-built Halifax B/GR Mk 2 srs 1	W1270-W1276; DT481-DT808	Aug 1942-Jan 1943
150	Halifax B Mk 2 srs 1	W7801-W7939; HR654-HR699	Aug 1942-Feb 1943
138	Rootes-built Halifax B Mk 5 srs 1	DG231-DG424	Aug 1942-Mar 1943
10	Fairey-built Halifax B/MET Mk 5 srs 1	DJ980-DJ999	Aug 1942-Jan 1943
81	Fairey-built Halifax B/MET Mk 5 srs 1	DK114-DK151; DK165-DK207	Nov 1942-Feb 1943
74	LAPG-built Halifax B Mk 2 srs 1	BB236-BB313	Nov 1942-Jan 1943

Unit	Representative Aircraft	Base
No 1 Group, Bomber Command		
103 Squadron	W1270, W7850, DT513	Elsham Wolds

best crews to mark targets with flares ahead of the main force. Arrival at the new base at Cellone near Foggia also brought the arrival of the first Halifax B Mk 2s equipped with Gee, H2S and the Mk 14 bombsight. By this time, Gee ground stations had been set up in Italy but their effective cover was limited over enemy territory, not only by the ranges involved, but also by enemy jamming. H2S was a search radar-set mounted in the Halifax with its scanner inside a protuberant blister on the belly of the aircraft. It presented the navigator with a 360° plan of the main radar-reflecting features on the ground beneath the aircraft out to a range of about 80nm, depending on height and terrain. It measured bearing and distance very accurately and when switched to a forward sector scan it could be used for blind bombing and target marking. It was not affected by the weather and it was not at that stage subject to jamming, but German night-fighters were being equipped with a device to home in on its transmission. H2S, however, had two major shortcomings: the first was, inevitably, a low rate of

serviceability especially when newly introduced into an overseas theatre without much back-up from the manufacturers and the scientists; secondly it was also far from easy to interpret and operate even by crews who had been back to England for specialist training on the equipment. Mountainous terrain which cast radar shadows coupled with intermittent or unreliable operation frequently made it difficult to get the best out of it. Nonetheless, with the use of Gee for part of the outward track and with H2S working in at least some of the aircraft, the results in finding and marking targets improved rapidly throughout 1944.

No 614's first marking operation was on 10 April 1944 and the target was the marshalling yards at Plovdiv, southeast of Sofia in the heart of Bulgaria. Eight Halifaxes took part and successfully illuminated the target with flares, returning without loss. Thereafter the squadron was to locate and mark a surprising variety of targets throughout Southern Europe for what had become the Mediterranean Allied Strategic Air Force. The nature of

Unit	Representative Aircraft	Base
No 3 Group, Bomber Command		
138 Squadron	DG252, DT543, DJ996, HR665, BB309	Tempsford
161 Squadron	DG245	Tempsford
No 4 Group, Bomber Command		
10 Squadron	DT520, W7867, HR691, BB249	Leeming/Melbourne
51 Squadron	DG638, DT693, BB253	Snaith
76 Squadron	W7805, DT511, BB237	Middleton St George/ Linton-on-Ouse
77 Squadron	DG250, DT579, DJ983, BB252	Elvington
78 Squadron	W1273, W7809, DT525, HR684, BB241	Middleton St George/ Linton-on-Ouse
102 Squadron	W1271, W7807, DT512, BB243, HR665	Topcliffe/Pocklington
158 Squadron	W7862, DT569	East Moor/Rufforth
No 4/6 Group, Bomber Command*		
408 Squadron	DG239, DT673, HR658, BB311	Leeming
419 Squadron	DT615, BB283	Croft/ Middleton St George
No 4 Group/HQ Coastal Command		
405 Squadron	W1274, W7802, DT507	Pocklington/Topcliffe/ Beaulieu
No 8 (Pathfinder) Group, Bomber Command		
35 Squadron	W7875, W7851	Graveley
No 18 Group, Coastal Command		
58 Squadron	DT636, BB277	Holmsley South
502 Squadron	HR675, BB310	St Eval
No 38 Group		
295 Squadron	DJ989, DG303	Netheravon

Canadian Squadrons became part of their own No 6 (RCAF) Group in 1942

these targets is indicated by the experience of one new Halifax crew which joined No 614 Squadron in the summer of 1944. Flg Off Hagues and his crew converted to the Halifax at Marston Moor and then went on to H2S training at Newmarket, where the airfield was right on the racecourse. They picked up a Halifax B Mk 2 srs 1a, JP241, equipped with H2S, from the Ferry Flight at Pershore and flew it out to Stomara near Foggia where No 614 was then based. They first joined C flight for further training and to familiarise themselves with the local terrain. Their first operation involved bomb aimer Roy Nash dropping a 250lb target indicator and 14×500lb bombs on the Brod oil refinery in Yugoslavia on the night of 14/15 July 1944.

Other targets then followed in rapid succession, good results often punctuated by the frustrations of H2S and bomb-release gear failures. This happened on their second operation on an oil refinery at Fiume in Italy when they were lucky to escape from two attacks by enemy night-fighters. In August they went to Valences in the Rhône Valley to attack more marshalling yards, to Ploesti in Rumania, to Hadju Boszormen in Hungary to attack an airfield, and to Marseilles in support of Operation Anvil, the Allied landing on the south coast of France. Other targets in that month were the Hermann Goering works at St Valentin in Austria, Szony and Miskolc in Hungary, then Pesaro and Ferrara nearer home in Italy.

In October 1944, No 614's role as a pathfinder squadron was officially recognised when selected crews were authorised to wear the coveted PFF badge. Thereafter, however, the squadron was more involved in actual bombing attacks rather than pure target marking, although the latter skill was several times displayed to good effect in the difficult art of bombing bridges. Meanwhile, the squadron had been converting to the Liberator and many operations in the winter of 1944-45 were by a combined force of Halifaxes and Liberators. The last operation by a Halifax Pathfinder was against an oil depot at Port Maaghera on 3 March 1945.

CHAPTER 5

ALL AT SEA

During 1942, the enduring battle against Admiral Doenitz's growing fleet of U-boats had taken a serious turn for the worse. More than six million tons of Allied shipping had been sunk and the number of U-boats destroyed was only about 10 — and the U-boat fleet now numbered 400. Shipyards in Britain and the USA were beginning to make up the losses but there was still an acute shortage of escort vessels and anti-submarine craft. In the autumn of 1942 the launching of the Allied invasion of North Africa — Operation 'Torch' — with its call for massive strongly protected convoys, had drawn heavily upon all Allied naval resources not least upon the escort vessels on the North Atlantic and Russian convoy routes. Admiral Doenitz wasted no time in exploiting this Allied weakness and in the month of November alone his 'wolf-packs' sank more than 600,000 tons. Most of these losses occurred in the area of the North Atlantic which could not be covered by aircraft patrolling from bases in Britain, Iceland or Newfoundland because of the limited range of the types of aircraft involved — Sunderlands, Hudsons, Whitleys and Wellingtons and a handful of Liberators — a region known at the time as the 'Atlantic Air Gap'. Aircraft patrolling over this enormous sea area were primarily concerned with forcing marauding U-boats to operate underwater where their speed and hence their radius of action was sharply curtailed. Some U-boats would be sunk in the process but the main U-boat killing area was in the Bay of Biscay while they were in transit to and from their bases on the French Atlantic coast. By the end of 1942, Coastal Command had established an effective system of patrols of the nearer areas of the Bay using Whitleys and Wellingtons equipped with a primitive form of search radar — Air-to-Surface Vessels (ASV) Mk 1 — and a specially developed aerial searchlight called a Leigh light for use at night. To cover the outer areas of the Bay, longer range aircraft were needed. Although Coastal Command had nine squadrons of Sunderlands and a

growing number of Liberators, these were desperately needed to help to cover the mid-Atlantic gap. As sinkings continued to mount, in October a small force of Halifaxes and Lancasters was detached from Bomber Command to help in the process of keeping the U-boats under pressure in the Bay while the North African landings were completed. The Halifax detachment comprised five B Mk 2s from No 158 Squadron and 15 from No 405. The aircraft arrived at Beaulieu in Hampshire on 24 October and flew their first anti-submarine patrol over the Bay three days later. It proved to be a highly successful detachment. Several U-boats were sighted and attacked and daylight raids were carried out against their bases. One Halifax crew of No 405 Squadron even tried its hand at a shipping strike by attacking a small convoy. The most successful attack on a U-boat was carried out by Flt Lt Palmer from No 405 Squadron on 27 November when he straddled *U263* (Lt Cdr Nölke) with a stick of depth charges and severely damaged it. The

Below:
This Halifax GR Mk 2 srs 1 (Special), 'J2' of No 502 Squadron, seen flying over St Davids at 2,000ft, has ASV Mk 3 radar fitted and the earlier, skirted, mid-upper turret.
J. Hochkins

detachment ended early in 1943 and by this time Coastal Command had two Halifax squadrons of its own: No 58 which formed at St Eval in December and No 502 which formed there in January.

In January 1943 Churchill and Roosevelt and their respective chiefs of staff met in Casablanca, and among other things set out their priorities for the future conduct of the war. It was agreed that 'the defeat of the U-boat must remain the first charge on the resources of the United Nations'. There could be no decisive invasion of Western Europe until the Battle of the Atlantic was won. The Germans for their part fully appreciated the crucial importance of their U-boat campaign. A week after Casablanca, Hitler promoted Doenitz to be commander-in-chief of the German Navy and ordered Albert Speer, his minister in charge of armaments, to give the highest priority to producing U-boats. At the strategic level the Germans had considerable advantages. They had broken the British naval codes and were able to read instructions sent to convoys. The 'wolf-packs' were fighting a form of guerrilla warfare — they had the initiative. They could group for a surprise attack, strike, disperse and disappear only to re-group for another surprise attack. Allied convoys, on the other hand, were slow and difficult to manoeuvre and control. Once located they could be under attack for days by concentrations of U-boats numbering some times as many as 70. The Allies for their part, through the Ultra code-breaking organisation at Bletchley Park, could read the German Enigma code and follow the signals traffic between Doenitz and his U-boats at sea. This was of immense value in routeing convoys to avoid U-boat concentrations and knowing the area where the 'wolf-packs' were operating. They also had a long-range HF/DF ('Huff-duff') system that took bearings on U-boat transmissions. There was also a similar system aboard Allied warships acting as escorts but none of these methods could actually locate an individual U-boat with the

accuracy needed to drop bombs or depth-charges on it. First find your guerrilla — then find your U-boat, this was the paramount tactical task and here the Allied sea and air forces were making steady progress when the Halifaxes joined Coastal Command.

The great weakness of the U-boats of World War 2 was that they were not true submersibles in the sense that modern nuclear-powered submarines are — capable of remaining submerged for indefinite periods. The 1943 vintage U-boat had to surface at regular intervals to charge the batteries required for running when submerged. Furthermore, cruising speed on the surface was between 12 and 15kt, that submerged between five and eight. A submerged U-boat also had limited visibility not just for locating its prey but also for the essential purposes of navigation in the wastes of the Atlantic. For these reasons the U-boats operated on the surface whenever they could, submerging only for attacking purposes or when Allied aircraft were in the vicinity. In areas

Below:
Coastal Command's No 58 Squadron Halifax 'O-Oboe' is seen here sporting the .5in Browning machine gun in the nose. This gun was belt fed and required extra bracing with metal struts to secure it in the Perspex nose. *J. Hochkins (via Mick Wright)*

Above:

Four-bladed propellers were found to add another thousand feet to the service ceiling of the Halifax, and to improve the rate of climb at high altitude. They were also beneficial to Mk 5 aircraft operating with Coastal Command on long endurance flights. *IWM*

where Allied air patrols were frequent — as in the Bay of Biscay — the usual tactic was to submerge during the day and surface at night. Thus the battle between aircraft and U-boat was a classic cat-and-mouse game. If the submarine saw or heard the aircraft, it would crash dive and invariably by the time the aircraft was in a position to drop its depth charges, the U-boat was safely under the sea. The distance at which even a surfaced submarine under way and making waves could be seen from an aircraft at the usual patrol height of about 2,000ft was rarely better than about seven miles in daylight, much less at night. The introduction of the Mk 1 ASV in 1942 meant that surfaced submarines could be located as far away as 20 miles depending upon the angle of approach and sea conditions and, of course, by night as well as by day, in bad visibility as well as good. The equipment itself was primitive — it looked only in one

direction — usually forward around to amidships — and gave only a coarse indication of whether the blip seen on the screen was to port or starboard of the aircraft's course and how far it was away in slant range. When the aircraft was very close, the blip disappeared altogether in the sea returns so there was no hope of using Mk 1 ASV for blind attacks. One needed to be able to see the U-boat and it was for this purpose that the powerful Leigh light was installed. Nonetheless, Mk 1 ASV was, as the crews said, a considerable advance on the Mk 1 Eyeball, and sightings increased steadily throughout the summer of 1942 reaching 120 in September. The advantage had clearly shifted to the cat — but not for long.

During the autumn, U-boats were fitted with a listening device called 'Metox' which worked on the 1½m transmissions of the Mk 1 ASV. It gave the crews an

advance warning of the approach of patrol aircraft at a longer range than the aircraft could hope to detect the U-boat, enabling it to dive to safety in good time. The effect upon the sighting rate was immediate — down to 57 in October. At the same time, shipping losses continued to rise. In the last week of the year, 20 U-boats attacked a single convoy, ONS154 with 45 ships, in the North Atlantic and sank 14 of them without loss. As the Admiralty wrote in a review in February 1943: 'Never before has the enemy displayed such singleness of purpose in utilising his strength against one objective — the interruption of supplies from America to Great Britain. The tempo is quickening and the critical phase of the U-boat war cannot be long postponed.' This, we might say, is the point where the Halifaxes came in. At the same time as the Halifaxes, the Mk 3 ASV came into service. The equipment was Bomber Command's new centrimetric H2S search

radar adapted to the maritime anti-submarine role. It was a great advance on the Mk 1. Not only did it give all-round search at greater ranges, more accurate indications of range and bearing and highly accurate sector scanning for the attack phase, it was also not detectable by Metox. By an unlucky chance, the first experimental deployment of the Mk 3 ASV, in a Leigh light Wellington of No 172 Squadron, resulted in the aircraft being shot down. *U333* (Lt Cdr Cremer) was charging his batteries on the surface at night in poor weather when without any warning from his Metox, the Wellington launched its attack. From this incident and the rise in the number of U-boats lost, the Germans realised that a new radar was being used and changed their tactics. They ran submerged at night and charged their batteries by day, intending to beat off air attacks with the additional AA guns they had fitted to the U-boats. The result was a

HP63 Halifax B/GR Mk 5 srs 1 (Special)
March to July 1943

Type
Heavy bomber, met and general reconnaissance aircraft

Power Plant
Four 1,220hp Rolls-Royce Merlin XX engines

Performance
Maximum speed: 254mph at 12,750ft
Cruising speed: 190mph at 15,000ft
Service ceiling: 22,000ft
Range: 1,900 miles

Armament
Four .303in Browning machine guns mounted in a tail turret, later some had a further four in the mid-upper position
Bomb load: 13,000lb

Weights
Empty: 36,000lb
Loaded: 61,500lb

Dimensions
Span: 98ft 8in
Length: 70ft 1in
Height: 20ft 9in

Entry into Service Mar-Jul 1943

No Built	Type	Serial Block	Constructed
101	LAPG-built Halifax B Mk 2 srs 1	BB314-BB446	Mar-Jul
45	LAPG-built Halifax B Mk 2 srs 1	JN882-JN926	Mar-Jul
100	Rootes-built Halifax B Mk 5 srs 1	EB127-EB276	Apr-Sept
49	Fairey-built Halifax B/MET Mk 5	DK223-DK271	Mar-Jul
152	Halifax B/GR Mk 2 srs 1	HR711-HR952	Mar-Jul
123	EE-built Halifax B/GR Mk 2 srs 1	JB781-JB974	Feb-Mar
223	EE-built Halifax B/GR Mk 2 srs 1a	JD105-JD476	Apr-Jul

Unit	Representative Aircraft	Base
No 3 Group, Bomber Command		
138 Squadron	JD171, JN921, BB378, JB871	Tempsford
161 Squadron	BB431, DK206, EB129	Tempsford
192 Squadron	DK246	Gransden Lodge

sharp increase in U-boat sightings and sinkings — and also in aircraft losses not only from the U-boat's quadruple 20mm cannons but also from long-range enemy fighter aircraft — mostly formations of Ju88s but including the odd Arado 196 seaplane. In May 1943 a total of 41 U-boats were sunk. Of these, eight were sunk by aircraft in the Bay, and Halifaxes had a hand in five of those sinkings.

On 7 May, *U663* (Lt Cdr Schmidt) making his way back across the Bay was sunk by a No 58 Squadron Halifax. Four days later, *U528* was sunk in the eastern Atlantic at 46°55′N 14°44′W by another No 58 Squadron Halifax when it attacked a convoy. Particularly successful in the hunt for U-boats was No 58 Squadron's CO, Wg Cdr W. E. Oulton (later Air Vice-Marshal, CB, CBE, DSO, DFC). On 15 May he scored his squadron's third kill for the month when he sank the supply submarine *U463* (Cdr Wolfbauer), flying Halifax HR746:M. Supply submarines, or

'milch cows' as they were known, had the job of replenishing the 'wolf-packs' at sea with fuel, torpedoes, food and supplies, thereby increasing their endurance and range. The only armament they carried was AA defence. Wg Cdr Oulton followed what had become standard tactics — an approach out of the sun with the nose gun raking the U-boat, a stick of six depth charges and further gunfire from the turrets. On this occasion, the U-boat sank in under two minutes after the attack had begun. Quite often, however, there were repeated exchanges of fire between aircraft and U-boat as there were on 31 May when the wing commander spotted *U563* on the surface. He dropped two sticks of depth charges at it in the course of over an hour and finally had to leave another No 58 Squadron Halifax and two Sunderlands to finish it off.

After their heavy losses in the Bay, the U-boats changed tactics again sailing in groups to give mutual AA support. This

Unit	Representative Aircraft	Base
No 4 Group, Bomber Command		
10 Squadron	JD105, JD322, HR922, JB930	Melbourne
51 Squadron	JD250, JN901, HR842, JB792	Snaith
76 Squadron	JD145, BB365, DK134, EB249	Linton-on-Ouse/ Holme-upon-Spalding Moor
77 Squadron	JD110, BB427, JB956	Elvington
78 Squadron	JD329, HR874, JB924	Linton-on-Ouse
102 Squadron	JD206, JN908, BB428, HR919, JB921	Pocklington
158 Squadron	JD246, HR837, JB789, JN884	Lissett
No 6 (RCAF) Group, Bomber Command		
405 Squadron	JD123, BB374, HR905, JB906	Leeming/ Gransden Lodge
408 Squadron	JD361, JB898	Leeming
419 Squadron	JD270, BB376, JB912	Middleton St George
427 Squadron	DK135, EB246	Leeming
428 Squadron	EB213	Middleton St George
431 Squadron	DK264	Tholthorpe
434 Squadron	DK261, EB219	Tholthorpe
No 8 (Pathfinder) Group, Bomber Command		
35 Squadron	BB368, HR878, JB785	Graveley
No 18 Group, Coastal Command		
58 Squadron	HR792	Holmsley South
502 Squadron	JD176, HR814, JB901	Holmsley South
No 38 Group		
295 Squadron	DG390, DK130, EB178	Holmsley South
No 205 Group, MEAF		
148 Squadron	JN888, BB421	Derna/Tocra
178 Squadron	BB414	Hosc Raui
462 Squadron	JN916, BB419	Gardabia/Hosc Raui
624 Squadron	JN898	Blida

Far left:
Halifax B Mk 5 srs 1 (Special), DG252:D of No 138 (Special Duties) Squadron, flown by Sqn Ldr Dick Wilkins when he was attacked by fighters over Holland, forcing him to ditch on 19 September 1943

new tactic made depth charge attacks by single aircraft extremely hazardous and Coastal Command countered it in two ways; firstly, it operated its own aircraft in groups and it improved co-operation between them and the Navy's new special escort groups of surface ships; secondly, it also armed some of its aircraft, notably the Halifaxes, with new 600lb anti-submarine bombs that could be dropped from higher altitudes than depth-charges and which, because of their stability after release, could be aimed with an ordinary bomb-sight. The tactics were soon tested. On 30 July, an outward-bound group of U-boats, *U461* and *U462*, both tankers, and *U504*, a standard attack boat, was sighted by a Liberator of No 53 Squadron which called in nearby aircraft — a USN Liberator, two Halifaxes, a Sunderland and a Catalina. The latter was sent off to bring in a surface escort group and the rest took it in turn to attack the U-boat group through a barrage of ferocious flak. The first Halifax flown by Flg Off Biggar of No 502 Squadron attacked from 1,600ft but missed with its bombs and was damaged by the flak. The USN Liberator and the Sunderland attacked together and the Sunderland sank *U461*. (By a curious coincidence, she was Sunderland 'U' of No 461 Squadron RAAF.) The second Halifax, also from No 502, damaged *U462* in his first bombing run and finished it off on his second; the escort group arriving in the nick of time, sank the remaining U-boat with gunfire.

For Doenitz, it had been a disastrous summer. Between May and July he had lost 90 U-boats and he was to lose a further 60 between August and October. He had little to see for his losses: in March he had sunk 90 Allied ships; in May, 40 and in June only six. The tide of the Battle of the Atlantic had turned irreversibly in the Allies' favour: Hitler's 'first line of defence in the West' had been broken, opening the way for the final assault on 'Festung Europa'.

CHAPTER 6

THE QUICK AND

James E. Johnson

THE DEAD

Left:
Although still without the rectangular fins and rudders, Merlin 22s made 'H-Harry' of No 78 Squadron, Breighton, officially a B Mk 2 srs 1a.
P. Finch

Below:
A No 462 Squadron, RAAF, Halifax Mk 3, LL599, flying low over the North Sea for a daylight raid on Europe in October 1944. This aircraft collided with a Lancaster over Essen later in the year. *Mick Wright*

'I first flew in a Halifax at No 1658 HCU based at Riccall, on 2 September 1943. Unfortunately my first crew were killed in a flying accident at night, when the rear gunner and myself were in hospital. I then took the place of the unfortunate wireless operator who had stood in for me and joined Flg Off Everett's crew. After completion of the Conversion Course we were posted to No 78 Squadron at Breighton, in mid-October 1943. Our first taste of operations came on 3 November when we went to Düsseldorf in Halifax Mk 2 "F-Freddie". We did a further six ops in Mk 2s taking us up to 19 December. (Incidentally, during this time our Skipper was promoted to Flt Lt.) On 21 January 1944 we picked up a Halifax Mk 3 from Holme-on-Spalding Moor, our parent station, and flew it back to base. The next few weeks were spent doing H2S training, cross country flights and we did our first operational flight in the new aircraft to Berlin on 15 February. Looking at my log book I see that my next op was not until 20 March to Kiel Bay, and then to Frankfurt on the 22nd. In the gap between 15 February and 20 March I believe some of the crew got a couple more ops in as stand-ins with other crews, which made our trip on 24 March 1944 the "unlucky thirteenth" for some.

'On the night of 24 March 1944, the target was Berlin. For the crew of "D-Dog" it was our fourth visit. The crew comprised: Flt Lt Eric W. Everett (pilot), Sgt Jock Stewart (navigator), Flg Off Joe Green (bomb aimer), Sgt Jim E. Johnson (wireless operator), Sgt Taff Jones (flight engineer), Sgt Ralph Graham (mid-upper gunner) and Plt Off Alan Sinden (rear gunner).

'We took off along with the other aircraft from our squadron and headed for Flamborough to join up with the main force and set course. To me it was always an awe-inspiring sight to see so many aircraft in flight at the same time all heading for the same target. After crossing the enemy coast there was the usual flak bursting all around and tracers streaking

55

Right:

'Z-Zooloo' NP995 of No 78 Squadron, actually survived the war, but it was a close-run thing. Bill Rodney, seen at the pilot's window, was 20,000ft over Montorgeuil in daylight on 24 June 1944 when another Halifax exploded. 'Z-Zooloo' was hurled upwards and almost inverted by the force of the detonation and had to dive and half-roll back into level flight.
Northern Echo
(via E. Pritchard)

Far right:

This highly decorated Halifax Mk 3, MZ296 of No 462 Squadron, Driffield, sets out on the crew's last operation of its tour in 1944, which was successfully completed. The aircraft was lost near Brussels on 15 October that same year.
RAAF

Right:

Doug Petty's 'W-William' of No 429 Squadron, RCAF, seen standing-by at Leeming for a mining operation. Of the 14 operations recorded beneath the pilot's window, six are for minelaying.

Centre right:

The rear gunner of a No 77 Squadron Halifax at Full Sutton. The Halifaxes are beginning to last a little longer, long enough for a photograph to be taken, and this probably explains the smile on the gunner's face.
S. C. Thorne

upwards, and we, like every other crew in that mighty air armada, each had our individual duties to carry out. Soon it was the last leg in to the target and Joe had just released the bombs, when we were hit by a burst from a fighter, which set our rest position on fire. What happened after that has never been quite clear, but I know some of us grabbed fire extinguishers and went back, and with the help of the Skipper's diving and weaving, the fire was put out. Taff, the flight engineer, then checked the damage and from that moment on we all knew we would never make it back home. We had been very badly damaged — fuel cocks shattered, bomb doors still open, port wheel down and the flaps half down. However, the Skipper battled with the controls and we limped on. Soon the port engine started cutting and finally stopped. By this time we were over Holland, but were losing height and we limped on until finally the Skipper gave the order to abandon aircraft. We all got out safely, and the last thing I saw while floating down to earth was our aircraft bursting into flames as it hit the deck. The time was approximately 12.30am; the place somewhere near Rockanje, south of the Hook of Holland. (This I learned much later.) My own personal experiences of the remainder of that night after hitting terra firma, minus my flying boots — I lost them as soon as I jumped — came more by instinct and the disciplines we had been taught should such an occasion as this occur. I ditched my chute and started walking away from the area. I

remember it was very cold and with no boots I decided to hide for the night. I eventually came across some farm buildings and got into a Dutch barn and hid amongst the hay. It was while lying there that the realities of life started drifting back and my thoughts turned to my family, my girlfriend Joan and the many dear friends back home, some of whom I had been with not 48 hours ago. I consoled myself with the knowledge that I knew I was safe and in one piece, and that sooner or later they would get to know too. The next thing I knew was being literally forked out of my hiding place by the farmer. He gave me some bread and cheese later but as he spoke no English and I spoke no Dutch, communication was impossible. He did however give me a pair of clogs to wear. Not long after that two Germans came and took me away. As the day progressed all but one of our crew, the rear gunner Alan Sinden were brought in. For us the war was over. We were then taken to a prison at Breda. From there to Rotterdam and then to Amsterdam, where

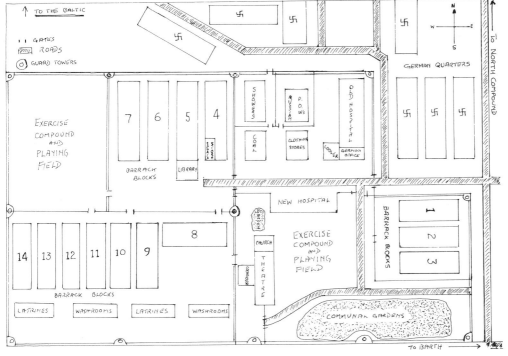

Left:
**'How long will we be here? —
How long before we hear from
home? Then we began to adapt
to life at Stalag Luft 1, Barth.'
This plan of the camp was copied
from the log-book of one of the
inmates.**

Right:

This is an unusual photograph considering that private cameras were forbidden. A No 77 Squadron Halifax is seen here during a daylight operation over Germany; the photograph was taken through the wireless operator's window. *S. Cook*

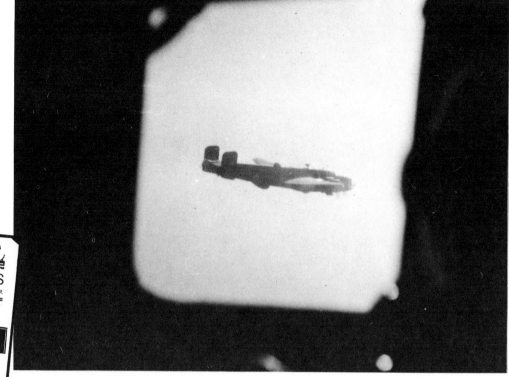

Below:

The *Barth Hard Times*, Vol 1, No 1, Last 1. This broadsheet was produced by the inmates of Stalag Luft 1 on the advent of their liberation by the Russian forces.

we were then taken by train to an interrogation centre in southern Germany and joined many more airmen who had suffered the same fate as us. We were at the Dulag Luft Oberheusel about three days before being transported by train to Stalag Luft I on the Baltic Coast due north of Berlin near the town of Barth. The journey took about four to five days and we arrived at Stalag Luft I at the beginning of April. The camp itself was situated close to a German radar school and mid-way between Rostock and Peenemunde, where the V-bombs were tested.

'On reflection, I suppose we must have looked a rather dirty and dishevelled lot, and there were a lot of us, as we entered the main gates of the camp. It was, if I remember rightly, primarily an American POW camp for officers and NCOs of the American Air Corps, now having to accommodate other nationalities as well, due, I assume, to the heavier aircrew losses incurred by the increased bombing

Right:

Harold Bertenshaw's crew of *Randy Andy*, of No 76 Squadron, Holme-upon-Spalding Moor, prior to being shot down during the 'Gisela' operation in Lincolnshire on the morning of 4 March 1945. Some 200 Luftwaffe night-fighters followed the returning bombers to their bases and shot 20 of them down.

Far right:

An English flight engineer, Jack Wilson, of York, flew with a Canadian HCU crew from Dishforth. Canadian rations extended to soft drinks, Caporal cigarettes and doughnuts. Jack is seen here enjoying all of these at once before he found himself swinging on his 'chute after being hit by a German night-fighter near base on Sunday, 4 March 1945.

raids. The next couple of days were taken up by having clean clothing etc being dished out, photographs and details taken for "Kriegie" identification cards and POW number — I still have mine — medicals and allocation of billets. After this, I suppose it was a case of making the best of a bad job and settling in, for we were here for the duration.

'Apart from the privation, the feeling of being surrounded by barbed wire, being continually watched from the guard towers, and that ever-nagging thought — "how long will we be here and how long will it be before we hear from home?", one soon adapted to this new way of life. Camp life on the whole was not too bad. We were not forced to work, although many volunteered, for our own benefit, such as coal parties, rations, etc. Each barrack block held on average about 180 men, and each block had its own security officer, mail officer, parcels, rations, equipment, coal and education officers. There were the usual roll calls morning and night, and as the nights grew lighter, we were not locked in the barracks so early. It was a very good summer, and many spent the time getting sun-tanned, and making the most of the good weather. There were the usual escape attempts, as were common in other POW camps, but without success, due to the continual searching for tunnels, etc by the "ferrets", the offenders having to spend some time in the "cooler".'

Looking back on the events of that night, James Johnson set his memories down in verse:

How the years have passed since that dark March night,
When 'D-Dog', one of hundreds took part in the flight,
How well we'll remember the last hours of that day,
Till at last we were off and on our way.
The navigators had their 'film show', crew briefing was o'er,
We all stood nattering at the briefing room door;
To the crew of 'D-Dog' old Greenslade was talking;
'Remember Jock, let's not hear of you walking'.
Crew buses loaded, whizzed round to dispersals;
The last minute checks need no rehearsals;
Kites all lined up, such a wonderful sight,
Then the Skipper's 'this is it' as he gets the green light.
We're off at last to join up with the stream;
Aircraft above us, below, on our beam;
From 'D-Dog', all around us, planes by the score,
All circling round Flamborough, awaiting the hour.
At precisely the hour Jock gave his course,
'D-Dog' sets it nose like a well trained horse
Obeying the commands of the Skipper's touch,
With whom we always felt safe, we will all surely vouch.
The time passed quickly, crossed the enemy coast;
And we, like others in that mighty air host,
Sat at the ready, searching the skies,
Watching flak and tracers like giant fireflies.
Another course set, then the last leg in,
The leg to the target, that dreaded Berlin;
The Pathfinders had been there to start up the show,
And the second wave in set it really aglow.
The flak's getting thicker as we approach the scene
With its colourful setting, reds, orange and greens;
Joe's down in position, his bomb sight ready,
'Bomb doors open' he calls, then 'left, left, steady'.
'Bombs gone', he shouts; then rat-a-tat-tat,
The crew's cry in unison, 'What the h--- was that?'
An enemy fighter beneath us went zipping,
With a burst from his guns through our fuselage ripping.
That one small burst set our rest position aglow,
Alas, for us, this was to be our last show.
But God had been kind, the fire was put out,
We could still make a few miles without a doubt.
How many of us thought those moments our last,
Till the fire was out and the danger past?
And back in our positions, sitting there,
Offered to God his own silent prayer?
Taff checked the damage, what a terrible blow,
To the port engines no fuel would flow;
Main fuel cocks shattered, port wheel down,
Bomb doors open and the flaps half down.
How well we'll remember our terrible plight,
Port engines cutting, the plane losing height,
And the Skipper's struggles to keep the plane aright
While we made our jumps into the pitch-black night.
Then as we floated down on to a foreign shore,
'D-Dog' plunged earthwards and with a might roar
Burst into flames, his job was done,
Amongst the aircraft missing, we were one.
For us, like many others, the fighting was o'er,
Picked up next morning — prisoners of war.
Fourteen months behind wire then at last we were free,
Flying home once more, our loved ones to see.
Many years have now gone since those 'happy' days
When the 'Powers That Be' sent us our different ways,
But I hope in our hearts these memories we'll retain,
Till some day, perhaps, we can all meet again.

HP59/63 Halifax B/A/MET/GR Mk 2/5 srs 1a
August to December 1943

Type
Heavy bomber, general reconnaissance, met and airborne aircraft

Power Plant
Four 1,480hp Rolls-Royce Merlin 22 engines

Performance
Maximum speed: 250mph at 13,000ft
Cruising speed: 205mph at 20,000ft
Service ceiling: 21,000ft
Range: 1,660 miles

Armament
Eight .303in Browning machine guns mounted in the mid-upper and tail turrets; a Vickers K gun was sometimes fitted in the nose
Bomb load: 13,000lb

Weights
Empty: Mk 2 srs 1a, 35,577lb; Mk 5 srs 1a, 36,177lb
Loaded: Mk 2 srs 1a, 60,000lb; Mk 5 srs 1a, 61,500lb

Dimensions
Span: 98ft 8in
Length: 71ft 7in
Height: 20ft 9in

Above:
Halifax B Mk 2 srs 1, JD467:V of No 102 Squadron, flown by FS McPhail during a raid on Kassel on 3/4 October 1943. It was finally shot down over Frankfurt in December 1943.

Entry into Service Aug-Dec 1943

No Built	Type	Serial Block	Constructed
33	EE-built Halifax B Mk 2 srs 1a	LW223-LW345	Aug-Oct
75	EE-built Halifax B Mk 3	LW346-LW446	Oct-Dec
38	LAPG-built Halifax B/GR Mk 2 srs 1a	JN941-JN978	Sept-Nov
80	LAPG-built Halifax B/GR Mk 2 srs 1a	JP107-JP207	Nov-Dec
96	Fairey-built Halifax B/Met Mk 5 srs 1a	LK626-LK746	Aug-Dec
87	Rootes-built Halifax B/Met Mk 5 srs 1a	LK890-LK999	Oct-Dec
42	Rootes-built Halifax B/A/ Met Mk 5 srs 1a	LL112-LL153	Nov-Dec
12	Halifax B/GR Mk 2 srs 1a	HR977-HR988	Aug
49	Halifax B/GR Mk 2 srs 1a	HX147-HX225	Aug-Oct
101	Halifax B Mk 3	HX226-HX357	Sept 1943-Jan 1944

Unit	Representative Aircraft	Base
No 3 Group, Bomber Command		
138 Squadron	JD154, LW275, LL119, HX161, LK743	Tempsford
161 Squadron	LK899, LL120	Tempsford
No 4 Group, Bomber Command		
10 Squadron	LW332, HX179, JN948	Melbourne
51 Squadron	JD118, LK827, LW286, HX350	Snaith
76 Squadron	LK910, LW363, LL140	Holme-upon-Spalding Moor
77 Squadron	JD110, LW269, LL138	Elvington
78 Squadron	JD108, LK829, LW225, JN974, JP118	Breighton
102 Squadron	JD111, LW330, HX158, JN947	Pocklington
158 Squadron	JD115, HR978, LW297, HX340	Lissett
466 Squadron	LW372, HX337	Leconfield
No 6 (RCAF) Group, Bomber Command		
405 Squadron	JD124, HR984, HX147	Gransden Lodge/ Topcliffe
408 Squadron	JD107	Linton-on-Ouse
419 Squadron	JD114, LW325, HX189, JN953, JP111	Middleton St George
420 Squadron	LK996, LW383	Tholthorpe
424 Squadron	LW347, HX314	Skipton-on-Swale
425 Squadron	LW394	Tholthorpe
427 Squadron	LK920, LL153, HX339	Leeming
428 Squadron	LK836, LW326, JN967, JP113	Middleton St George
429 Squadron	LW285	Leeming
431 Squadron	LK833, LL150	Tholthorpe/Croft

Unit	Representative Aircraft	Base
433 Squadron	LW361, HX272	Skipton-on-Swale
434 Squadron	LK916, LL134	Tholthorpe/Croft
No 8 (Pathfinder) Group, Bomber Command		
35 Squadron	LW343, HR987, HX160, JN954, JP121	Graveley
No 18 Group, Coastal Command		
58 Squadron	HR982, HX178, JP165	Holmsley South
502 Squadron	HX175, JP164	Holmsley South
517 Squadron	LK962, LL117	St Davids
No 19 Group, Coastal Command		
518 Squadron	LK960	Stornaway/Tiree
No 38 Group		
295 Squadron	LK651	Hurn
298 Squadron	LL147, LK652	Tarrant Rushton
No 205 Group, MEAF		
148 Squadaron	JP179	Derna/Tocra
624 Squadron	JN941, JP176	Blida

61

CHAPTER 7

METAMORPHOS

By the autumn of 1942 losses of Halifaxes both on operations and in flying accidents around base had risen alarmingly. Careful analysis revealed three causes — the problem of rudder overbalance which A&AEE had noted during the aircraft's Service trials, reducing operational performance and some shortcomings in the training of new captains. Of these three, the rudder overbalance problem was to prove the most intractable. What was happening was this: when the rudder was used heavily to keep the aircraft straight, especially at the lower airspeeds, it could swing sharply over to extreme right or extreme left and stall, meaning that the aircraft was out of control in the lateral plane. If it happened on take-off, the aircraft would swing violently off the runway, if airborne it could sideslip into the ground or turn on to its back with the same result. If the overbalance occurred at altitude, the Halifax could go into an irrecoverable spin. Not only was the pilot physically incapable of straightening an overbalanced rudder, even the use of full rudder trim was either inadequate or aggravated the problem. The greatest

difficulty occurred if there was a loss of engine power, especially on take-off, and particularly if an engine failed on the port side where airscrew torque contributed to a tendency to roll to the left.

During 1942, various remedies had been tried. The movement of the rudder was restricted by the introduction of mechanical stops — but these became distorted and worn with use. A variety of aerodynamic solutions were then tried and finally bulbous noses were fitted to the rudders and after trials, made an official modification (No 413) to all Halifaxes in service and on the production line. This measure, too, proved only to be a short-term palliative and losses from rudder-overbalance persisted. The Halifax rudder problem became a matter of special study by the Bomber Performance Testing Flight at A&AEE, Boscombe Down, headed by Sqn Ldr D. Clyde Smith DSO, DFC. Two production Halifaxes, W7922 and W7917, both from No 103 Squadron were used for a variety of investigations into Halifax performance. W7917 was flown from Boscombe Down on 4 February 1943 by Flt Lt Reiss accompanied by a flight

Below:
Seen here in January 1942, W1005, an English Electric-built B Mk 2, joined No 102 Squadron and later No 1652 Heavy Conversion Unit, Marston Moor, where it was crash-landed by Flg Off Hagues.
London Transport

Left:
B Mk 2 srs 1, W7676, operated with No 35 Squadron from May to August 1942, when it was lost over Nuremberg. Sometimes the rudders overbalanced with such force that the rudder was whipped away in the slipstream, taking the top fin with it.
RAF Museum

Left:
This No 102 Squadron Halifax swung on landing at Dalton, and one leg of the undercarriage collapsed. Swings on take-off were almost impossible to correct due to the shortcomings in the design of the fins. *IWM*

Below:
London Passenger Transport began to produce the Halifax aircraft at Leavesden from the end of 1941. One of its buses shows very clearly the size of the Halifax. *London Transport*

engineer, FS Fielding and a civilian scientist, Mr J. J. Unwin, to conduct rudder trials at altitude. Observers on the ground saw the Halifax dive, go into a flat spin and then crash. From the wreckage it was discovered that the rudders had overbalanced with such violence that the top half of one of them had broken away. After further trials at A&AEE and by Handley Page, the entire rudder assembly was redesigned to give a 40% increase in the area of the fin, changing the profile from an arrow-head to a rectangle. The new assembly was fitted to the prototype Halifax B Mk 3 which was then under test and found to be an acceptable solution to the problem of overbalance and it was introduced on to the production line of all Halifaxes together with a massive modification programme of those already in service in mid-1943. Eventually some 600 aircraft were fitted with the new assembly.

But the rudder problem, serious as it was, was only part of the shortcomings of the Halifax as discerned in late 1942. In common with almost all other aircraft in front-line service, the early marks of Halifax were suffering from what might be called the 'Christmas-tree' syndrome. This was the outcome of a host of additions to all-up weight and all-up drag imposed by operational demands, but usually not compensated for by an increase in engine power with the result that performance suffered. Take-off runs were protracted to a dangerous extent, the aircraft climbed slowly and its ceiling was reduced as was its cruising speed. Examination of a Halifax B Mk 2 of No 10 Squadron showed what the problem was — all-up weight had risen by over 5,000lb. This was not helped either by the fact that when carrying the maximum load of two 4,000lb MC bombs, the bomb doors had to be partly open. Additional weight came from the added dorsal turret, and from other additions to internal equipment like armour plate. Extra drag also came from many sources

Above:

The first London Aircraft Production Group-produced aircraft in the BB series are shown off at a distinguished gathering at Leavesden in January 1942.
London Transport

Centre right:

The Maharajah of Nawangar visited No 35 (Pathfinder) Squadron at Graveley in October 1942. The photograph also shows evidence of another drama — in the search for an answer to Halifax crashes, the nose turret was to be removed. As can be seen here, they were disarmed and sealed as an interim measure. *Fox Photos*

Right:

L9515 was a test aircraft fitted with a new low-drag mid-upper turret, more powerful engines and a solid, neatly faired nose to be made in Perspex for the B Mk 2 srs 1a aircraft. Note the extended inboard nacelles.
Flight International

— not least the dorsal turret — and from the exhaust shrouds and less obvious sources like the rough black paint put on to stop the aircraft glinting in searchlights, and de-icing paste on the leading edges of control surfaces. During the autumn of 1942, the Halifax squadrons undertook fewer operations while their aircraft were cleaned up. Some squadrons did away with the dorsal turret altogether as they had done earlier with the nose turret. Others removed various items of armour plate and odd fittings like the barrage-balloon cable cutters and de-icing paste on the leading edges of control surfaces — in all cases preferring higher performance as more likely to contribute to their survival. Later there was a general change of dorsal turret by the introduction of the shallower and smaller Boulton Paul Mk 8 turret in the Halifax B Mk 2 srs 1a

As a result of these various measures, the performance of the Halifax B Mk 2s in the squadrons was improved, but only marginally. What was required was more engine power, and although various trials

Above:
The instrument panel of the Halifax B Mk 3 with the throttle and airscrew pitch levers prominent in the centre.
R. Hines

Centre left:
'D-Dog' of No 102 Squadron seen here at Pocklington during October 1942, was the mount of FS Dick Hubbard. It took a long time to remove the nose and mid-upper turrets, and the large heavy flame dampers are still apparent as the two outboard engines are run-up. This is a rare photograph as very few of these aircraft and crews survived operations for long.

Left:
Wg Cdr Smith and crew of No 78 Squadron based at Linton with the *Saint,* **LK645. The aircraft is the Halifax B Mk 2 srs 1 (Special) with shorter flame dampers and no nose or mid-upper turrets; the 'Tollerton' nose fairing shows up well against the sky.** *Mick Wright*

65

were carried out during 1943 to fit more powerful Merlins and improved propellers, none proved practical in view of the successful development of the Halifax B Mk3 fitted with four Bristol Hercules XVI engines each giving 1,615hp compared with the Merlin's 1,390hp. The first prototype Mk 3 flew in July 1943 and went into squadron service in November. During the winter of 1943-44, Halifax losses again rose disastrously and in January 1944, squadrons equipped with the Merlin-engined marks — the B Mk 2s and Mk 5s (Dowty undercarriage) were permanently suspended from operations against German targets. There was no such restriction upon the B Mk 3 which not only restored the Halifax's performance but went on to vindicate its reputation.

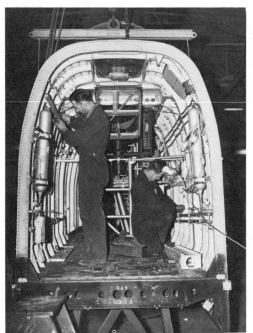

Far left top:
London Passenger Transport-produced B Mk 2 BB249 went to No 10 Squadron, then to No 158 and was lost over Gelsenkirchen in July 1943 operating with No 102 Squadron, Pocklington.
Fox Photos

Centre left:
Women mechanics are seen at work here on the undercarriage of London Passenger Transport-built BB252, delivered to No 77 Squadron. It soon passed to No 10 Squadron at Melbourne and was lost 'Gardening' (laying sea mines) on 9 January 1943, skippered by Sgt Fish. The Royal Netherlands Air Force found its remains during 1974.
Fox Photos

Far left bottom:
BB250, seen here at Chiswick in September 1942, failed to return from Stuttgart on 11/12 March 1943 whilst serving with No 405 Squadron RCAF, Leeming.
Fox Photos

Left:
London Aircraft Production Group (LPTB) produced the B Mk 2 srs 1a. A H2S scanner dome can be seen behind women mechanics in this view at Leavesden in late 1943.
Fox Photos

67

HP61 Halifax Mk 3
January to June 1944

Type
Heavy bomber and airborne
aircraft

Power Plant
Four 1,675hp Bristol
Hercules XVI engines

Performance
Maximum speed: 277mph at
6,000ft
Cruising speed: 225mph at
20,000ft
Service ceiling: 20,000ft
Range: 1,770 miles

Armament
Eight .303in Browning machine
guns in mid-upper and tail turrets
and provision for one Vickers
K gun in the nose. Some RCAF
units carried a .5in machine gun in
place of H2S in the ventral
position
Bomb load: 13,000lb

Weights
Empty: 38,332lb
Loaded: 65,000lb

Dimensions
Span: 104ft 2in
Length: 71ft 7in
Height: 20ft 9in

Entry into Service Jan-Jun 1944

No Built	Type	Serial Block	Constructed
225	Halifax B Mk 3	LV771-LW195	Jan-Mar
15	Halifax B Mk 7	LW196-LW210	May-Jun
43	Halifax B Mk 7	NP681-NP723	Jun-Jul
411	Rootes-built Halifax B/A/ Met Mk 5 srs 1a	LL167-LL542	Jan-Jun
60	Rootes-built Halifax B Mk 3	LL543-LL615	May-Jun
86	LAPG-built Halifax B/GR Mk 2 srs 1a	JP220-JP338	Feb-Jun
86	LAPG-built Halifax B Mk 3	MZ282-MZ378	Mar-Jun
104	Fairey-built Halifax B Mk 3	LK747-LK887	Jan-Jun
85	Fairey-built Halifax B Mk 3	NA492-NA587	Apr-Jul
40	EE-built Halifax B Mk 3	MZ500-MZ539	Mar-Aug
185	EE-built Halifax B/A Mk 3	LW459-LW724	May-Jun

Above right:
**'L-Love', HR928, a B Mk 2
srs 1a of No 35 (Pathfinder)
Squadron, was flown by Sqn Ldr
Alec Cranswick. The HR series
of airframes were the first to use
the new rectangular fins and
rudders which solved the rudder
lock-over problem once and for
all.** *RAF Museum*

Right:
**A Halifax B Mk 6 operating with
No 102 Squadron at Pocklington.
With new Hercules 100 engines,
Halifax performance reached a
peak in the B Mk 6.** *R. Lyne*

68

Unit	Representative Aircraft	Base
No 3 Group, Bomber Command		
138 Squadron	LL192	Tempsford
161 Squadron	LL183	Tempsford
No 4 Group, Bomber Command		
10 Squadron	MZ532, NA506, LW717, LL588	Melbourne
51 Squadron	LK885, LL328, MZ507, NA493, LV778, LW461	Snaith
76 Squadron	LK873, LL237, NA522, LW573, MZ309, LV869	Holme-upon-Spalding Moor
77 Squadron	LL239, MZ701, NA520, LW179	Full Sutton
78 Squadron	LK840, MZ516, NA495, LW501, LL546, LV788	Breighton
102 Squadron	MZ644, NA502, LL581, LW143	Pocklington
158 Squadron	LK826, MZ533, NA519, LW459, LL604, LV771	Lissett
346 Squadron	MZ709, LL551	Elvington
347 Squadron	LL507	Elvington
466 Squadron	MZ816, LL615, LV781	Driffield
578 Squadron	LK797, MZ508, NA501, LW586, LL548, LV937	Burn
640 Squadron	LK757, MZ500, NA492, LW549, LL543	Leconfield
No 6 (RCAF) Group, Bomber Command		
420 Squadron	LK884, MZ502, LW197, LL550, NP682	Tholthorpe
424 Squadron	MZ754, LW460, LV780	Skipton-on-Swale
425 Squadron	LK796, MZ525, NA505, LW467, LL576	Tholthorpe
426 Squadron	LK879, MZ589, NA518, LW117, NP684	Linton
427 Squadron	LK900, LL194, MZ756, LW548, LV821	Leeming
429 Squadron	LK800, MZ864, LW685, LV913	Leeming
431 Squadron	MZ509, NA498, LV951	Croft
432 Squadron	LK764, MZ504, NA500, LW595, LL432, NP688	East Moor
433 Squadron	LV797	Skipton-on-Swale
434 Squadron	LL247, MZ716, NA510	Croft
No 8 (Pathfinder) Group, Bomber Command		
35 Squadron	LV782	Graveley
No 100 (Bomber Support) Group, Bomber Command		
192 Squadron	LK780, MZ501, NA494, LW613	Foulsham
No 18 Group, Coastal Command		
58 Squadron	JP296	St Davids
502 Squadron	JP297	St Davids
517 Squadron	LL220	St Davids/Brawdy
No 19 Group, Coastal Command		
518 Squadron	LL296	Tiree
520 Squadron	LL195	Gibraltar
No 38 Group		
298 Squadron	LL217	Tarrant Rushton
644 Squadron	LL228	Tarrant Rushton
No 205 Group, MEAF		
148 Squadron	JP284	Brindisi
462 Squadron	LL609	Celone
614 Squadron	JP241	Celone
624 Squadron	JP231	Brindisi/Blida

Far left:
Halifax B Mk 3, LV907:F of No 158 Squadron was flown by many crews until *Friday the 13th* retired with 128 operations to its credit in 1945.

CHAPTER 8

HALIFAX VC

H. D. Wood

Flg Off H. D. Wood flew as an air gunner in Halifax LK979:E of No 578 Squadron when it took part in the disastrous raid on Nuremberg on 30 March 1944. His captain was Plt Off C. J. Barton and this is his story of that night:

'At 10 minutes past 10 on 30 March 1944, the weather was cloudy with occasional showers, and visibility was moderate. A total of 14 Halifaxes of No 578 Squadron were detailed for the trip to Nuremberg, two of these were cancelled before take-off. Finally, 12 aircraft set out between 2min and 26min past 10. Engine trouble caused two Halifaxes to abandon their mission: one landed at Snetterton Heath and the other returned to Burn. Thus 10 aircraft and their crews represented the squadron and bombed Germany, including "E-Easy" in which I occupied the mid-upper turret.

'After crossing the enemy coast to the usual welcome from flak and searchlight emplacements, I several times witnessed the result of German fighter activity as streams of coloured tracer cannon shells appeared in the sky and a British bomber flared into flames, fell into a fiery curve and dropped like a large ball of fire from the sky. The blazing path through the clouds, which was followed by a brief but bright flash lighting up the cloud carpet, told its all too vivid story. Occasionally an exchange of tracer would appear, .303in bullets against the German cannon shells, and from these contests it mostly was the bomber which fell away. Sometimes but rarely, the ball of fire was smaller as a fighter fell into the clouds, though the illumination beneath the clouds cheered those of us left to fly on.

'We flew unmolested on the long leg across Germany until we were approxi-

Right:
Framed by the gaunt and tattered sails of the windmill at Melbourne, Flt Lt Gordon Culverhouse banks 'S-Sugar' of No 10 Squadron on to course for the coast and another sortie over Germany. *IWM*

Below:
Plt Off Barton's crew: left, standing, Sgt J. Kay, wireless operator; Flg Off Crate, bomb aimer; Plt Off C. J. Barton, pilot; Sgt L. Lambert, navigator; and Sgt M. Trousdale, flight engineer. At the front are Sgt F. Brice, rear gunner, and Sgt H. D. Wood, mid-upper gunner.

mately 70 miles from Nuremberg. Cy Barton, our pilot, had just instructed that we should keep a sharp look-out, as soon we would be turning on to the course which would take us over the target. We were in a steep bank to port, a move taken to provide an opportunity for the area below us to be checked, when there were a series of bangs, a voice called out an evasive action command, the Halifax shuddered, went into a slight dive and the intercom became dead. Cy took the required corkscrew action but we had been hit in the starboard inner engine and the nose by a Ju88 attacking from the starboard bow.

'When I heard the evasive action call I rotated my turret, at the same time elevating my four Browning .303in machine guns and fired blindly to the rear: only one gun operated, the others were frozen fast. During a turn to port I spotted the Ju88 beneath us and with my one Browning I fired a long burst with it, but the Ju88 flew away into the darkness and out of sight.

'Although we were without means of speaking to each other we did have an emergency method of communication, in the form of an intercall light, and by pressing a button it was possible to send messages. Early in our training days as a crew we had devised our own code, using Morse, for contacting each other. The call for Cy to resume course was the letter "R" or a series of . - . (dot-dash-dot), these were sent and we resumed course. Moments later the Ju88 reappeared on our port beam and I sent a series of dots, this was the signal for Cy to resume the corkscrew action, beginning with a diving turn to port. During this, an Me410 joined the fight from up front and I saw the tracer it fired fly harmlessly over our heads to the rear. I had a brief glimpse of the Messerschmitt in silhouette as it sped past.

'We lost the Me410 and Ju88 and I sent Cy the "resume course" signal. He brought the Halifax back to straight and level flight; when first attacked we were at our maximum height, at the end we were down to 9,000ft.

'It was during the use of the intercall light that the bomb-aimer, navigator and wireless operator/air gunner misunderstood one of the signals and baled out. In spite of this Cy flew on and, as we thought, bombed the target indicators shining over Nuremberg. We did not find out until many years later that our bombs were in fact dropped on an unhappy Schweinfurt.

'The starboard inner engine had been vibrating furiously and evidently had been badly damaged. Eventually its propeller, which was red hot, tore loose and flew up and away into the night, looking like an enormous Catherine Wheel. The engine did not catch fire but threw sparks back briefly. These ceased and the engine died.

'After dropping our bomb load Cy flew well past the blazing town before turning on to a direct heading for home. We had once before landed at the emergency aerodrome at Woodbridge, and it is likely that Cy had this in mind when setting course. Using his captain's map and with the stars and compass to steer by he flew the Halifax across the enemy territory, avoiding bunches of searchlights en route. During this part of the journey, and despite an absence of power from the starboard inner engine, Cy managed to increase our altitude so that when we crossed the French coast we were at 13,000ft.

'We were well into the return journey when Maurice Trousdale, our flight engineer, came down the fuselage and told me what had happened. We still had a long way to go and we were without three very important members of our crew. My first reaction was to ask about the fuel position and when Maurice told me that we had sufficient to see us back home I opted to press on. This coincided with votes from Cy and Maurice, they too voted for the return attempt. Shortly after this I left my turret, on instructions from Cy, and made my way further down the fuselage to Fred Brice, in the rear turret, where I told him about the situation and the decision to carry on.

'Immediately following I went up front to tackle the navigational aids in an attempt to plot our position. Cy had insisted that each crew member should have some experience of the work in the aircraft of the others, and on the ground I had achieved some success using the Gee set. Unfortunately the set must have suffered the same fate as the radio, which was shattered, and despite all my efforts I was unable to secure any guide. The underside of the navigator's desk was badly holed and the maps inside the draw were torn to shreds by exploding cannon shells.

'When I descended the steps into the nose of the aircraft I was met by a forceful

72

stream of air which came into the plane through the square hole in the floor, left when the escape hatch was jettisoned prior to the navigator, bomb-aimer and wireless operator/air gunner baling out.

'It was still dark when we crossed the enemy coast and after a long time over water it was suggested that if some searchlights avoided earlier had surrounded Frankfurt (as at that time we had thought), and as we were heading due west, we could be flying over the English Channel. It was, in the circumstances, decided that we should turn north. Had we but known it we were at that time not more than 20min flying time from the emergency aerodrome at Woodbridge. We maintained the new course until we crossed some lights in the sea, which were taken to be convoy marking lights. At this point Cy returned to a westerly heading, and as he did so the grey of dawn became brighter so that we were able to see a Beaufighter fly past us. Hurriedly using the Very pistol we fired off the distress signal, but the Beaufighter pilot, having identified us, flew on into the morning mist and out of sight.

'Like all Allied aircraft we carried an IFF set which was designed to identify us as friendly, but this was out of action. The Beaufighter had been sent out to intercept an unidentified aircraft approaching the coast and we had been recognised by him. Searchlights had been raised and although our radio and intercom were not working, we were able to receive the squeaker sounds emitted from these; the ground defences failed to recognise us and we were fired upon. Cy as a result turned on to a reciprocal course and flew back out to sea. In the nose I connected up the Aldis lamp and was signalling SOS; I was also sending a message to say we were friendly. The firing stopped and I made my way back, avoiding the open escape hatch, and as I reached the cockpit Cy called to me to "Get back quickly, we're going to crash!" The fuel pipes from one of the petrol tanks had been severed during the attack, and when Maurice switched over, the fuel ran out instead of into the engines.

'I rushed back down the fuselage, climbed over the rear spar, and had just settled in my crash position when the first bump came. I was knocked out and when I came round it was to the sound of Maurice's voice urgently calling to Fred to "Get off me bloody leg". I looked over and saw Fred trying to get out of the fuselage through the escape hatch above the crash position. (Maurice had taken the starboard side crash position and was badly injured in the crash when the flap accumulator burst, and for several days he was on the danger list.)

'In our descent, and despite strenuous efforts, Cy was unable to avoid the end of a row of houses, one was demolished and its neighbour slightly damaged. The momentum carried the Halifax into the yard of Ryhope Colliery (near Sunderland) where it broke into several parts and that carrying Maurice, Fred and I came to rest at the foot of a hill.

'Cy survived the crash for 30 minutes, so a very pretty nurse told me, and he was saved much suffering when claimed by the Maker he loved so dearly. He was conscious briefly before he died and his last words asked after Maurice, Fred and me. We very regrettably injured a miner who was on his way to work, and to our great sorrow another was killed. This part of the fateful occasion I did not learn about until many years later.

'We were helped out of the fuselage by a group of miners and taken to their first aid room, where we were given steaming hot cups of very sweet tea. It remains in my memory after all these years how kind and how compassionate the miners were to us.

'Realising that our squadron commander would want to know that we were back, I asked if I might be permitted to use the colliery 'phone. After a long time spent trying to convince the telephone operator that it was imperative I be put through to squadron headquarters, but to no avail, I

HP61 Halifax Mk 6
July 1944 to February 1945

Type
Heavy bomber, airborne and met aircraft

Power Plant
Four 1,680hp Bristol Hercules 100 engines

Performance
Maximum speed: 290mph at 9,000ft
Cruising speed: 230mph at 20,000ft
Service ceiling: 22,000ft
Range: 2,500 miles

Armament
Eight .303in Browning machine guns and a Vickers K gun in the nose
Bomb load: 12,000lb

Weights
Empty: 38,300lb
Loaded: 65,000lb (some cleared to 68,000lb)

Dimensions
Span: 104ft 2in
Length: 71ft 7in
Height: 20ft 9in

Above:
Halifax B Mk 6, NP763:N of No 346 Squadron, Free French Air Force, produced September 1944. The aircraft survived the war and was scrapped during 1949.

Entry into Service Jul 1944-Feb 1945

No Built	Type	Serial Block	Constructed
184	Rootes-built Halifax B/A/ Met Mk 3	MZ945-NA263	Aug 1944-Jan 1945
319	EE-built Halifax B Mk 3	MZ540-MZ939	Aug
59	EE-built Halifax B Mk 3	NP930-NP999	Sept
141	EE-built Halifax B Mk 3	NR113-NR290	Aug 1944-Feb 1945
95	LAPG-built Halifax B Mk 3	MZ390-MZ495	Aug-Nov
80	LAPG-built Halifax B Mk 3	PN365-PN461	Nov 1944-Feb 1945
95	Fairey-built Halifax B/A Mk 3	NA599-NA704	Jul-Nov
41	Fairey-built Halifax B Mk 3	PN167-PN207	Oct 1944-Feb 1945
157	Halifax B Mks 3, 6, 7	NP736-NP927	Aug-Dec

Unit	Representative Aircraft	Base
No 3 Group, Bomber Command		
161 Squadron	LL534	Tempsford
No 4 Group, Bomber Command		
10 Squadron	NA627, NP994, LL588, MZ398	Melbourne
51 Squadron	NA626, NP933, PN184, MZ401, MZ566	Snaith
76 Squadron	NA623, LL578, MZ460	Holme-upon-Spalding Moor
77 Squadron	PN175, NA109, LL555, MZ393	Full Sutton
78 Squadron	NP930, NA164, LL546, MZ391, MZ557	Breighton
102 Squadron	NA599, NP950, PN176, LL581, MZ426	Pocklington
158 Squadron	NP876, NA194, MZ408, MZ567	Lissett
346 Squadron	NA615, PN170, LL551, MZ472	Elvington
347 Squadron	NA606, NR153, PN167, LL587, MZ489	Elvington
462 Squadron	NA622, NR119, PN168, LL610, MZ457	Driffield
466 Squadron	NP931, PN181, NA199, MZ395	Driffield
578 Squadron	NA601, NR150, LL548, MZ485, MZ556	Burn
640 Squadron	NP923, PN182, NA222, LL543, MZ394	Leconfield
No 6 (RCAF) Group, Bomber Command		
408 Squadron	NP744	Linton-on-Ouse
415 Squadron	NA600, NR156, PN174, LL594, MZ476	East Moor
420 Squadron	NA610, NR207, LL550, MZ471	Tholthorpe
424 Squadron	NP936, MZ418	Skipton-on-Swale
425 Squadron	NA612, PN173, LL576, MZ466	Tholthorpe
426 Squadron	NP737, MZ469	Linton-on-Ouse
427 Squadron	NP941, MZ423	Leeming
429 Squadron	NP943, NA179, MZ424	Leeming
431 Squadron	MZ405	Croft

Unit	Representative Aircraft	Base
432 Squadron	NP736, LL547	East Moor
433 Squadron	NP935, MZ417	Skipton-on-Swale
434 Squadron	MZ420	Croft

No 100 (Bomber Support) Group, Bomber Command

171 Squadron	NA673, NR244, PN169, MZ491	North Creake
192 Squadron	NP970, NA187, MZ449	Foulsham

No 18 Group, Coastal Command

517 Squadron	LL485	Brawdy
520 Squadron	NA136, LL518	Gibraltar

No 19 Group, Coastal Command

58 Squadron	NA226	Stornaway
502 Squadron	PN199, NA262	Stornaway
518 Squadron	PN187, NA142, LL514, MZ462	Tiree

No 38 Group, Transport Command

96 Squadron	PN185, NA232	Leconfield
296 Squadron	NA638	Earls Colne
297 Squadron	NA637, NP794	Earls Colne
298 Squadron	NA613, MZ955	Tarrant Rushton
644 Squadron	NA636, MZ957	Tarrant Rushton

Left:
In high spirits, Plt Off S. McDonald (*left*) and his crew of No 466 Squadron pose for the camera on their return to Driffield from Berlin on 21 January 1944. Other crews were less fortunate: 22 Halifaxes failed to return that night.
Australian War Memorial

asked her to contact the wing commander and request that he telephone me. Before and after an operation calls in and out of the camp were not allowed, which was why I had difficulty getting through. Wg Cdr Wilkerson came on the line eventually and I told him about our misfortune. He asked about Cy; at that time I was unaware that Cy had been mortally injured, and I told him that we had all survived.

'From the colliery we were transferred to Cherry Knowle Hospital and placed in the emergency ward under the care of the wonderful Sister Herbert and her lovely nurses. Fred and I had back injuries, whilst Maurice needed several blood transfusions.

'Two events emerged from this operation which are difficult to explain: firstly, prior to take-off, whilst waiting for the crew bus to take us out to our aircraft, Cy used his torch to test us in the Morse emergency intercall light signals. He had not checked on this previously; secondly, what prompted me to leave the nose after signalling with the Aldis lamp? Had I delayed it many minutes it is certain I would not be writing this.

'Maurice received an immediate award of the Distinguished Flying Medal, for the part he played in bringing us back. Fred and I received ours some little while later. Cy Barton, the pilot, and whom this story is all about, received the Victoria Cross posthumously.'

Meanwhile the war went on.

YORKSHIRE'S OW

79

| Year | | AIRCRAFT | | Pilot, or | 2nd Pilot, Pupil | DUTY |
Month	Date	Type	No.	1st Pilot	or Passenger	(Including Results and Remarks)
—	—	—	—	—	—	— Totals Brought Forward
Aug.	2	HALIFAX	E	SELF	CREW	OPERATIONS. HAMBURG.
	5	HALIFAX	G	SELF	CREW. F/S. SCHOFIELD	FORMATION
	22	HALIFAX	H	SELF	CREW	OPERATIONS LEVERKUSEN.
						Ju. 88 SHOT DOWN. CONFIRMED.
	23	HALIFAX	E.	SELF	CREW SGT. AINSWORTH	OPERATIONS. BERLIN
	27	HALIFAX	E	SELF	CREW	OPERATIONS. NUREMBURG. 3 ENEMY N/Fs. ʙ⸌ ATTACKED. ATTACK BEATEN of
	29	HALIFAX	E	SELF	SGT. AINSWORTH CREW	RETURN FROM STANTON HARCOURT.
	30	HALIFAX	A V	SELF	CREW	OPERATIONS. BERLIN. ENGINES 4/S MÜNCHEN GLADBACH
	31	HALIFAX	A.	SELF	CREW	OPERATIONS. BERLIN. ENGINES. U/S

SUMMARY FOR AUGUST 1943
UNIT. 10 SQDN.
DATE. 4ᵗʰ Sept. 1943.   A/C TYPE HALIFAX
SIGNATURE. EBGoodall.

EB Dunn S/Ldr.
O.C. "A" FLT.   Plus 7½ hrs

GRAND TOTAL [Cols. (1) to (10)]
589 Hrs. 30 Mins.   Totals Carried Forward

Top:

A group of three Halifax B Mk 2 srs 1a of No 158 Squadron, Lissett, set course for Germany. The odds against at least one of them failing to return were high. *IWM*

Centre right:

The flying log-book of Flt Lt E. B. Goodall of No 10 Squadron which records a series of operations over Hamburg, Leverkusen, Berlin, Nuremberg and München Gladbach. On one occasion a Junkers Ju88 night-fighter was shot down, and on another a return was made with one or more engines out of action. *E. B. Goodall*

Right:

'G-George' of No 408 'Goose' Squadron, RCAF, stands by to receive its HE and incendiary load at Linton on 10 August 1943.
Public Archives of Canada

Left:
**Three RAAF Halifaxes are seen
here being serviced in the hangar
at Driffield under powerful
arclights.**

Below:
**The Halifax Mk 5 srs 1a became
available in March 1943; this
one, *Zombie IV*, belonged to
No 408 'Goose' Squadron,
RCAF, based at Lington-on-
Ouse. At view the Halifax Mk 5
srs 1a was identical to the Mk 2
srs 1a, apart from the Dowty
landing gear.**
Public Archives of Canada

Right:

During the war years women filled many of the ground jobs on RAF stations normally held by men. In this photograph a lady crew bus driver is seen at Leeming. *D. Petty*

Below:

As soon as aircraft landed, petrol bowsers would race to dispersals and replenish the Halifaxes' empty tanks. A Matador bowser is seen here at Leeming with a No 429 Squadron aircraft. *D. Petty*

Top right:

At Tholthorpe *The Fiery Queen* **took to the air. She was carried aloft by a Halifax Mk 3 of No 425 'Alouette' Squadron, RCAF, which was designated as a French-Canadian unit.**

Far right top:

With a bomb log stretching almost off the aircraft, a quotation from St Luke adorns this No 432 Squadron, RCAF Halifax at East Moor. *W. E. Miller (via Mick Wright)*

Bottom right:

This Halifax named *Trixie*, **of No 466 Squadron, RAAF, was hit by a night-fighter which left a damaged forward bomb bay and a cowling hanging, but** *Trixie* **managed to land safely.** *F. Nicholson*

Far right bottom:

Embraceable U **was a Halifax B Mk 7, NP742, of No 408 'Goose' Squadron, RCAF, based at Linton. Many of the Canadians used the Black Swan public house in York as a watering hole, so the use of a foaming tankard to remind the crew of what awaited them on return from ops was particularly apt.** *J. Muirhead (via Mick Wright)*

Left:
This No 462 Squadron machine made it back to a hard fast landing at Driffield.

83

CHAPTER 10

'PREPARE TO DIT

From time to time throughout the long Bomber Command offensive, intrepid reporters from newspapers and the BBC flew on operations with bomber crews. Here is the transcript of a recording made by the BBC in 1943 reporting the experiences of a No 78 Squadron crew based at Breighton near Selby, Yorkshire, flying Halifax Mk 3, JD157, on an operation against Gelsenkirchen in the Ruhr Valley. (The rather bizarre sound effects are the BBC's own idea of what bomber operations sounded like.)

Announcer: Into battle: The fighting spirit of the United Nations.

Effects: *Up 'Lilliburlero' and out.*

Announcer: Tonight we tell the story of a journey from the Ruhr — the story of a crew of seven young men in a Halifax, one of a great force of bombers which recently attacked Gelsenkirchen. Their captain was a sergeant pilot from Ayrshire.

Jock: We were all sergeants in that crew, and we were flying together for the first time. Three of us were Scots: myself — the lads called me Jock, of course — the wireless operator and Sandy the bomb-aimer. Sandy was 29, the old man of the party.
Well, we got to the Ruhr all right, flying over thick cloud, and the fun started as we were over the target . . .

Effects: *Drone of aero engines.*

Jock (on intercom): Now ready, Sandy. I'm going down. Then I'll straighten out, giving you a level run. Carry on.

Effects: *Accelerated aero engines; flak.*

Navigator: That's more flak coming up. Gosh! They ought to see us now all right.

Mid-upper gunner: We're in a searchlight fix.

Jock: Then we'll give 'em a present of this lot. Bomb doors open.

Sandy: Bomb doors open, Jock. Just keep her like this.

Effects: *Flak; a crash; stuttering engines.*

Engineer: Look out! That hit us! The inner

port engine's burning. Feather that prop, Jock.

Jock: Take it easy now, take it easy. The engine's cut out, but everything's under control. Carry on, Sandy and snap into it.

Sandy: Steady, Jock, steady. Hold her. That's it! Bombs gone!

Gunner: Boy! Did she buck when the lot left her.

Wireless operator: You won't see the bursts in that mess. There's hardly a dark spot left.

Effects: *Flak*

Jock: And there won't be a dark spot left up here if we don't get out of it. I'm heading for home pdq. Hullo! The bomb doors have jammed. That flak got 'em.

Engineer: What about the emergency gear, Jock?

Jock: That's jammed too. We're in for a nice trip back — on three engines and with the bomb doors slowing us down.

Navigator: That's fine. You could climb out and pick daisies at this speed.

Wireless operator: All we need, Skipper, is a good strong headwind, just to cheer us up.

Navigator: Don't worry my lad. We've got that too.

Narrator: So with the bomb doors open and the speed considerably reduced, the damaged Halifax sets course to England on three engines.

Effects: *Drone of labouring engines.*

Navigator: We ought to reach the coast in about 15 minutes, Skipper.

Jock: It'll be a pleasure to see it. We'll be lucky to get back for a lunch at this rate.

Engineer: Try and boost it up, Jock. I've got a date with a corporal after dinner.

Jock: A corporal! WAAF or RAF?

Engineer: WAAF, of course.

Sandy: A corporal! The man's slumming!

Mid-upper gunner: Mid-upper here, Skipper. Fighter closing in on the starboard beam.

Rear gunner: It's a ME110, Jock. Here it is!

Effects: *Bullets: MG fire.*

Mid-upper gunner: He's turning in again. Swing her to starboard, Jock.

Effects: *Zoom of planes.*

Rear gunner: He's after our tail. Coming in now.

Effects: *MG fire; splintering noise.*

Rear gunner: Rear gunner here, Jock. (*grunts*) He's put the guns out.

Jock: Are you hurt?

Rear gunner: Yes, I think so. (*grunts*) A bit.

Mid-upper gunner: He's coming back. Better start weaving, Jock.

Effects: *MG; splintering noises.*

Wireless operator: Sparks here. Fire in the oxygen tubes. The cabin's hit.

Mid-upper gunner: Keep her steady, Jock! He's coming round. Hold your horses!

Effects: *MG burst.*

Mid-upper gunner: Got him! Got him! He's burning! He's going down!

Effects: *Whine of plane going down.*

Jock: Good work, laddie. You all right back there?

Rear gunner: (*grunts*). No, I can't move. The turret's jammed.

Jock: We'll dig you out. Upper, go along and look after him. How are you getting on with that fire, Sparks?

Wireless operator: The extinguisher's smashed. I can't get the flames out. I can feel the heat coming up through the floor.

Narrator: The wireless operator and the bomb-aimer eventually manage to smother the flames. The upper gunner hacks away at the jammed doors of the rear turret and releases the wounded rear gunner. The badly damaged Halifax drones slowly on, steadily nearing the French coast . . .

Engineer: Aircraft ahead, Jock. Looks like a Focke Wulf.

Jock: All right. It's no good staying up here at this speed. We'll go right down and dust the waves off going back.

Effects: *Power dive, tapering into steady drone.*

Mid-upper gunner: That's shaken 'em off. Struth! What's our height? Six feet?

Jock: I don't know. The instruments don't feel very well. Navigator: got any idea of a course? The compasses aren't working.

Navigator: What about getting a radio fix?

Wireless operator: With what? The set's full of holes.

Navigator: Well, your guess is as good as mine, Jock. We ditched the maps getting the fire out, but I'd say that if you keep her nose straight ahead we might cross the coast around Margate.

Engineer: Margate! Gosh! Put me down at Dreamland with that corporal, Jock. That's all I ask.

Mid-upper gunner: Hullo, Skipper, upper here. Land ahead.

Jock: Good.

Engineer: There it is, Jock. I can darned nearly see that corporal.

Jock: Keep an eye out for a landing field.

Mid-upper gunner: There's a cloud bank over the coastline.

Effects: *Drone of engines; spluttering.*

Jock: That's the port outer engine gone. It's seized up.

Engineer: That would happen.

Jock: Take your ditching positions. I'm going to try landing near the coast. In the drink.

Effects: *Drone of engines; more spluttering.*

Engineer: Inner starboard engine cut out, Skipper.

Jock: I know, I know. We've still got one left, haven't we? How far are we off the land?

Navigator: I'd guess a mile.

Jock: We won't make it. But we'll try.

Effects: *Engine with splutter: engine cuts out.*

Jock: Here we go!

Effects: *Windrush of plane; crash of water; lapping of waves.*

Jock: Open the escape hatch. Get on the port wing and get the dinghy out. Someone help the rear gunner.

Sandy: I'll look after him. Come on lad. Put your arms round here: That's it; you'll be all right.

Navigator: Dinghy's no good, Jock. It's in ribbons. It looks like a swimming job to me.

Jock: You'd need to be a pickled herring to swim in a sea like this. That coast may not look so far in the moonlight, but it's too far for any of us. I'll try a Very light.

Effects: Explosion and rocket noise of a Very light.

Sandy: That's a bad light for the complexion. You look quite green without your make-up on, Jock.

Jock: If this wing doesn't stop rolling I'll be greener still in a few minutes.

Mid-upper gunner: I never did like being on the sea. I'd rather be in it. I'm going to swim. I reckon I can get that far.

Operator: Same here. I'll come with you. We'll send you a rowing boat if ever we get there. So long!

Gunner: So long!

Effects: Two splashes, as of men diving; lapping of waves.

Engineer: Gosh! This is worse than a switchback.

Jock: Just keep a good grip and don't worry. They'll have seen our light from

the coast. They'll pick us up. How are you, gunner?

Rear gunner: I'm not so bad.

Jock: You'll be all right. A few days in hospital, perhaps, but you'll be all right, laddie. Just relax; we've got hold of you.

Effects: *Speedboat in distance; waves.*

Sandy; What's that, Skipper?

Jock: Just another aircraft getting home, I guess.

Sandy: Wait a minute! It isn't. That's no aircraft! They must have seen us. That's a rescue launch. Send up another light.

Effects: *Very light; speedboat; waves.*

Jock: There she is! You can see the wake. They'd better hurry up. We won't float much longer. I wonder how deep it is. I never learned to swim.

Engineer: You'll get a free lesson now, Jock. That ought to appeal to the Scotsman in you. Send 'em another flare.

Rear gunner: Look out! I'm slipping!

Effects: *Splash; lapping of waves; speedboat.*

Jock: He's overboard. Chuck him a line.

Navigator: I'll go in; wait a second.

Jock: Ahoy there!

Effects: *Speedboat; loud; spluttering engine; stops.*

Sailor: Ahoy there!

Jock: Wounded man overboard. Can you help him first?

Sailor: We'll get him. Put that beam on, Jim. There he is.

Effects: *Chugging of boat at slow speed.*

Sailor: Give us a hand with him. That's right. Over you come. Mind his leg. That's it. Get some blankets on him. Hi there! Grab this line. We'll tow you in.

Jock: Okay.

Sailor: You can wade ashore in another 100yds.

Effects: *Chugging of speed boat at slow speed; slight bump.*

Jock: That's it, lads, back home and broke. We've grounded.

Shout: (off) Hi, there!

Engineer: That'll be Sparks and upper gunner. Still swimming for it.

Effects: *Chugging of boat.*

Jock: They're picking 'em up alright. Come on. Let's get wet.

Engineer: I always did like a nice paddle. Here goes. Gosh! It's that corporal's lucky day. She darned nearly lost me.

Effects: *Up 'Lilliburlero' — peak and out.*

Announcer: *That's how a crippled Halifax returned from the Ruhr.*

CHAPTER II

SPECIAL OPERA

The term 'Special Operations' was applied to a variety of air force activities conducted in support of several organisations engaged in undercover or clandestine warfare within enemy or enemy-occupied territory. These ranged from the delivery of single agents for the Secret Intelligence Service (SIS or MI6) by parachute or actual landing, through the delivery of groups of agents, instructors and radio equipment by similar methods for SOE (the Special Operations Executive, formed to organise resistance and sabotage), to the dropping of arms and supplies to resistance groups throughout Europe, the parachuting in of Special Air Service teams on sabotage missions, and support for MI9 in the setting up of escape networks.

Although at times such operations were carried out by ordinary bomber squadrons or, for example, during the build-up for the invasion of Normandy by the airborne squadrons of Nos 38 and 46 Groups, most of them were conducted by 'Special Duties' (SD) squadrons equipped with a variety of aircraft types for what became a highly professional and hazardous role.

The first of these SD squadrons was No 138 which formed at Newmarket in August 1941 with the one flight of Lysanders and one of Whitleys; the latter, lacking the range to operate over Poland were augmented by Halifaxes in October 1941. These aircraft, all B Mk 2s, were sent to Ringway for special modification. A special parachute hatch was fitted, as was a winch for recovering static lines, and special fairings to protect the tailwheel, fins and rudders from static lines and containers. These Halifaxes were initially flown by Polish crews who, during the long dark winter nights went as far east as Warsaw, a round trip of some 2,000 miles, to supply the very active Polish Home Army. The first sortie took place on 7/8 November 1941 in L9612 and was flown by Wg Cdr Rudkowski. The drop was successfully completed but strong headwinds and icing were encountered on the way back and Wg Cdr Rudkowski crashlanded in neutral Sweden. The aircraft was

destroyed but the crew survived and was back on the squadron early in 1943.

No 138 Squadron moved to Tempsford near Sandy in Bedfordshire in March 1942 to join a second SD squadron, No 161, which had been formed there a month earlier. It also had a flight of Lysanders and one of Whitleys but did not receive its Halifaxes until October 1942. This coming together under one roof of both SD squadrons also put them under the direct control of the Assistant Chief of Air Staff (Intelligence) in Air Ministry rather than Bomber Command, although No 138 continued for some time to fly ordinary bombing sorties under the auspices of No 3 Group — an arrangement to placate 'Bomber' Harris over the 'loss' of his precious Halifaxes. The move also made Tempsford the primary RAF 'cloak and dagger' airfield, a role it fulfilled for the rest of the war. And as the activities of SOE steadily expanded into the Mediterranean and the Balkans, the first overseas SD flight, No 1575, equipped with Halifaxes and Lockheed Venturas, was formed at Tempsford in May 1943. It operated over Corsica, Sardinia and Italy from a number of bases in North Africa and became No 624 (SD) Squadron in November 1943 when its missions extended into Czechoslovakia. Then from February 1944, preceding the invasions, it operated exclusively over southern France. A second SD squadron, No 148, was formed in North Africa early in 1943 and had both Halifaxes and Liberators. It operated over southern Europe and the Balkans and later moved to Brindisi in southern Italy. For operations over Poland, a Polish SD squadron, No 301, also equipped with Liberators and Halifaxes, was formed in November 1944 on the same base.

Special duties operations were highly individual affairs with none of the mass briefings and mass take-offs of Bomber Command. With the lives of dozens of agents and freedom fighters at stake, the need for secrecy and security was paramount and all information was passed on a

Right:

B Mk 2 srs 1, W7773, produced by Handley Page, is seen here on a check flight at the end of June 1942. The aircraft was lost on operations with No 138 (Special Duties) Squadron on 30 October 1942. Note the large asbestos exhaust shrouds intended to shield the unhealthy exhaust glow. *Flight International*

Below right:

No 148 (SD) Squadron was also operational in the Western Desert; *Maid of the Mountains* **is seen here at Derna with air and ground crews.**

ONS

strict 'need to know' basis. Crews were briefed individually, knew nothing of other squadron activities, and usually only the pilot and navigator knew the location of the Drop Zone (DZ) in case captured crews inadvertently gave away vital information. Crews also operated alone and unaware of what other crews were doing. Finding isolated fields in the heart of enemy territory was a difficult and dangerous business in the absence of navigational aids — although some use of Gee and Rebecca/Eureka was made — but especially in south and east Europe, total dependency on map-reading and the 'Mk 1 Eyeball' for the drop itself was essential. Inevitably, this meant keeping contact with the ground by flying at low altitude in all sorts of weather and all sorts of terrain, often at the limits of aircraft radius of action despite additional fuel tankage and reduced equipment. As one SD crew member put it: 'Normally we were on our own, below 10,000ft because we carried no oxygen and no armament, looking for a special field in some country or other . . .'.

Below:
These Halifax B Mk 5 srs 1 (Specials) of No 76 Squadron at Holme-upon-Spalding Moor have been refuelled, bombed-up and towed to the end of the runway in order to save fuel for a long-range mission. *IWM*

Besides the high risks entailed in such low level flying at night, there were the special risks involved in trusting that the reception party on the ground was what it seemed and friendly — an aircraft at low altitude and low speed in a known position was inevitably a sitting duck for flak and night-fighters. As events over Holland in 1943 cruelly demonstrated, the links between SOE in London and its agents in the field were both tenuous and vulnerable. Communication was by brief cypher W/T signals on one side, verification being

Above:
On 19 September 1943 two aircraft from No 138 (SD) Squadron set out for Holland on a re-supply mission. The Germans were waiting for them: one crashed and the other, DG252, was so badly damaged that Flt Lt Dick Wilkins had to ditch after dropping his cargo of arms and agents on the DZ.
Gerrie J. Zwanenberg (via Mick Wright)

largely dependent upon correct cyphering, procedure and the recognition of keystrokes. Once an agent's cover was blown and his equipment and documents captured, months would pass before the arcane and complicated bureaucracy of SOE headquarters woke up to the fact that their organisation had been taken over by the enemy. This was despite firm promptings from the RAF Statistics and Losses section who pointed out the price No 138 Squadron was paying in blood. What had happend in Holland was that the first two agents dropped in November 1942 fell into German hands. The enemy promptly set up a spoof organisation code-named 'Nordpol'. They continued the deception for nearly a year, picking up agents and shooting down the aircraft that brought them in as they pleased. Losses on No 138 mounted steadily. Between March and September 1943, 22 aircraft were lost, four in August alone and a further seven in September, all on operations over Holland. This finally alerted SOE to what was happening and further operations were abandoned. This was SOE's greatest failure during World War 2.

There were also other hazards to be faced by SD crews flying over the partisan areas of Yugoslavia. Alfred Elkes was the rear gunner of a No 148 Squadron Halifax operating out of Brindisi, Italy, early in 1944:

'Halifaxes engaged on SOE operations were fitted with a large aperture in the mid-fuselage through which personnel, goods or equipment requested by the partisans could be delivered to them. Of necessity we had to operate at very low altitude and frequently down in deep valleys to avoid being seen by Jerry. The Halifax was a heavy aircraft and it wasn't always easy to gain height quickly which meant that there was a fair chance that we could be shot down by rifle fire. Unfortunately at that time there was deadly rivalry between Tito's communist partisans and those of the royalist, General Mihailovich, and after the drop had been made, it wasn't at all unusual for which ever side had taken delivery to open fire on us simply to prevent the next drop going to their rivals. My job was to discourage this practice by well-aimed bursts from the turret and regrettably some very stupid partisans paid a high price for their folly. If only they had had the good sense to unite, what a difference it might have made to their war.'

In February 1944, the Halifax in which Sgt Elkes was flying crashed into a mountainside in Montenegro in bad weather and he was the only survivor. He was a POW in Stalag 5b until repatriated in February 1945. The rest of his crew, four Australians, one Canadian, one Welshman and another Englishman are all buried in a communal grave in a small town called Setanja some miles inland from Scutari on the Adriatic coast.

———————————

Hostility from the underground forces was, however, a rare exception and like their counterparts in Bomber Command, many crashed SD crews were helped to escape or evade capture. FS Tadeusz Mecznik was the captain of Halifax BB309:T of No 138 Squadron which was returning from a supply drop over Poland on 17 September 1943 when it was attacked and shot down by a night-fighter over Zealand in Denmark. FS Mecznik was in the rest position and the second pilot, Sgt Kasprazak, was flying the aircraft when the attack came. He attempted to crash-land but skidded some 800ft across a frozen field before crashing into a small farmhouse and bursting into flames. Most

of the crew and the farmer's family were killed but the rear-gunner, Sgt Roman Pochta, turning his turret sideways and rolling out as the aircraft skidded, escaped unhurt. As he ran from the fire, he met the Polish-born wife of a neighbouring farmer who sent him to hide with the farm hands. FS Mecznik also escaped but was badly injured. He came-to the next day in Ringsted hospital where his broken left leg and right arm had been set safely. Sgt Pochta was not so lucky. He was found by a German search of the area after the bodies of Waselewski, Michalski, Bardzo, Pachlewicz and Kasprazak had been found in the wrecked farmhouse. Ironically, the Germans also found three other bodies — entangled in the remains of high-tension cables and their wrecked night-fighter. A low pass to confirm a kill had brought victor and vanquished together.

The Rev Svend Jacobsen, the pastor of the community of Slagelse, was confronted next morning by an irate grave-digger who had been hauled out of bed at 3am by German troops who took him to the cemetery and demanded to be shown a place to bury five bodies. Under protest he pointed out a place and was allowed to go back to bed. Svend Jacobsen knew of the previous night's crash and realised that the hurried and furtive burial was an attempt by the Germans to avoid the Danish people paying tribute to dead Allied airmen as had been their custom. Besides offending the rules of Christian decency, it was also a breach of the Geneva Convention. He sent a protest to his bishop and the following afternoon conducted a

Above:
Partially opened parachutes and supply containers stream out from a height of 800ft to land near the cross in the centre of the picture. Resistance men rush about in the snow to retrieve the supplies before the enemy can get near them on 7 February 1945. *Crown Copyright*

service at the graveside in English and Latin. By the end of the day the site was covered in flowers. In November 1943 the bodies were reburied and the grave properly marked. Meanwhile, FS Mecznik was recovering in hospital. The Danish doctors kept a special eye on him, and on the evening of 7 November they fed sleeping pills to the other patients in the ward, and smuggled a disguised Mecznik to a waiting ambulance which took him the 40 miles to Copenhagen. Two days later he was taken out to a ship bound for Sweden by a Danish police launch.

Although in return for German promises on their national independence and integrity, the Danes had apparently remained passive under occupation since 1940, resistance seethed beneath the surface. After German moves to take greater control of the Danish economy in the late summer of 1943, the Danish government resigned and from the end of August the Danes were openly at war with Germany. The senior SOE agent in Denmark was Dr Flemming Muus who in October had travelled through Sweden to London for a conference at SOE HQ in Baker Street to set up a supply network for his growing resistance movement. He made one attempt to return by parachute but was frustrated by bad weather and on 11 December 1943 he took off from Tempsford in a No 138 Squadron Halifax BB378:D, flown by Flt Lt Barter. He was to be dropped on a DZ in Zealand and the Halifax also carried 12 containers which were to be dropped in a prominent lake on the east of the island, Lake Tisso. The Halifax was picked up by German radar and a Bf110 was scrambled from Kastrup to intercept it. Dr Muus was sitting on the edge of the parachute hatch when the fighter attacked and in the subsequent evasive action was unable to jump. The Halifax was hit and set on fire but not before the rear gunner, Sgt Mould, had shot down the night-fighter. Flt Lt Barter crash-landed successfully and all the crew escaped. Dr Muus took command and told the five NCOs in the crew to walk northwest and contact either a doctor or a priest who would be likely to have a telephone to contact Copenhagen. After walking some distance, however, the NCOs met a farmer who was not quite aware of what was going on and they finished up in German hands. The officers were luckier. With the help of Dr Muus they were hidden in the house of a Dane who was living in America which was amply supplied with food and fuel. Dr Muus left the airmen in the hands of a local landowner, Count Scheel, who provided them with shirts, suits and overcoats and they enjoyed a dinner of roast chicken listening to warnings on the German-controlled radio of the dire consequences to any Danish national who helped an Allied airman. The Count's brother living in the town of Roskilde, contacted the local 'Falck' rescue service — an underground network using ambulances — and that afternoon Flt Lt Barter and his two companions were picked up and taken to Copenhagen. A few days later they met Dr Muus again and a week later were in Sweden on their way home.

Above:

This photograph is very rare because it shows Halifax A Mk 5 srs 1a aircraft of No 148 (SD) Squadron flying together in formation, a most unusual occurrence. *RAF Museum*

CHAPTER 12

PHANTOM MEAS

Although the 'wizard war' of electronic counter measures and counter-counter-measures had gone on steadily since 1940, until the formation of No 100 Group in November 1943, there was no force capable of carrying out major and co-ordinated jamming and deception of German defences. Most of the devices that had been introduced — Monica, Mandrel and Window were carried by individual bombers for their own defence. There was also a single squadron — No 192 — which specialised in ferreting out electronic data on German defences by flying with the bomber force and recording the characteristics of German radar and radio transmissions. The squadron had Wellingtons and Mosquitos on its strength as well as a small force of Halifaxes. A second squadron equipped with Halifax Mk 3s, No 171, joined No 100 Group in the summer of 1944 and a Stirling squadron, No 199, also converted to

Halifaxes. These aircraft were fitted with batteries of Mandrel jammers directed against the German early warning radars. Their function was to set up a screen of Mandrel jamming that effectively obscured all movements coming from behind it. To confuse enemy defences still further, some 24 or so 'spoof' aircraft flying a special pattern and dropping Window at timed intervals would emerge from behind the Mandrel screen and create the image on German radar that they were the main force of 500 or more bombers. Meanwhile, the real main force — also dropping Window — was on its way elsewhere, leaving the German night-fighter controllers to decide where they should commit their increasingly limited night-fighter force.

In December 1944, a third Halifax squadron, No 462, joined No 100 Group and whilst waiting for its aircraft to be fitted with 'ABC' — 'Airborne Cigar' —

Right:

This is the image produced on the H2S radar screen of the area around Steyr and Linz in Austria.

Below right:

In this rare photograph, 'R-Roger' of No 462 Squadron, RAAF, carries its full array of aerials: the masts above and below the fuselage are 'Airborne Cigar' transmitter aerials; the automatic 'Window' layer lies aft of the H2S dome below 'R-Roger'. Under the rear turret is the arrow aerial of 'Monica'. No 100 Group retained 'Monica' long after Bomber Command had discontinued its use in order to draw off German night-fighters from main force bombers. *R. Hines (via Mick Wright)*

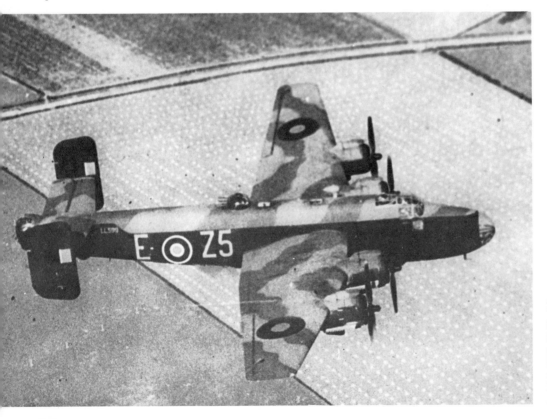

Left:
'E-Easy', LL599, of No 462 Squadron RAAF, returning from a daylight sortie over corn stooks in a Yorkshire field to land safely at Driffield. 'E-Easy' collided with a Lancaster over Essen on 23 October 1944. *RAAF*

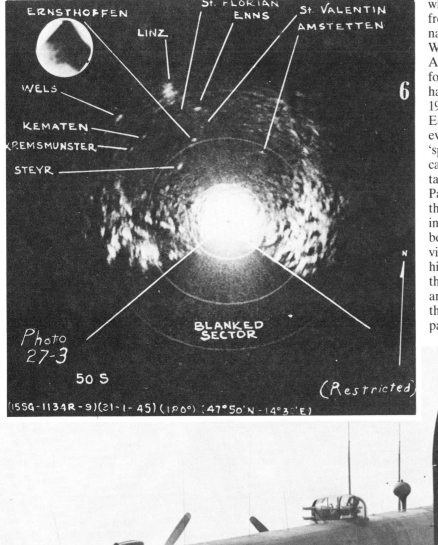

ERNSTHOFFEN
LINZ
St. FLORIAN
ENNS
St. VALENTIN
AMSTETTEN
WELS
KEMATEN
KREMSMUNSTER
STEYR
6
BLANKED
SECTOR
Photo
27-3
50 S
(Restricted)
N
(155G-1134R-9)(21-1-45)(180°)(47°50'N-14°30'E)

which jammed the German fighter control frequencies and required a massive external aerial array, took part in Mandrel/Window spoof operations. No 462, an Australian squadron, had been a main force bomber unit in No 4 Group since it had been reformed at Driffield in August 1944 following its return from the Middle East bomber force. The Australians added even more teeth to the No 100 Group 'spoof' technique, first of all by insisting on carrying bombs into their alternative targets and later by simulating both Pathfinder target marking using flares and the Master Bomber technique by employing the same RT frequencies. As the bombing campaign was about to end in victory, these spoof tactics had become highly sophisticated. No 100 Group used them to draw enemy night-fighters into areas where its own Mosquitos fitted with the new AI Mk 10 were on offensive patrol.

Flt Lt Ron Hines, an Australian, was a pilot on No 462 Squadron based at Foulsham, Norfolk, and recalls these final operations of the war in Europe. On Easter Monday, 2 April 1945, he was the captain of Halifax 'N-Nan', MZ913, briefed to take part in a Mandrel/Window spoof raid on the Luftwaffe night-fighter base at Stade near Hamburg, and to simulate a main force attack with Pathfinder markers and follow up with bombs. As was usual in Halifax Bomber Support squadrons — the official designation of No 100 Group units — the standard Halifax crew of seven was augmented to eight by the addition of a 'Special Operator' to work the jamming equipment. To the crews he was known as the 'Spare Bod'. Often he was German-born, and flak and fighters were just the beginning of his worries should the aircraft crash in occupied Europe.

'We saw our first searchlight beams and tracer as we approached the heavily defended island of Heligoland. Before we reached the target area, the bomb aimer had turned on the master switch that controlled all the bomb bays. It was positioned near the door leading into the nose of the aircraft.

'Just before we started our run up to the target the navigator said he was going to the toilet and was asked to check the master switch on his way. He had gone back without his oxygen bottle so was a little woozy on his return, and on checking the master switch he turned it off.

'Over the target the bomb aimer called, "Bombs Away" and as I turned to starboard the aircraft felt lighter and bombs were bursting below. Shortly after, the flight engineer went through his drill of checking the bomb bay and advised that all bombs were gone. On returning to base I made the worst landing ever in a Halifax, after levelling out at 50ft she just dropped in. Later whilst we were having a nip of rum in the de-briefing room some ground staff came in and asked, "Who was flying 'N-Nan' tonight?" "I was", I said. They then informed me I had landed with all my bombs still on board.'

On 10 April 1945 he flew 'N-Nan' to Berlin.

'Our "spare bod" hopped into the aircraft and who should it be but my old mate, Vic Chaffer. The last time I saw him was at Boggabri, New South Wales, in 1940 when I left the Bank of New South Wales and was introducing him as a junior. A great reunion at a questionable time, I thought, as he disappeared down the fuselage and no time for reminiscences over bank affairs.

'On starting up I found the magneto on the port outer engine was dead; this had given us trouble on the last trip. Eventually we got things sorted out, but we were the last to take off and 10 minutes late, too. I forgot to sign Form 700 but again it was too late. We set course off the end of the runway and didn't get the undercarriage up for 10 miles. Old Nan was in a bad way as she had flown many trips before we inherited her but I really liked her because she was good to handle and she had got us back from our first trip. Little did I realise this would be the last trip in her — 10 days later we flew her down to St Athan in Wales. Eventually we managed to get up to 6,000ft and just below the clouds and we opened up. Suddenly we were at the front of our squadron and flying over Hastings, again not knowing that we would be down there the following day making big time with the locals.

'Dozens of Lancaster aircraft were sitting in all round us and as we left the coast cumulus cloud towered to the north and south, luckily leaving a break in the middle right on our course. It was a wonderful sight, all those aircraft coming up from all over England, and as we flew out to sea they all seemed to converge into the narrow course between the cloud. It

was still daylight when we crossed into France and saw towns everywhere that were just a mass of craters. It got dark as we climbed above cloud; we seemed to be all on our own apart from the shadow of a Lancaster or the glowing engine exhausts of a Halifax above. Now the clouds were glowing beneath us with a hue that gently pulsated from explosions on the ground. Directly below was the front line battle area. Every night it seemed to be a bit further towards Berlin but never quite far enough. We were both in the same war and I felt for them — they could not go back to a pair of clean sheets every night as we did.

'The main force target that night was Leipzig and we were to make a spoof raid on Berlin to draw night-fighters away from the main force and to where our Mosquitos were intruding. Our mid-upper gunner, Jerry O'Donoghue, reported a fighter aircraft to our rear so I did a quick "corkscrew". On our ETA we dropped the flares finding we had overshot the target by at least 10 miles. Soon navigator Ray Philbrick judged we should be over Potsdam and the set-operator, John Sibbald, confirmed this on his radar. As I turned to port I could see the outline of the target below us, then the one million candle-power flare lit the earth and sky like daylight and for about two minutes we hung about like ducks on a pond. As we headed back you could see the rest of the

HP61 Halifax Mk 7
January to March 1945

Type
Heavy bomber, airborne and
cargo aircraft

Power Plant
Four 1,675hp Bristol
Hercules XVI engines

Performance
Maximum speed: 277mph at
6,000ft
Cruising speed: 225mph at
20,000ft
Service ceiling: 20,000ft
Range: 2,225 miles

Armament
Eight .303in Browning machine
guns and a Vickers K gun; later,
four .303in and two .5in
Brownings plus the Vickers K gun
in the nose
Bomb load: 12,000lb

Weights
Empty: 38,500lb
Loaded: 65,000lb

Dimensions
Span: 104ft 2in
Length: 71ft 7in
Height: 20ft 9in

Entry into Service Jan-Apr 1945

No Built	Type	Serial Block	Constructed
31	Halifax C Mk 8	PP217-PP247	Mar-Apr
23	Halifax B Mk 6	TW774-TW796 (renumbered PP142-PP164)	Jan-Feb
37	Halifax B Mk 6	PP165-PP216	Jan-Mar
70	EE-built Halifax B/Met Mk 3	RG345-RG446	Jan-Mar
20	EE-built Halifax B Mk 7	RG447-RG479	Jan-Mar
24	EE-built Halifax B Mk 6	RG480-RG513	Mar
42	EE-built Halifax B Mk 6	RG527-RG568	Mar
36	Rootes-built Halifax B/A/Met Mk 3	NA275-NA310	Mar-Apr
55	Rootes-built Halifax A Mk 7	NA311-NA380	Mar
46	Fairey-built Halifax B/A Mk 7	PN208-PN267	Feb-Mar

Unit	Representative Aircraft	Base
No 4 Group, Bomber Command		
10 Squadron	RG345	Melbourne
51 Squadron	RG446	Snaith
76 Squadron	RG568, PP172	Holme-upon-Spalding Moor

squadron's flares going down along our inbound track. We kept on weaving until they went out. The wireless operator picked up an echo on "Fishpond" (the tail radar) but it was probably one of our own Mosquitos as, after a corkscrew, it disappeared.

'Just after our turning point the darkness was soon spitting clusters of bright green markers over Leipzig down to port of us. The work of the Pathfinder Lancaster crews was the opening scene for the main act, putting a torch to the bonfire. Within a few seconds all hell started to break loose and we had to fly back through it! On course just to starboard of Dessau, shells were bursting in amongst the red and green target indicators as if trying to put them out, the big "cookies" were starting to come down and explode, masses of searchlights turned night into day and I

seemed to be able to see anything on the ground I cared to look at. Heavy flak was bursting at about twice our height and I could see the aircraft coned in the searchlights as they crossed the target over Leipzig. From 18,500ft the city looked like a patch of bubbling molten steel as petrol and gas tanks blew heavenwards. Above it was almost a balancing scene as heavy flak exploded in a box-like pattern into which the main bomber stream had to go.

'In between was a mass of material going up with a lot more coming down, all of which was exploding, flaring or burning. We seemed to be hours getting over the mess but there was a 50mph headwind blowing. The Rhine seemed miles away, but eventually we found ourselves over France where the cloud was patchy and we could see well-lit cities beneath. Automatic pilot "George" was working well so

Unit	Representative Aircraft	Base
77 Squadron	RG346, PN379, PP208	Full Sutton
78 Squadron	RG434, PP168	Breighton
102 Squadron	PP171	Pocklington
158 Squadron	PN380, PP167	Lissett
346 Squadron	RG543, PN365	Elvington
347 Squadron	PP165	Elvington
578 Squadron	RG353	Burn
640 Squadron	RG549	Leconfield

No 6 (RCAF) Group, Bomber Command

408 Squadron	RG450, PN223	Linton-on-Ouse
415 Squadron	PN367	East Moor
420 Squadron	RG347	Tholthorpe
425 Squadron	RG350	Tholthorpe
426 Squadron	RG449, PN226	Linton-on-Ouse
432 Squadron	RG451, PN224	East Moor
433 Squadron	PN229	Skipton-on-Swale (converted to Lancaster, Feb 1945)

No 100 (Bomber Support) Group, Bomber Command

171 Squadron	RG357, PN372	North Creake
192 Squadron	RG430	Foulsham
199 Squadron	RG373, PN375	North Creake
462 Squadron	RG379, PN391, PP214	Foulsham

No 18 Group, Coastal Command

517 Squadron	RG380, PN392	Brawdy

No 19 Group, Coastal Command

58 Squadron	RG359	Stornoway
502 Squadron	RG351, PN368	Stornoway
518 Squadron	RG362, PN377	Tiree

No 38 Group, Transport Command

96 Squadron	RG371, PN394	Leconfield
187 Squadron	RG356	Merryfield
298 Squadron	NA310, PN244	Woodbridge
644 Squadron	NA342, PN251	Tarrant Rushton

No 205 Group, MEAF

301 Squadron	PP215	Brindisi

Far left:
Halifax B Mk 7, LW210:Y of No 426 'Thunderbird' Squadron RCAF, crashed with Flt Lt T. Emerson at the controls on Nunthorpe Estate, York, on 5 March 1945 after icing up.

Below:
Halifax 'Q-Queenie' is seen here being serviced at Foulsham in early 1945. *R. Hines*

I started to take a rest but this was quickly ended as the revs on the port inner engine began to fluctuate, then the engine cut as Jim Bowden, our engineer, was changing petrol tanks. I was getting very tired so I took one of the issue "Wakie Wakie" tablets (Benzedrine) that I thought I could do without. The navigator said it would take us two-and-a-half hours to get to base, so imagine my dismay when our fuel turned out to be far lower than I thought — we had only an hour-and-a-half left. My first thought was to land at Juvencourt as had been suggested at briefing, with the prospect of a break in Paris! Further calculations were made and it was found we could just reach the master diversion airfield at Manston in Kent. If we didn't, we could bale out or ditch and after what we had seen this would not have been too bad. To add tension to the crew, "N-Nan" then became enveloped in a good demonstration of St Elmo's fire. It zig-zagged over the cockpit windows and danced around the props and wings as all we were going to see of Paris vanished behind us. As we came to the English Channel the whole of the UK seemed to be clouded over with the exception of the little peninsula on which Manston is situated. We could see it for miles with its cone of searchlights. The flarepath was extensive and very well lit — like coming into Luna Park. Suddenly all four engines cut — I advised the crew on baling out or ditching or something as we dropped — just as quickly they picked up again. The flight engineer nearly broke both legs as they made contact with the main spar while he was diving for the fuel cocks. Something had failed in the changeover.

'Contact with Manston was dead on and it was quite a simple matter getting in although I had to overshoot once (luckily not twice), and I thought the landing was quite good considering it was on the green and white flarepath on the left-hand side of the runway. The runway was over 3,000yd long and on reaching the end of it, through a mass of coloured lights, we were guided by a green Aldis lamp mounted on a Jeep for another mile or more round the loop. We booked in at the control tower and then had a good supper, the mechs reporting that Nan was covered all down the port side with oil and all the bearings of the port outer had gone. The engine would have to be replaced. Its oil tank was found to be 11 gallons short which meant empty and there was one-and-a-half minutes of petrol left. I did not need to wonder who had kept us in the air. After a good night's sleep and reading the account of the big

raid on Leipzig in the papers, dressed in a variety of flying clothing, Margate claimed our interest. We spent lunchtime having a sing around a piano in a tavern and on to a dance in Hastings. Wg Cdr Paul, the squadron commander, arrived with an

Above:
Behind the flight engineer's compartment, the H2S operator sat facing forward on the port side. *Mick Wright*

Above left:
'W-William', an ABC-equipped B Mk 3 of No 462 Squadron RAAF, takes off from Foulsham.
R. Hines (via Mick Wright)

Left:
Ron Hines often flew 'N-Nan', MZ913, although the aircraft was known to her crew as *Jane*.
*R. Hines
(via Mick Wright)*

aircraft to pick us up, all too soon. When I got back to my hut at Foulsham, my mate "Bitsey" Grant had started to sort out my gear prior to sending it home. No one had told him where we were.'

Flying a new aircraft coded 'P-Peter', Ron Hines was to carry a load of flares and target indicators to Magdeburg on the night of 8 April 1945:

'The highlight of this trip was my take-off. As we taxied round to the north/south runway I said to the crew members nearest to me: "How about standing in the cockpit tonight to watch the take-off?". I was first to the end of the runway with Scott's aircraft close behind, and as I eased the throttles forward I knew I was not someone to watch doing anything. Not enough accent on the starboard throttles was the beginning and very nearly the end as "P-Peter" swung towards the control tower. We had quite a turn of speed on, adding to which the runway had a decidedly downhill tilt. I did not trust the brakes to put us right as we would have probably hit the tower. On seeing a long grassy stretch in front I pushed the four throttles full on — went through the FIDO installation tail up and downhill, to lift off with the tower on my left and the top of a large hangar on the right.

'My crew members were quite petrified and I was sure would never be the same again, but I felt quite confident in what I was doing. In the rear turret, Frank Hughes was perplexed as he watched the runway disappear at 45° instead of seeing an end view of it. Scotty in the aircraft behind nearly had a heart attack, meanwhile anyone who could get out of the control tower did, very rapidly; the washing lines were reported full of underclothing the following day.

'Daylight stayed until we reached the target; although it was a long dirty trip with thick clouds, we did see a large war memorial over France. At Magdeburg there was a beautiful exhibition of lights and colours like daylight. We circled the flares for a while, much to the annoyance of Frank in the rear turret who apart from myself was the only one who knew what was going on all the time. All went well on the return until we had just passed London. The weather began to clamp and we were diverted to Tangmere. There were at least another seven Halifaxes, some Tempests, Liberators, Fortresses and Mosquitos all dotted about the airfield and oddly enough, even some German aircraft.

'It was a cold night and we had to spend some time looking for food and bedding but the ground staff were very helpful. The next day we had an hour's flight to Foulsham where I was interviewed by Wg Cdr Paul. He asked me what had gone wrong with the take-off so I told him I was a little short in the legs to reach the rudder pedals. He advised me to carry a couple of cushions on the next trip.

'Next morning the local newspapers carried complaints about the noise of bombers returning from operations and wanting them re-routed elsewhere. Boy! was my mid-upper mad?'

On 10 April, Ron Hines flew 'Q-Queenie' on a spoof raid on Dessau. The main bomber force attacked Leipzig again.

'Take-off was at 6.40pm and we went into Germany at 3,000ft on automatic pilot; apart from some near misses by Lancasters and vapour trails above us we were early all the way, through flak at the target to bomb on the red and greens.

'Heading home over the North Sea a stretch of solid cumulus cloud ran from north to south, the view from our height of

Above:
'T-Tommy' sets course over Foulsham with Ron Hines at the controls. *R. Hines (via Mick Wright)*

18,500ft and 10 miles away helped me make up my mind about climbing over it. A very stupid idea, probably it meant going down into the blackness in front of us and the tops looked quite inviting. We entered cloud a few thousand feet from the top and flying on instruments only, it took less than a minute for the aircraft to begin icing up. I called the navigator for a reverse course and slowly began to turn to port as pieces of ice thumped their way down the fuselage sides. I glued my eyes to the artificial horizon, keeping the nose slightly down as I slowly turned on to course, momentarily checking the altitude at intervals. Frozen in this attitude we dropped through some warmer air. At an altitude of less than 50ft the white capped North Sea flashed beneath us. I was thankful for all the blind flying I had done in the Link Trainer and, not least, for being over the sea when it happened. With help from the wireless operator, we flew straight into Foulsham, no trouble at all; it was nice to talk over the intercom with my crew and they spoke as if nothing had happened to cause concern. We lost one aircraft that night, that of Alf Ball and crew in a Mk 3, NA240, which had been to Leipzig, but we were back first and into bed first too.'

With a load of flares, incendiaries, Window and two 500lb bombs, his 'Old Mate' Vic Chaffer as the 'Special Operator', Ron Hines went to Boizenberg on the Elbe near Hamburg and back in 5hrs 5min on 13 April 1945.

'The main force attack was on Kiel. It was Friday the 13th and when we arrived at "X-X-Ray" it was parked in dispersal number 13. It was a short but rotten trip. We had a surging port inner and went in below Hamburg and on downwards through France and Belgium — we were first home. Berlin, in "P-Peter", the next night we had an eight-hour trip to Jüterbog southeast of Berlin, carrying 500lb bombs and Window. A long trip, 750 aircraft over Berlin wiped out Potsdam, we dropped four 500 pounders just south of Berlin for the sake of morale of the ground boys. Mass of aircraft over France which we crossed at 2,000ft just below a cloud, a great deal of static electricity all over the aircraft, "George" behaved well. We came back from the target lit up like a Christmas tree by German white fighter beacons with their more worrying attendant aircraft. John Sibbald picked up one on radar at 1,500yd but the gunners missed it. It was a good trip home, we were first again landing where we found another crew was missing, that of Andy Anderson. We think he may have landed in France.'

On the 18th the target was Gardelegen, again loaded with flares, incendiaries and Window, 'spare bod' Vic Chaffer in 'Z-Zebra':

'One of several raids on southern Germany, we took off at 12 minutes past midnight. The weather was hazy but good, the aircraft was very stiff to handle even out of autopilot and I had some trouble with the port outer. Heavy flak over the target as we saw tracers, possibly a kite going down. On our return we found yet

Entry into Service Apr-Jun 1945

No Built	Type	Serial Block	Constructed
65	Rootes-built Halifax A Mk 7	NA392-NA468	Apr-Jul
38	Halifax C Mk 8	PP259-PP296	Apr-Jun
44	EE-built Halifax B Mk 6	RG693-RG736	May-Jun
84	EE-built Halifax B Mk 6	RG583-RG679	Jun

Unit	Representative Aircraft	Base
No 4 Group, Bomber Command		
76 Squadron	RG583, RG656	Holme-upon-Spalding Moor
77 Squadron	RG584	Full Sutton
78 Squadron	RG650	Breighton
102 Squadron	RG585	Pocklington
158 Squadron	RG593, RG639	Lissett
346 Squadron	RG587, RG654	Elvington
347 Squadron	RG625, RG645	Elvington
640 Squadron	RG589	Leconfield
No 38 Group, Transport Command		
190 Squadron	NA414	Great Dunmow
298 Squadron	NA392	Tarrant Rushton
620 Squadron	NA406	Great Dunmow
644 Squadron	NA399	Tarrant Rushton
Miscellaneous		
G-AHYH	PP261	
1361 HCU	PP284	

HP61 Halifax B Mk 3 (modified)
April to June 1945
Type
Heavy bomber and radio countermeasures aircraft
Power Plant
Four 1,675hp Bristol Hercules XVI engines
Performance
Maximum speed: 290mph at 9,000ft
Cruising speed: 230mph at 20,000ft
Service ceiling: 22,000ft
Range: 1,260 miles
Armament
Eight .303in Browning machine guns and a Vickers K gun in the nose
Bomb load: 12,000lb
Weights
Empty: 38,300lb
Loaded: 65,000lb
Dimensions
Span: 104ft 2in
Length: 71ft 7in
Height: 20ft 9in

another crew, Loder from "A" Flight, had been lost in a collision over the target.'

A new sort of Window which the Americans called 'Chaff' was carried by Ron Hines when he flew 'T-Tommy' in the Heligoland-Wilhelmshaven area on 22 April.

'There was a terrific wind across The Wash around 18.00hrs and all Bomber Command operations were cancelled at the last minute. We went on a spoof paratroop raid towards the German coast dropping the "Chaff" all the way in. There was a full moon, consequently it was very bright. It was a very exhilarating trip; although we should not have gone.'

Ron Hines' last trip was to Munich on 24 April 1945:

'We were the guinea pigs on this one. It was a test to find out what the Germans had left in the way of fighters, flak and what have you. All we got were searchlights until the cry, "Weave, Skipper, Weave!" rent the air. A Mosquito from 100 Group approached from the starboard stern, flew in beside us and waggled his wings, all in full moonlight too. Frightened the hell out of the gunners.'

All Australian personnel were posted home in May 1945 and No 462 Squadron was disbanded.

Above:
Halifax B Mk 3, MZ913:N of No 462 Squadron RAAF, No 100 (Bomber Support) Group. Flt Lt Ron Hines used this aircraft in an attack on Stade, Easter Monday 1945.

CHAPTER 13

OF SEA AND SKY

From the end of 1943 Halifaxes fulfilled a vitally essential if rather unglamorous role on meteorological patrols out of a variety of remote and also rather unglamorous locations. Throughout World War 2, the uncertain climate of Western Europe and the relatively primitive navigation and blind flying aids then available put a premium on accurate weather forecasting in the conduct of the Allied bombing campaign against Germany, and from 1943 onwards made it a vital element in the planning for the invasion of Europe. But the accuracy of forecasting was totally dependent upon the prompt and timely receipt of weather data from the Western Approaches to the British Isles — the Atlantic cradle of Europe's weather. Some data came from ships but it was limited in scope and subject due to many radio security restrictions. Most came from Coastal Command aircraft operating in the area but this, too, was restricted by their need to operate at low altitudes, and to them weather reporting was inevitably secondary to their main role of hunting U-boats. Specialist meteorological observation flights had been set up as early as 1940 and later several of these Blenheim-equipped flights came under the control of Coastal Command. One of them, No 1404, which by then operated Hampdens, Hudsons and Flying Fortresses, received the first specially adapted meteorological Halifax in December 1943. Met Halifaxes were at that time Mk 5s modified by Cunliffe Owen at their factory in Eastleigh, Southampton. The nose gun was removed and a special station in the nose forward of the navigation table was installed for an additional crew member — a meteorological observer. (Met observers were usually qualified after short spells at gunnery and navigation schools and had been given specialist training in meteorology. They wore a distinctive half-wing bearing the letter 'M'.)

Among the special equipment fitted was a highly accurate outside air temperature and humidity gauge with an external probe sticking out from the starboard side of the

Below:
No 517 (Met) Squadron flew this Met Mk 5 srs 1 (Special) from Holmsley South during 1943. The ASV radome can be seen beneath the fuselage.
Via Flt Lt Ling

Left:
A Halifax Mk 3 from No 517 (Met) Squadron flying over St Davids.

nose. There was also a sophisticated radio altimeter which by comparison with the standard barometric altimeter, made it relatively easy to calculate sea level pressures. There was also additional navigation equipment — Loran, a long-range fixing aid, as well as Gee, ASV and a highly accurate drift meter, the American B3. To provide the extended range required, extra fuel tanks were fitted into the bomb bays.

No 1404 Flight became No 517(Met) Squadron and moved to Brawdy in Pembrokeshire in February 1944. Other met squadrons were No 518 Squadron based at Tiree, No 519 Squadron at Wick and later at Leuchars, No 520 Squadron based at Gibraltar and No 521 Squadron based at Chivenor. (The last did not however receive its Halifaxes until December 1945 — a fact which perhaps serves to illustrate the enduring value of the long-range weather reconnaissance service which Halifaxes did so much to pioneer. Indeed, the service they established continued long after the war. The last Halifax in front-line service with the RAF was a Met Mk 6, RG841, which flew with No 224 (Met) Squadron at Gibraltar until March 1952. Flying Met Hastings, the RAF continued weather reconnaissance sorties until August 1964 when space satellites took over.)

For the Met Halifaxes during the last two years of the war, weather reconnaissance sorties followed precise routes and were given code-names and allocated to specific squadrons. Each route was then flown twice every 24 hours, except No 518 Squadron which flew four. No 518 Squadron based at Tiree in the Western Isles, for example, flew 'Bismuth' patrols. They followed a triangular pattern — 550nm due west from base, northeast for 400nm then back to base. Each leg was divided into numbered 'stations' at 50nm intervals. The aircraft flew a series of climbs to the midway point, crossing each station at a predetermined barometric pressure level. The second half of the leg was a complementary series of box descents and sea level pressure was measured every 100nm. At the end of the outward leg the aircraft then made a spiral climb to 20,000ft, descending and climbing again in a pattern — and so on throughout the sortie which frequently lasted more than 10 hours. Not only was careful and accurate flying and navigation absolutely essential, but the sortie was also flown daily regardless of the weather. During the whole of 1944, No 518 Squadron only failed to take-off on two days and then

because of snow on the runway. But losses were high — No 518 Squadron lost eight aircraft during the year.

Here is the story of a met sortie in 1945 as told by a met observer with No 518 Squadron:

'Our route was flown four times every 24 hours, different crews flying one sortie per night or day, and at 9pm GMT on 25 January 1945 the duty officer called on ours. A rapid dash to put on as much clothing as possible above and below our aircrew underwear before a good meal and a ride in a truck to the briefing.

'Met operations, signals, intelligence and duty officers pass on their information to us then off to the safety equipment section for Mae Wests, parachutes, survival rations and what have you. On to a truck for a check with Air Traffic Control followed by another run out to the aircraft where I climb into the nose and check all the instruments. The Halifax turns on to the runway and the navigator and I sit on the main spar as the pilot shoves the throttles through the gate. As soon as we are airborne, we are able to go forward into the nose. Very soon we are on a westerly heading out from Tiree Island and following an operation known as "Bismuth" over the Atlantic, climbing steadily. Every 50nm a full weather "actual" is taken — types of cloud, height, temperature, humidity — all is seen and logged. The report is passed to the wireless operator who codes it and sends it back to base by W/T, usually just when the pilot is taking another dive through cloud to sea level. More measurements are taken and again on the winding climb back to operational altitude back once more to sea level for another series of measurements. The climb to find the upper winds are often made through cloud and the cry "Oxygen on!" rings through the aircraft while the navigator has to cope with 150mph winds and the pilot with the resulting turbulence. At the turning point our height is 19,000ft and although it is colder, there is mercifully less buffeting. Flying back to base in the early morning means flying dead into the rising sun, its rays beating on the Halifax. Although I can observe a much greater distance, right into the clouds way below, the wings and engines gleam new and metallic and make my eyes sore. For some 30 observation positions and 10 hours in the air the aircraft has bumped through cloud where everything is dark and wet then out into blinding sunshine again. It was somewhere about here one early morning when there was a

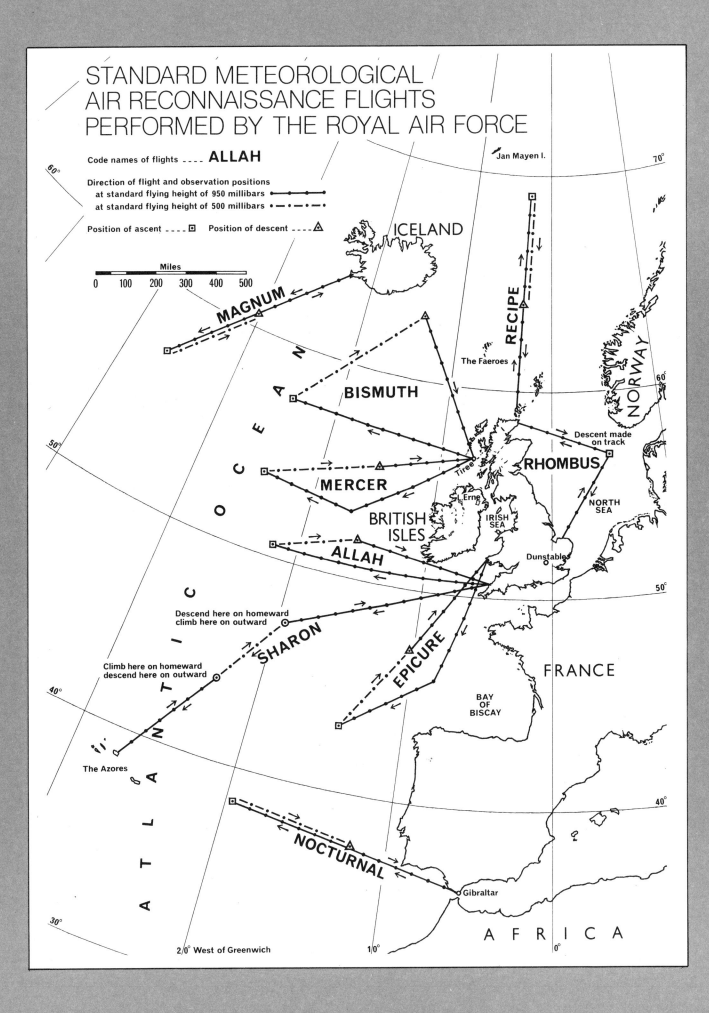

Above:
Having served with No 433 Squadron RCAF, Halifax LV839 went to No 517 (Met) Squadron based at Brawdy and is seen here flying low over the Atlantic.
Crown Copyright (via R. Gunst)

Right:
A Met Mk 3 of No 518 Squadron was caught by a gust of wind on landing at Tiree and overshot the runway. The aircraft was written off.

sudden flash and I saw log books and charts flying through the air in a lashing wind; an icy blast was searing through the aircraft.

'The nose of the aircraft had gone. We looked out as much as we could but there was no sign of any other aircraft and in the cloud we could not see any shipping either. We reached the conclusion that it had been a lightning strike. (Which it later proved to be — the metal plug replacing the nose gun had not been bonded to the aircraft.) I held onto the seat in the nose, the slipstream like a solid wall, occasionally plucking at me as I bent double to keep warm in the sub-zero temperature. I was thinking about another of our aircraft that went missing the other day in about the same place — 300 miles from base. The ASV would see us home just as soon as we could get in range of a coastline. Suddenly there was a lifting movement in the aircraft and it began to balloon up into a weather front. That was all we needed! Ice began to form on the wings and we sank lower and lower. We were only some 200ft off the sea, which looked considerably lumpy, when there was an instant silence. I thought my ears had gone with the cold but in a few seconds I realised the engines had stopped, all four of them.

'I felt numb when I heard the Skipper shout "Transmit!", the white tops of the waves were by now much nearer and I couldn't get back out of the nose as the second pilot was helping the Skipper and standing in the way. The nose of the Halifax lifted and the slipstream fell away, we slowed right down and I could see the water and sky, when all four engines burst into life at the same time; white tops and grey/green sea moved away from us. Later sitting on the main spar and feeling the wheels touch and touch again on the runway made me feel warm and very, very tired. Fat, lumbering crewmen collected boxes and papers, instruments and parachutes, their beards glistening in the early morning light, the flight truck was there with its cheery driver. Another met sortie was over. Our results have been sent all round the airfields and will be used for the basis of weather forecasting of systems crossing the United Kingdom for the next 12 hours. Soon another Halifax and crew will be rolling out on to the runway and climbing out to sea, but I knew where I would be!'

Left:
After 10 hours in the air over a lonely sea followed by a bumpy ride in a truck, a Met Halifax crew is de-briefed. There followed breakfast, maybe a shower and bed, then out once again in 12 hours' time.
R. Gunst

CHAPTER 14

AIRBORNE OPER

Unlike the Germans, the British were latecomers in the techniques of airborne warfare and though the German successes in Norway and the Low Countries in 1940 led to the establishment of the Airborne Forces Development Unit in October 1940 to carry out experiments with parachutes and gliders, little had been achieved towards building up a British airborne force until the Germans hammered home the 1940 lesson again with their airborne conquest of Crete in May 1941. As Churchill put it in a memorandum to the Chiefs of Staff: '. . . The gliders have been produced on the smallest possible scale, and so we have practically now neither the parachutists nor the gliders . . . A whole year has been lost and I now invite the Chiefs of Staff to make proposals for trying, so far as is possible, to repair the misfortune.'

The Chiefs' response was to set in train a plan to form two parachute brigades and a glider force big enough to lift 10,000 men and their equipment. The gliders would be built by the furniture trade to avoid interfering with the production of bombers and fighters and there were to be three types — the Hotspur (already in production) which could carry eight men; the Horsa which could carry either 25 men or a Jeep towing a gun; and a very large glider capable of carrying a tank, later known as the Hamilcar. Again, unlike the Germans who had a fleet of Ju52s, or the Americans who had the DC3, the British had no readily available transport aircraft suitable for easy and rapid conversion to the airborne role. It was proposed, therefore, to adapt 10 medium bomber squadrons to paratroop-dropping and glider-towing duties. And thereby hangs a tale. The term 'medium bomber' meant the twin-engined types — Hampdens, Wellingtons and Whitleys — which at the time formed the bulk of the front-line squadrons in Bomber Command and which were in the process of being replaced by Stirling, Halifax and Lancaster 'heavy bombers'. Of the mediums, the Hampden was totally unsuitable, the Wellington whilst having a large

fuselage for carrying paratroopers was of geodetic construction — a sort of aluminium basket — which could not be cut to provide adequate paratroop exits. Furthermore, when AFDU tried it as a glider tug, the 'basket' was found to stretch alarmingly! This left only the slow and ageing Whitley and later trials showed that the Whitley could not tow a fully loaded Horsa — let alone the massive Hamilcar. Luckily there was available a spare bomber design also built by the piano and furniture industry which was to become a highly effective paratrooping and glider-towing aircraft, the Armstrong Whitworth Albermarle. But only a four-engined aircraft would be able to tow the Hamilcar. The first Halifax to join AFDU at Ringway in October 1941 was B Mk 2 srs 1, R9435. For the airborne role it was necessary for all aircraft to be able to drop paratroops as well as tow gliders, so R9435 was modified by having a hatch cut in the floor of the fuselage. Trials with dummy parachutists soon revealed problems with the static lines used to deploy the parachutes. When the dummies were dropped the lines streamed back under the fuselage and tended to wrap around the tailwheel or become entangled with the rudder — a dangerous occurrence in either case. It was also difficult to retrieve the lines when the retrieval stick had been dropped and a special winch had to be fitted. But the

Below:
The Hamilcar with an all-up weight of 15½ tons and a 110ft wing span, was towed into Normandy by the Halifax on D-Day, carrying 17-pounder anti-tank guns and Jeeps. This photograph was taken from the rear turret of the Halifax tug.

Right:
The first troops into France on D-Day arrived by Horsa gliders; one sporting invasion stripes is seen here being towed by a Halifax A Mk 5 with four-bladed propellers.

main snag was the effect of the slipstream on the departing paratroopers. At worst it could cause his parachute to twist risking a fatal 'Roman Candle' or, at best, cause him to 'ring the bell' on exit — bang his parachute pack on one side of the hatch and his face on the other. The toothless 'Halifax grin' is said to have been only too common at AFDU until special wind-shields were fitted in front of the hatch. Thus although Halifaxes were to be used operationally for dropping paratroopers — notably the pathfinders who marked the DZs in Normandy on D-day — they made their main contribution towing gliders.

The Halifax had no problems in towing the Horsa glider when trials began at Snaith in Yorkshire in January 1942 and in February of that year the first Halifax/Hamilcar flight took off from Newmarket. By the end of May, seven Halifaxes were engaged in glider-towing trials mostly with the Hamilcar. The Halifax/Horsa combination was, however, the first to go into action — in one of the most imaginative and tragic coup-de-main actions of the war — the raid on the Norsk Hydro heavy water plant at Vermok some 60 miles due west of Oslo in Norway.

The British had known for some time that the Germans, like the Allies, were engaged in research that could lead to the development of a nuclear weapon. They also knew that enemy atomic research was heavily dependent upon supplies of 'heavy water' — an isotope of hydrogen with twice its mass known as deuterium — which was scarce and extremely difficult to produce in quantity. One important source was the Norsk Hydro plant in Norway and by 1942 German demands were rising steadily. If the Allies were to stay ahead in atomic research, it was vital that the Norsk plant should be put out of action and its stock destroyed. The problem was how best to do it. The plant lay in a deep valley with sheer wooded sides rising to 3,000ft and overshadowed by Gaustatoppen, a mountain some 5,400ft high. The heavy water plant itself was sited on a rock shelf over 1,000ft above the river. It was an

exceedingly difficult target to locate and bomb and virtually impossible for a parachute landing. It was decided therefore to launch an assault with glider-borne specialist troops who would land some distance away on a LZ marked out by Norwegian agents. To locate the LZ, a new radar homing device known as Rebecca/Eureka was to be employed. This comprised a portable radar beacon — Eureka — which would be smuggled into the Norwegians who would set it up on the LZ. When triggered off by radar transmissions from the aircraft, the Eureka gave a response which showed up on the Rebecca screen as a left-right steer and distance to go. In flat terrain it had a range of about 80nm and, later in its history, was accurate enough for use as a blind approach aid. Unfortunately, as in all such devices, its signals could be blanked off by mountains and rocks.

For the operation, code-named 'Freshman', two teams of highly skilled technicians were drawn from the Royal Engineers, 16 in each team and all volunteers. Three Horsa gliders were allocated, flown by experienced members of the Glider Pilot Regiment and two RAAF pilots. The RAF supplied three Halifaxes and two crews from a special detachment of No 38 Wing. After intensive training, the force called the 'Washington Party' moved to Skitten in Scotland and the operation was launched on the night of 19/20 November 1942.

The first combination, flown by Sqn Ldr Wilkinson, took off at 17.50hrs followed by the second, flown by Flt Lt Parkinson, 20min later. Both made their landfall in Norway but only one Halifax, the first, returned to Skitten. It had reached the LZ area but Rebecca was not working and the LZ could not be found by map-reading because of cloud cover. The combination iced up in the cloud and eventually the tow rope parted and the glider went down just north of Stavanger. This was all that was known until after the war when a full account of what happened could be pieced together. Flt Lt Parkinson's combination crashed into the mountains of southern Norway, the glider hitting one range, the tug the next. No one will ever know why. There were no survivors. In the glider, three were killed on impact and the rest were captured and shot by the Germans on Hitler's personal orders. All the Halifax crew died in the crash. The first glider from Sqn Ldr Wilkinson's combination, also crashed into a mountain-side. Eight of the 17 occupants were killed at once and four were injured. All were captured by the Germans. The four injured were poisoned by a German doctor on the orders of the Gestapo. The five unhurt were shot by the Gestapo on 18 January 1943. The Norsk Hydro plant was later destroyed by agents of the SOE working with members of the Norwegian underground.

The first glider towing squadron under No 38 Wing of Army Co-operation Command was No 295, based at Netheravon and equipped with Whitleys. In February 1943 the Whitleys began to be replaced by Halifaxes and the squadron moved to Holmsley South in the New Forest near Beaulieu. The surrender of the Axis forces in North Africa in May was followed by intense preparation for an airborne landing in Sicily and No 295 was quickly involved. In an operation code-named 'Beggar', it was required to tow unladen Horsa gliders to North Africa, picking them up at Hurn and flying them through Portreath in Cornwall some 1,200 miles across the Bay of Biscay to Sale in Morocco, at a time when enemy fighters

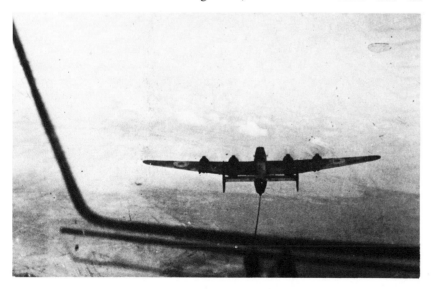

were active along most of the route in their ceaseless battle against Coastal Command. From Sale the Horsas had then to be towed to Kairouan in Tunisia, another 1,000 miles through sand, dust and scorching heat. Twenty-one Horsas eventually reached North Africa to take part in the airborne assault on Sicily — an operation which came very close to failure. Of some 137 gliders released by British and American towing aircraft — seven Halifaxes among 28 Albermarles and 109 Dakotas — 69 landed in the sea, 56 were scattered over the island. Only 12 landed on the LZ — all Horsas.

During 1943 the expansion of the airborne forces and the necessary air force 'lift' continued apace. No 38 Wing became a Group with nine squadrons — four of Albermarles, four of Stirlings but only one of Halifaxes — No 298, formed at Tarrant Rushton in Hampshire in November 1943, specifically to tow the giant Hamilcar glider. In March 1944, a second Halifax squadron, No 644, was formed. It too had a crucial role — it perfected the technique of precision landings by coup-de-main Horsas which captured the bridges over the Orne and the Caen canals prior to the Normandy landings.

After the successful invasion of Europe, the No 38 Group Halifaxes were employed on a variety of SOE operations as well as others of a similar clandestine nature involving the SAS and occasionally towing gliders. Both squadrons were also involved in the ill-fated landings at Arnhem — Operation 'Market Garden'. At that time, one of the Albermarle squadrons, No 296, was converted to the Halifax in preparation for the final airborne operation in Europe — Operation 'Varsity', the Rhine crossing.

Tom Staniforth was a flight engineer on No 296 Squadron at the time:

'We were based at Earls Colne in Essex and we were the headquarters squadron of No 38 Group. Other squadrons in the Group at the time were next door at Great Dunmow — our circuits overlapped — and at Tarrant Rushton and Brize Norton. Our aircraft were Halifax GT Mk 3s with Hercules engines. The squadron commander was a remarkable man in the same mould as Douglas Bader — Wg Cdr Musgrove. Like Bader, he had two artificial legs but he flew the Halifax just like any other pilot. It must have been difficult sometimes, especially when towing gliders, not that this prevented his crew from making sarcastic remarks if a

take-off was erratic. I am also told that they usually lit their post take-off cigarettes from matches struck on his legs.'

'At this time, operations carried out by No 38 Group were many and varied — dropping SAS men behind enemy lines on special operations, supplying the underground forces in Norway — a task which invariably involved trips of 12 to 14 hours in the air and a heavy reliance on long-range tanks. These operations usually called for 20 canisters in the bomb-bays and a couple of 300lb panniers — huge rectangular baskets — which had to be literally kicked out of the parachute hatch when the red light came on — one of my jobs as flight engineer. We also kept in practice towing gliders, but it wasn't something we had to do operationally very often. We had done it at Arnhem but that was before I joined the squadron. We towed them again on Operation "Varsity" — the Rhine crossing on 24 March 1945. Each Halifax towed a single Horsa glider — we called them "matchboxes" — which carried 20 fully-equipped airborne soldiers. With all the practices, we got to know our bunch very well.

'Wing Commander Musgrove had been put in charge of our part of the lift — Nos 296 and 297 Squadrons towing 60 Horsas between us — we lined them up the night before on the runway at Earls Colne — an incredible sight. We took off at 07.30hrs and the LZ was near a place called Wesel on the German side of the Rhine. By the time we arrived with the rest of the enormous gaggle of gliders and tugs at about 10.30hrs, the defences were fully alert and as we trundled along at 500ft, they shot at us with everything including rifles. We released our glider and made a wide sweep over the dense wood which must have hidden a large number of enemy troops so we let go the heavy glider tow rope in the hope that one of the massive fittings on the end would lay a German low.

'The Rhine crossing was a great success and several planned re-supply trips were cancelled. In due course the occupants of our glider returned to Earls Colne and told us their story. When they landed they were promptly surrounded and made prisoner and put to digging foxholes. Then another Horsa landed, the Germans surrendered — and they finished digging the foxholes for our lads.

'That night we had a hell of a party and the wing commander was seen swinging from the rafters at one point. He was later awarded the DSO for his part in the operation — and thoroughly deserved it.'

CHAPTER 15

POSTWAR HALI

Above:
Capt G. N. Wickner's *Waltzing Matilda* at Castel Benito on its trip to Australia. The aircraft was ex-NR169 of No 466 Squadron, RAAF, and became G-AGXA for the flight.
Flt Lt Ling

Top left:
'H-Harry', a B Mk 6 of No 102 Squadron at Pocklington, sporting No 4 Group's daylight identification markings of two horizontal red tail bands.

Left:
PP317 was built by Handley Page as a C Mk 8 but was found to be surplus to requirements and was given the civil registration G-AIID, but painted G-AHYI! To add to the confusion another Halifax received the same treatment.

Far left top:
The HP70 was called the Halton; G-AHDS had the service airframe number PP277 and flew 436 sorties on the Berlin Air Lift.

Far left bottom:
The only Halton 2 to be built was PP336 owned by the Maharajah of Gaekwar and used as a VIP transport. On 10 April 1951 an engine fell off in flight and the aircraft landed at Stansted, where it was written off.
J. D. R. Rawlings

Above:
Halifax A Mk 9, RT796, served with Nos 47 and 295 Squadrons until written off at Fairford in February 1948. *RAF Museum*

Left:
A weather-beaten collection of Halifaxes from No 644 Squadron line up prior to embarking parachutists at Qastina, Palestine, in January 1946.
K. Burchett

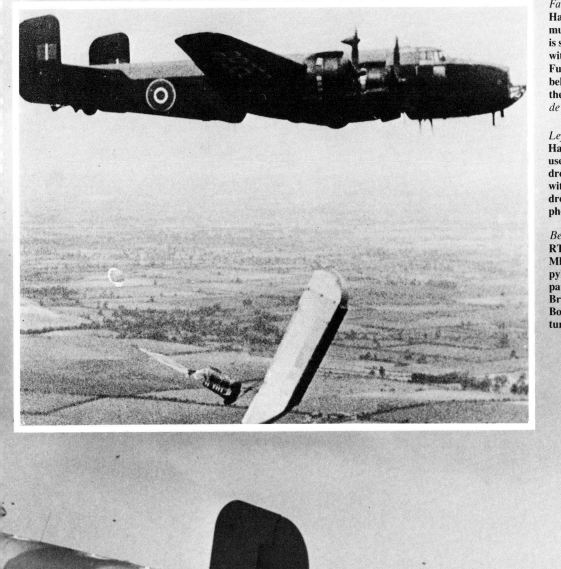

Far left:
Halifax B Mk 6, RG820, with multiple spray bar attachment, is seen here on engine icing trials with de Havilland in 1948. Fuselage reinforcing can be seen behind the cockpit to withstand the impact of the ice.
de Havilland

Left:
Halifax A Mk 7, PP350, was used in a series of tests in dropping containerised weapons with paratroops. Some were dropped free as shown in the photograph. *Crown Copyright*

Below:
RT760 was the third production Mk 9 complete with glider tug pylon and fairing near the parachute exit. Note the .5in Browning machine guns in the Boulton Paul Type D rear turret. *Flight International*

Top:
Halifax A Mk 9, ex-RT888 and G-ALOR, became Egyptian Air Force No 1157 and was almost certainly destroyed by the time of the Suez action.

Above:
Paras enter an A Mk 7 of No 644 Squadron at Qastina, Palestine, during January 1946.
K. Burchett

Above:
Halifax Met Mk 6, RG836, seen here at Luqa, Malta, was one of the last to fly with the RAF and served with No 224 Squadron, Gibraltar. *R. C. Sturtivant*

Left:
Hundreds of feet above a tranquil landscape, parachutists stream out of this Halifax A Mk 9.
Royal Aeronautical Society

HP71 Halifax A Mk 9
July 1945 to 1952

Type
Paratroop transport and glider
towing aircraft

Power Plant
Four 1,675hp Bristol
Hercules XVI engines

Performance
Maximum speed: 285mph at
6,000ft
Cruising speed: 195mph at
10,000ft
Service ceiling: 20,000ft
Range: 2,270 miles

Armament
Two .5in Browning machine guns
in tail turret

Weights
Empty: 37,800lb
Loaded: 65,000lb

Dimensions
Span: 104ft 2in
Length: 71ft 7in
Height: 20ft 9in

Entry into Service Jul 1945-1952

No Built	Type	Serial Block	Constructed
44	Fairey-built Halifax B/A Mk 7	PN285-PN343	May-Oct 1945
31	Halifax C Mk 8	PP308-PP338	Jun-Aug 1945
40	Halifax A Mk 7	PP339-PP389	Aug-Nov 1945
5	Halifax B Mk 7	RT753-RT757	Nov 1945
145	Halifax A Mk 9	RT758-RT938	Oct 1945-1946
96	EE-built Halifax B/Met Mk 6	RG749-RG879	Jun-Sept 1945
25	EE-built Halifax B/Met Mk 6	ST794-ST818	Sept-Dec 1945

Unit	Representative Aircraft	Base
No 18 Group, Coastal Command		
224 Squadron	RG838, ST804	Gibraltar
517 Squadron	RG780	Chivenor
521 Squadron	RG823	Chivenor

Top left:
**Halifax A Mk 9, RT796, of No 47
Squadron coded MOHDP. It saw
service in Palestine during 1946.**

Top right:
**Halifax C Mk 8, PP310, was
converted to a Halton and named
Falkirk in the BOAC fleet in July
1946.**

Right:
**LV838 was a converted Halifax
Mk 3 which was modified to
Mk 6 standard and then to
C Mk 8 with a removable belly
container. This container could
be winched up and down and
was designed to be exchanged
with a loaded one for quick
turnaround, although it was
never used.**

Unit	Representative Aircraft	Base
No 19 Group, Coastal Command		
202 Squadron	RG830, ST798	Aldergrove
518 Squadron	RG831, ST818	Aldergrove
No 38 Group, Transport Command		
47 Squadron	RT759	Fairford
102 Squadron	RG789	Pocklington
190 Squadron	PN286	Great Dunmow
295 Squadron	RT903	Fairford
301 Squadron	PP322	Chedburgh
304 Squadron	PP321	Chedburgh
620 Squadron	PN291, PP341	Great Dunmow/Aqir/ Cairo/Aqir
644 Squadron	PN302	Tarrant Rushton/ Qastina
No 205 Group, MEAF		
113 Squadron	RT786	Aqir
298 Squadron	PN289	Mauripur
Miscellaneous		
1 PTS	RT840	Ringway

HP70 Halifax C Mk 8

Type
Transport aircraft

Power Plant
Four 1,800hp Bristol Hercules 100 engines

Performance
Maximum speed: 304mph at 9,000ft
Cruising speed: 200mph at 10,000ft
Service ceiling: 25,000ft
Range: 2,710 miles

Weights
Empty: 37,760lb
Loaded: 65,000lb

Dimensions
Span: 104ft 2in
Length: 73ft 7in
Height: 20ft 9in

Below:
The battered remains of Halifax B Mk 7, PN323, retained by Handley Page for radio installation aerial tests. The forward fuselage is preserved at the Imperial War Museum.
Handley Page

CHAPTER 16

IN MEMORIAM

During 1984 one of the few Royal Air Force memorials in the country was unveiled near the former No 158 Squadron airfield of Lissett in the old East Riding of Yorkshire and 100 or so ex-members attended the service. It was from Lissett that the Halifax *Friday the 13th* flew its 128 operations leaving behind only its bomb-bedecked nose panel to be displayed in the Royal Air Force Museum at Hendon. That panel tells the story of the aircraft and perhaps that of Bomber Command's Halifaxes as a whole.

Halifax LV907 was taken on charge at Lissett on 10 March 1944 and given the letter 'F-Freddie'. This was a rather dubious honour despite the celebrated wartime film of the same name, because at Lissett during the previous 12 months no less than eight Halifaxes bearing the letter 'F' had been lost, and no 'Freddies' had completed tours.

An upside down horseshoe, a ladder over the entry door, a broken mirror and a skull and crossbones were added, to LV907 a large white tombstone was also originally painted on the nose with all the crew's names on it, but later had to be taken off because it shone in the search-lights. A scythe dripping with blood was also painted around the skull and cross-bones with the motto 'as ye sow, so shall ye reap 1944-194*'. As *Friday the 13th* survived each successive operation, so the 'bomb log' on the nose was extended. A key was added for the 21st operation and the usual array of decorations awarded to the crews — DFCs, DFMs, a DSO for 80 operations, a VC for 100 — was added to the aircraft's nose. *Friday* also achieved the unusual distinction among Bomber Command Halifaxes of surviving long enough to require a major inspection. At the end of the war it was displayed on Horse Guards Parade in London and then sent to be scrapped.

More memorials appear every year, but a little known RAF remembrance is sited in St Botolph's Church at Graveley. It commemorates all personnel who served with No 8 Group Path Finder Force,

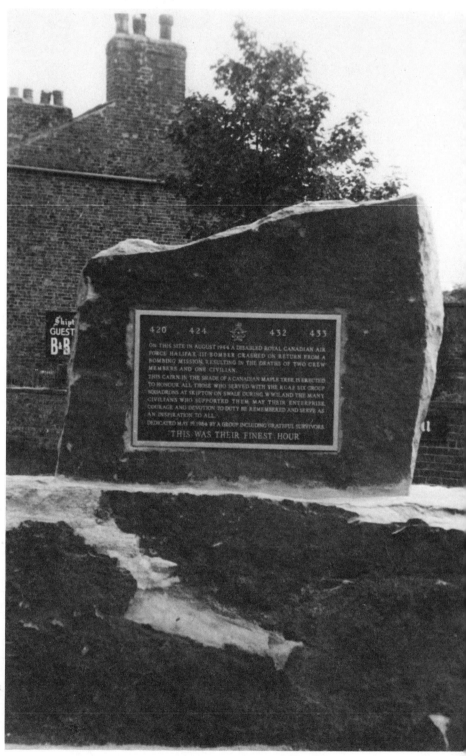

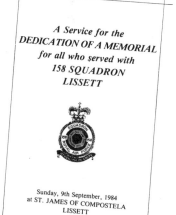

Far left:
Some 40 years on, veterans of the RCAF placed this memorial at Skipton-on-Swale during 1984 to honour the enterprise, courage and devotion to duty of all those who served with No 6 Group during World War 2.
P. Thorkildsen

Centre left:
This distinctive memorial to the Free French bomber squadrons stands on the edge of the airfield at Elvington, Yorkshire.
Brian J. Rapier

Left:
During September 1984 one of the few RAF memorials was unveiled at Lissett, wartime home of the Halifaxes of No 158 Squadron. *P. Thorkildsen*

Below:
The Order of Service for the dedication of the memorial to No 158 Squadron at Lissett.

A Service for the
DEDICATION OF A MEMORIAL
for all who served with
158 SQUADRON
LISSETT

Sunday, 9th September, 1984
at ST. JAMES OF COMPOSTELA
LISSETT

operating out of Graveley from 1942. Until March 1944, No 35 (Madras Presidency) Squadron flew Halifax aircraft alongside Mosquitos of No 692 Squadron, to lead 'Main Force' bombers to targets.

There is another memorial at Elvington, near York, to members of Nos 346 and 347 Squadrons which is looked after by members of the former Free French Air Force. There is a Royal Canadian Air Force memorial at Skipton-on-Swale and an avenue of oak and maple trees has been planted at Tholthorpe to commemorate the Canadian squadrons which served on the base. A second Royal Air Force plaque is to be sited at Pocklington in the near future.

The greatest memorial to the Halifax and those who flew it is the Mk 2 srs 1, W1048, 'S-Sugar', now in the Royal Air Force Museum; many regret that it cannot be restored to its former glory. Nowhere is this feeling stronger than in Yorkshire where the 500-strong Yorkshire Air Museum is planning to show a typical bomber airfield at work during World War 2 complete with a 'live' Halifax. Fuselage and engines have turned up from some most unlikely places, the RAF has some parts in store and others may be refurbished by the aircraft industry. The Yorkshire Air Museum is based at the former No 77 Squadron/Free French Air Force base at Elvington. There the control tower and several other airfield buildings will house a period canteen, a library and photographic displays as well as a bookshop and art gallery — all dedicated to bringing back a Halifax to the heart of 'Halifax Country'.

Right:
'The thin blue line' — VE-Day with No 10 Squadron at Melbourne.

Centre right:
RG815, a modified B Mk 6 called *Mercury*, was used for a round-the-world tour by the RAF Radio School during 1946-47 and is seen here at Shaibah, Iraq on Friday 15 November 1946.
K. Burchett

Below:
After May 1945 many flights were laid on for groundcrews to see the effects of the Allied bombing offensive; these were known as 'Cook's Tours'. Here a Mk 6 of No 102 Squadron, Pocklington, is prepared for one of these flights. About to embark on his very own 'Cook's Tour', FS S. R. Cook stands fifth from right.

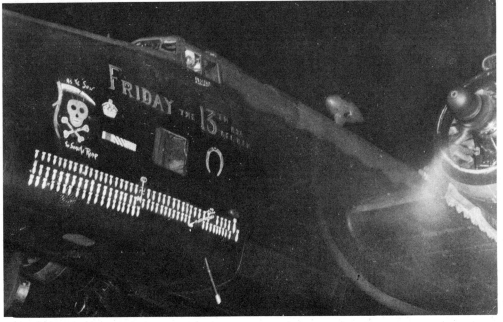

Above:
LV907 was named *Friday the 13th* and is seen here with its crew at the end of their tour.

Left:
Probably the best known Halifax, *Friday the 13th*, is seen at Lissett on return from its one hundredth operation — it was the first Halifax to achieve a century.

In memoriam
With the recent death of AVM Donald Bennett CB,
CBE, DSO, one of the RAF's most determined wartime
leaders has been lost. As commander of No 8
(Pathfinder) Group from 1943 to 1945, Bennett's name
will forever be linked with the exploits of the PFF
Halifaxes and their crews over occupied Europe. *IWM*

BOOK TWO

WELLINGTON AT WAR

Wellington
at war

Chaz Bowyer

Contents

Cover: Wellington III, Z1572, VR-Q, of No 419 ('Moose') Sqn, RCAF, circa May 1942. *C. E. Brown*

Title page: In Indian skies. Two of 99 Sqn's Wellingtons in the 'Forgotten War' zone, 1944. *IWM*

Left: Trolley train of 250lb GP bombs waiting for loading to a 149 Sqn Wellington at Mildenhall, while refuelling is completed.

Introduction

Any student of the RAF's bomber effort during 1939-45 can be forgiven if, after reading the wealth of literature published since then, he/she reaches the conclusion that the vast bulk of that effort was undertaken by Lancasters, Halifaxes, and/or Mosquitos. No one could deny the superb contributions made by all those aircraft, yet it is too often forgotten that until any of those designs appeared on the operational scene in significant numbers, ie until well into 1942, the full responsibility for carrying the air offensive into German skies was undertaken by several pre-1939 designs of twin-engined bombers. These included the Blenheim, Hampden, Whitley, and — especially — a design which was destined to remain in first-line operational service throughout the war and, incidentally, be built in greater quantities than *any* other RAF bomber during those years — the Vickers Wellington.

Universally nicknamed 'Wimpy' after the hamburger-gulping trencher-man J. Wellington Wimpy in the prewar Popeye strip cartoon series, the ubiquitous Wellington ultimately undertook every role and duty possible for an aircraft of its configuration. Primarily a bomber, it became equally effective as a submarine hunter-killer, torpedo-strike weapon, reconnaissance vehicle, freight-wagon and supply-dropper, VIP transporter, all-round trainer, ambulance, and general communications hack. Its strength of construction became a byword in aircrew circles, and many hundreds of crews owe their lives to the Wimpy's ability to absorb frightening battle damage and still 'bring 'em back alive'. In effect, the Wellington was almost the last of the RAF's 'cloth-bombers' — metal-constructed with fabric skinning — yet most ex-Wimpy crews would swear that it was the greatest such design.

The Wellington's origin can be traced to an Air Ministry Specification, B.9/32, issued to tender on 20 October 1932, for a new, twin-engined, monoplane, medium bomber for the RAF; a specification which also 'gave birth' to the Handley Page Hampden and Harrow bombers. With amendments and modifications in subsequent years, mainly for greater weight parameters and increased power, this AM Spec eventually spawned the Vickers B.9/32 prototype, serialled K4049. It made its first flight on 15 June 1936 at Brooklands, and in the same month it was proposed to call the new design Crecy, though this title was changed to Wellington three months later. K4049 commenced its flight trials and immediately displayed excellent potential, resulting in the issue of AM Spec 29/36 in February

1937 for a redesigned production version, the Mk 1 Wellington, for Service use. Before completion of its flight testing, however, K4049 was totally destroyed in a flying trial on 19 April 1937, breaking up in mid-air. In its Mk 1 production configuration the Wellington incorporated many necessary Service requirements and additions, including enclosed, power-operated gun turrets in the nose, belly and tail positions, bomb bay installation, *et al*; the first production example, L4212, making its first flight on 23 December 1937, fitted with two Bristol Pegasus XX engines.

The first RAF unit to commence re-equipment with Wellingtons was No 99 Squadron, based at Mildenhall, Suffolk, which received its first example, L4215, on 10 October 1938. Nine more squadrons began re-equipment before the outbreak of war — Nos 38, 149, 9, 148, 115, 37, 75, 214, 215 in chronological sequence. Thus, in September 1939, eight Wellington squadrons comprised the total strength of No 3 Group, Bomber Command, while the remaining pair (Nos 75 and 148) were Group Pool units with No 6 Group. By May 1945 a total of 73 Squadrons and a myriad of training or other specialised Flights or units were to have flown Wellingtons in some guise. Production of Wellingtons commenced in 1937 and was to continue until October 1945, during which period 11,460 production Wellingtons were built — the greatest number of *any* British bomber *ever* produced. The Wellington remained in RAF service after the war — mainly Mk X variants flown as trainers or airborne classrooms — until the type's ultimate retirement from RAF livery in late March 1953. Only one solitary example of a complete Wellington now exists; MF628, a Mk X built in 1944, which, after a chequered career, was finally handed over to the RAF Museum, Hendon, on 26 October 1971, where it may be viewed today in splendidly refurbished state.

The history of the Wellington has yet to be recorded in fully comprehensive form, and I would emphasise immediately that this volume is in no way intended to masquerade as any such 'biography' of that superb old lady. Its theme — as in all titles in this particular series — is simply a sincere evocation of the Wimpy, of the type of men and women who flew or tended her and, I hope, an authentic recreation of contemporary 'atmosphere' of the Wellington's hey-day. Towards that purpose I have been helped by the extraordinary generosity of many, many ex-air and ground crews who served with Wimpys during the years 1938-45; all of whom volunteered accounts, anecdotes, information, and the loan of precious photographs and documents. The list is long, and therefore detailed as a separate appendix in the rear of this book. In addition I received totally selfless and immediate practical help from a number of friends and colleagues. Of these I would mention particularly R. C. B. 'Chris' Ashworth, Roy Bonser, Jim Crowshaw, Sid Finn, E. 'Ted' Hine of the Imperial War Museum Photo Library, Phil Jarrett, Eric Morgan, Ken Munson, Bryan Philpott, Bart Rijnhout, Bruce Robertson, Ray Sturtivant, and G. S. 'Stu' Leslie. And no book of mine can fail to illustrate the skill and expertise of Dave Gray of Walkers Studios, Scarborough, who constantly produces splendid reproductions of faded and ancient photographs for use in illustration. To each of those mentioned I offer an open hand of sincere gratitude.

Chaz Bowyer
Norwich, 1982

Below: Wellington LN323 sets off to bomb a target in Italy, 1944. *IWM*

Roots

Above: Father-Figure. The first Wellington prototype, K4049, in its original configuration, June 1936. Engines are 915hp Pegasus Xs. *Vickers Ltd*

Left: K4049 being trundled over the River Wey toll-bridge at Brooklands. All aircraft bearing RAF roundels were not required to have the toll charged . . . *Vickers Ltd*

Above: L4212, the prototype Wimpy Mk 1, taking off from Brooklands on its first flight, 23 December 1937, piloted by Mutt Summers. *Vickers Ltd*

Right: Barnes Wallis's geodetic design illustrated by these Mk 1 Wimpy fuselages in the Weybridge erecting shop, 1939. *Vickers Ltd*

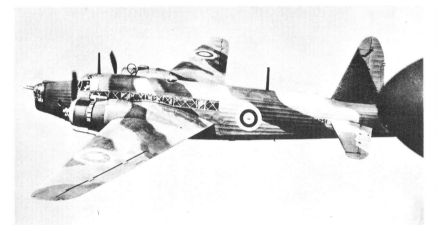

Above left: Close-up of the 'basket-weave' construction; an internal view from the nose position, with pilot's position in foreground. *Vickers Ltd*

Above: L4250, the prototype Wellington Mk II at Brooklands, fitted with Rolls-Royce Merlin Xs, which made its first flight on 3 March 1939. Later used for experimental 40mm cannon trials, L4250 ultimately became a training airframe (3477M) in December 1942. *Vickers Ltd*

Left: L4251, the prototype Mk III Wimpy, which first flew on 19 May 1939. Engines were Hercules HEISM two-stage supercharger units. *Vickers Ltd*

Right: P9238, a Mk 1c converted to become the Mk III production model, with improved Hercules engines. The Mk III Wimpy became a prime strike aircraft for Bomber Command from 1941. *Vickers Ltd*

Below: R1220, the Mk IV prototype, viewed just after roll-out from the Chester factory, late 1940. Engines were 1,050hp Pratt & Whitney Twin Wasps. First RAF deliveries of production examples began in June 1941. *Vickers Ltd*

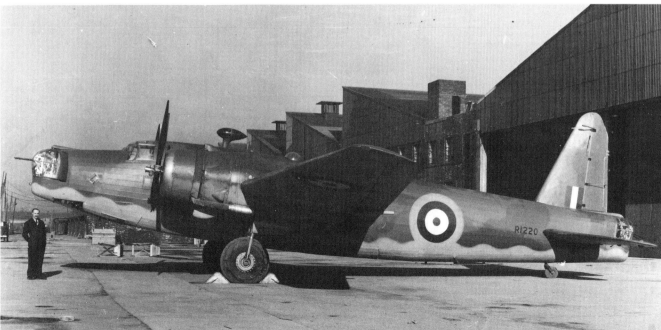

Above: L4250, the prototype
Mk II, fitted experimentally
with a 40mm Vickers cannon
mid-upper turret, and twin fin/
rudders, January 1942.
Vickers Ltd

Right: The same machine,
with 40mm cannon
installation, but with normal,
single fin/rudder, and rear gun
turret location faired over.
Vickers Ltd

Below: Postwar view of a
Wellington T10 trainer,
NC425, of No 7 Air Navigation
School (ANS), 1948. Note
retention of front and rear gun
turrets here.
*Sqn Ldr D. J. Munro via R.
Bonser*

Above: Shark-nose. Wellington
Mk VI, DR484, fitted with RR
Merlin 60 engines and Type
423 bomb gear. Designed for
high altitude bombing, with a
pressure cabin housing entire
crew of four. This particular
machine was eventually
reduced to spares on
21 December 1942.
Vickers Ltd

Above: A Wellington B10 of No 1689 Flight.
via R. C. B. Ashworth

Right: Hybrid. Wellington II, Z8570, fitted with Merlin 62 main engines, and a tail-installation of a Whittle jet engine, at Bruntingthorpe, 1944

Below: Wellington LN175, a Mk X modified for testing Rolls-Royce Dart turbo-props later used in the Vickers Viscount et al. *Vickers Ltd*

Right: Last of the Breed. Wellington X, MF628, the sole surviving complete Wimpy in the world. Built in 1944, it was ultimately handed over to the RAF Museum, Hendon on 26 October 1971, where, in splendidly refurbished state, it may be viewed today.
Vickers Ltd

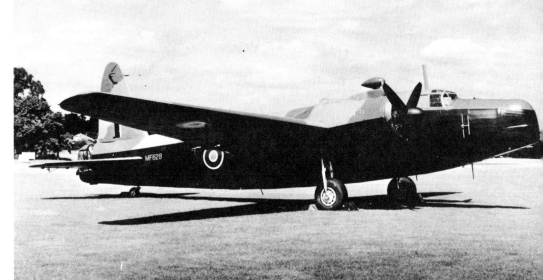

In the Beginning

Flying Officer (later, Group Captain) A. Montagu-Smith was the 99 Squadron adjutant when he flew a Wellington for the first time on 8 November 1938. His account of his personal reactions and experiences during those early days probably mirror most contemporary pilots' views of the first Wimpys:

'With the introduction of the Wellington into RAF squadron service in the autumn of 1938 a whole new era of military flying began for the pilots of Bomber Command. Until then the night bomber force consisted mainly of squadrons equipped with the Handley Page Heyford; a 100mph biplane with open cockpit, fixed undercarriage, and simple instrument panel — in fact, merely a refinement of the bombers used in France towards the end of World War 1. The Wellington was something entirely new.

'To the pilots of No 99 Squadron at Mildenhall, Suffolk, who were the first to receive the type, the changeover was exciting. Squadron pilots collected the first aircraft from Weybridge in October 1938, and caused some concern by arriving back at Mildenhall after dark, thus necessitating night landings. As one of the first officers to fly a squadron Wellington — L4220 on 8 November 1938 — I found it to be an exhilarating occasion, albeit somewhat claustrophobic due to the unfamiliar enclosed cockpit. Handling the aircraft required a very different technique from that of the Heyford. For the first time one had to operate a retractable undercarriage — which could easily be

Below: Wimpy crew about to board their aircraft, July 1940.
Sport & General Agency

forgotten; flaps had to be used, while the full instrument panel was a source of wonderment. Until then one had relied upon the elementary turn-and-bank indicator; now an artificial horizon had to be got used to. In the Heyford the pilot sat high, on a level with the upper mainplane, but in the Wellington, with its short under-carriage, one seemed very near the ground.

'The final weeks of 1938 and first eight months of 1939 kept the pilots of 99 Squadron busy becoming efficient in operating the new aircraft, and in early 1939 the tempo of life at Mildenhall increased noticeably. The two resident squadrons, Nos 99 and 149, flew their Wellingtons by day and night continuously to achieve operational standards. For example, during April and May I carried out 35 various training sorties. On 25 May, during an exercise with the Fleet in the English Channel, flying L4297, I suffered a burst fuel pipe which necessitated a forced-landing at RAF Gosport. The consequent one-engine approach and landing was effected without difficulty, but it must be admitted that the let-down from 10,000ft with only one serviceable engine created a moment or two of distinct uneasiness. Gosport was more or less in a built-up area, and I knew that my approach with a heavily-laden aircraft had to be right first time — I could not go round again.

'In the summer of 1939 the Wellington squadrons were ordered to practise daylight, low-level flying, which seemed to indicate a possible change in the operational role. Anyway, it provided an excuse to indulge in ''contour-chasing'', and Wellingtons were to be seen low-flying all over Southern England. It was fun, but very tiring when kept up for a couple of hours or so. Then on 18 July 1939 an exercise of some magnitude was planned to begin. All the serviceable aircraft of No 3 Group, Bomber Command, led by the Air Officer Commanding (AOC), Air Commodore A. A. Thompson, set off from their respective bases in East Anglia for a formation ''showing-the-

Top right: Sqn Ldr Montagu-Smith briefs his pilots of A Flt, 221 Sqn, at Bircham Newton, 1941. *C. Beaton/Air Ministry*

Right: Navigator's office in a 221 Sqn Wellington, Bircham Newton, 1941. *C. Beaton/Air Ministry*

Above: Peace Hazard. A 99 Sqn Wellington, bearing the unit's prewar codes VF, which had its tail fabric strip off in flight. Its pilot, Sgt Atkinson, was killed in action when serving with the Path Finder Force in later years. *S. C. Atkinson*

Right: War Hazard. Tail damage to Wellington T2739 of 99 Sqn, after an encounter with a German nightfighter, early 1941. *PNA Ltd*

Below: Czech Threesome. Mk 1cs of 311 (Czech) Sqn, late 1940. Aircraft 'M' was R1410 which later served with 25 OTU and failed to return on 25/26 June 1942; 'K' was R1378 which crashed on 3 March 1942; while 'A' (T2541) also served as 'O-Orange' on 99 Sqn at one period. *Imperial War Museum*

flag'' flight to France. However, bad weather south of London forced a change of plan, which was communicated to each aircraft of this very large formation by wireless — we did not have R/T. As a Flight Lieutenant now, I was leading a section of B Flight, 99 Squadron, in Wellington L4220. The result of this last-minute change of plan was chaotic. The new orders cancelled the French trip and substituted a tour along the south coast of England instead. As we flew west the weather got steadily worse, with low cloud and poor visibility, until it was difficult to even see the nearest aircraft ahead. Eventually I received a ''return to base'' signal from my wireless operator. At the same time, to my alarm, out of the gloom came a number of Wellingtons on a reciprocal course! These belonged to the leading squadrons returning home, having jumped the gun by following the leader before the signal had reached all aircraft. With Wellingtons gaily passing on either side of me, the scene can well be imagined — I can still remember the look of horror on the face of my second pilot-cum-navigator, Flg Off Hetherington, a New Zealander. However, we were able to extricate ourselves from this shambles, and miraculously there were no collisions.

'On 1 September 1939, in Wellington L4247, with the rest of 99 Squadron, I moved from Mildenhall to Newmarket Heath, which was to be our war station. During September and October training continued, although on a number of occasions the squadron ''bombed up'' and stood by for operations which were eventually scrubbed due to political reasons. Remember, at that period of the war bombing of the German mainland was forbidden. Thus, when 99 Squadron carried out its first sortie of World War 2 on 30 October, the target was the German Fleet reported somewhere in the Heligoland Bight. I took off in L4297 but bad weather on reaching the German coast prevented the squadron from sighting any enemy ships, and we recrossed the North Sea to Mildenhall after an uneventful flight. Much of the flight home was after nightfall and I can recall the problems of finding Mildenhall in a blacked-out countryside. All aircraft on this sortie had been ordered to land at Mildenhall for debriefing, but there was little control, if any, from the ground, with the result that there were numbers of

Wellingtons circling the Mildenhall district in the dark with pilots trying to identify the correct beacon.

'On 14 December 1939, No 99 Squadron set off on its second war sortie for the German coast with a full complement of 12 aircraft ie two flights of six — the normal size of a peacetime squadron. Strong opposition from enemy ships and aircraft was encountered and five Wellingtons and their crews were lost, while a sixth crashed on return, killing or injuring its crew members. This experience put 99 out of action for some time, while three squadron air gunners were recommended for and eventually awarded Distinguished Flying Medals.

In the winter of 1940 it was decided to form the first Wellington squadron for anti-submarine operations in Coastal Command, and on 21 November 1940 No 221 Squadron was reformed at Bircham Newton. In the following month I was posted to 221 Squadron and, as a Squadron Leader, was appointed commander of A Flight,

and because of my Wellington experience found myself as the unofficial squadron instructor. Our first aircraft were mainly cast-offs from bomber units for training and conversion use. Early in May 1941 the squadron became operational, and I flew to the new base at Limavady, Northern Ireland, on 2 May in Wellington W5671. We had by then received our new aircraft, fully equipped with ASV appendage including external antennae. All this extra equipment necessarily increased the overall weight of the aircraft considerably, and when carrying depth charges they felt very sluggish after take-off until speed had been built up.

'On 15 May 1941, flying in Wellington W5671, my crew and I located and attacked a U-boat well out in the Atlantic. This was 221 Squadron's first action, and (I believe) the first attack on an enemy submarine by a maritime Wellington in the war. It was an exhilarating moment for me as we dived in to the attack to release our

Top: Wellington Is, L4367 and L4369 of 75 Sqn during war exercises in August 1939. The white cross markings represented the 'Westland' ('friendly') forces of these war games.

Above: 75 Sqn Wimpys (L4367, nearest and L4370) at 12,000ft during the August 1939 war exercises.
Sport & General Agency

Above: L4221, BK-U, of 115 Sqn prior to the war. By 1944 this aircraft had been converted to a DWI anti-mine sweeper, and crashed in November that year, killing its crew.

depth charges, which hit the water near the U-boat but not close enough to create any visible damage. However, morale received an excellent boost and the squadron felt that it was seriously 'in business'. There followed a period of intensive flying, with trips of nine and ten hours out over the Atlantic forming a regular pattern of life. All sorties were carried out at fairly low level, which meant ploughing through all sorts of unpleasant weather conditions, and we were usually pretty tired men after such long flights. On 10 June and again on 12 June 1941, my crew and I found boatloads of survivors from torpedoed merchant ships out in the Atlantic. These were heart-rending scenes and we were gratified that on both occasions we were able to help rescue the unfortunate sailors by directing naval vessels to the relevant locations.

'By August 1941 the squadron had moved to St Eval, Cornwall, to help cover the Bay of Biscay, and on 5 August, in Wellington W5732 over the Bay, we attacked our second U-boat which was sighted on the surface. As we flew away after our attack we could see patches of oil and some pieces of wreckage floating on the sea. Although not sunk, we heard later that the submarine had been sufficiently damaged to force it to return to its base in France for repairs. We also received a congratulatory signal from the AOC, 19 Group. Our third attack on a U-boat came on 11 September 1941, again in the Bay of Biscay, but no positive results were seen.

'Two days later, on 13 September, in Wellington W5671, I flew my last sortie with 221 Squadron, and it proved to be very hectic. While on anti-submarine patrol well down in the Bay of Biscay we were intercepted by a Junkers Ju88 long-range fighter. As he closed in behind us for the attack I climbed at full throttle for cloud cover 2,000ft above. The Wellington responded well and we gained the safety of the overcast before the Ju88 pilot could get within lethal range. We all breathed a sigh of relief as I settled down for some ten minutes of instrument flying. When I let down below cloud and resumed my original course, with no Ju88 in sight, both engines of the Wellington stopped! The explanation was simple. In the excitement of avoiding the enemy fighter, we had forgotten to change over petrol tanks at the correct time. The effect on my crew was electric! I shouted, "Petrol cocks!" and there was a rush for the midway position in the aircraft. My second pilot had got there first and switched tanks. In the meantime, without any power, we were rapidly losing height and I was contemplating a ditching with a definite lack of enthusiasm. However, with less than 1,000ft to go both engines roared back to life again — the wonderful Wimpy had not let us down, and on completion of the patrol we returned to base to fly another day. In my own case, this was the end of my operational tour of duty with 221 Squadron. Sadly, after some 500 hours of Wimpy flying with Nos 99 and 221 Squadrons, I never flew a Wellington again.'

Above: L4304 of 148 Sqn in early 1939 livery. It later served with 75 Sqn, 15 OTU and 11 OTU before being struck off RAF charge on 19 November 1944. *Crown copyright*

Right: No 149 Sqn's Wellingtons (nearest, L4272, LY-G) over Paris on 14 July 1939 (Bastille Day). An ex-9 Sqn machine, L4272 later became OJ-C with 149 Sqn, served with No 9 BATF and No 3 OTU, before becoming instructional airframe 2875M in December 1941. *C. E. Brown*

Below: No 9 Sqn Wellingtons flying near Honington in early 1940, with ventral 'dustbin' gun turret extended under nearest aircraft N3000. This machine was later to see service with Nos 9, 40 adn 311 Sqns, then 12 OTU, 28 OTU, the Central Gunnery School (CGS) and the Air Transport Auxiliary (ATA), before being struck off RAF charge on 19 November 1944. *via T. Mason*

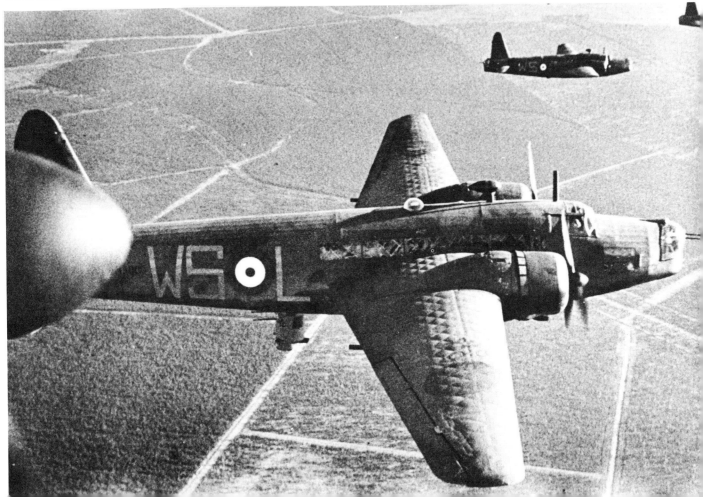

Early Days and Nights

Group Captain J. R. 'Benny' Goodman DFC, AFC completed 40 operational sorties in Wimpys during 1940-41 when, as a junior sergeant pilot, he commenced a lengthy and distinguished career. His account of just some of the varied facets of a Wimpy pilot's life during the first two years of the war give emphasis to the near-primitive conditions endured by the crews of Bomber Command then — and no less the courage and determination of those pioneering crews in the air offensive against Nazi Germany:

'I joined 37 Squadron — the "37th Foot" — at Feltwell, near Thetford, as a sergeant pilot in the middle of August 1940, when the Battle of Britain was at its height. Within a few days the squadron, indeed the whole of Bomber Command, was at instant readiness for operations against a German seaborne invasion, expected at any time. This meant that all personnel were confined to the station, and all aircraft were bombed up to maximum capacity with 18 250lb GP bombs. I was allocated as second dicky to the crew to Plt Off Herbert Ashton Clark, an ex-flight sergeant fitter who had turned pilot during the pre-war expansion of the Service. Not only was Nobby Clark very knowledgeable about what made aircraft tick, but he was also a first class pilot and navigator. If there is any one man to whom I have to be grateful for the fact that I survived two tours of ops in Bomber Command, that man is Nobby Clark. (He survived the war as a Wing Commander, DSO, DFC and became a farmer).

'Being on standby did not mean that we sat around waiting for the invasion fleet to set sail from Channel ports. In fact we hammered away at the German barges and also made regular sorties against targets in Germany. However, the squadron armourers were hard-pressed, because they were constantly bombing up or de-bombing aircraft. For example, an aircraft on standby, loaded with 18 250lb bombs, if it was detailed for normal operations, would need to be de-bombed and a mixed load of 500-pounders and incendiaries substituted. When it returned from its sortie, the aircraft would then again be loaded with 18 250lb bombs and resume its standby state.

'Our operational briefings covered three categories of target; the primary, the secondary, and something called SEMO or MOPA. The aim was to attack the primary if possible, but if for any reason this proved impossible — bad weather *et al* — then we were expected to go for the secondary, which would be similar in character though in a different area. If we could not find either of these targets then we would resort to SEMO or MOPA — meaning "Self-evident military objective" or "Military objective previously attacked". If no target in any of these categories could be found, then our strict orders were to bring the bombs back — remember, this was 1940; later in the war there was no such thing as bringing bombs back from Germany.

'One night be were briefed to attack the marshalling yards at Hamm, a favourite German target in those days. We duly arrived over the Ruhr but could not find Hamm, despite a good moon and diligent searching. The Ruhr smog was everywhere and also obscured the secondary target. After sculling around for a while at 3,000ft, we saw a train puffing along beneath us and we descended and identified it as a goods train. We decided this was a SEMO — indeed, it was a perfect target because it could neither stand and fight or run away. We made our bombing run straight along the railway line and dropped a stick of HE and incendiaries on the line of trucks, then turned away and flew well clear to await developments. These were not long in coming. Our incendiaries had

Right: No 37 Sqn Wellington crew, August 1940, Feltwell. From left: Unknown rear AG, Sgt J. R. Goodman (2/P), Plt Off H. A. Clark (Capt), Sgt W. W. W. Smith (Obs), Sgt 'Ginger' Jones (W/Op), and Sgt Ken Rutherford (AG, later killed in action). Note ice damage from props on fuselage fabric.
Grp Capt J. R. Goodman

Below: Wimpy T2888, 'R-Robert' of B Flt, 99 Sqn at Newmarket, November 1940 — the 'Jinx Kite' referred to in the text.
Grp Capt J. R. Goodman

Bottom: Crew of Wimpy T2888 'R-Robert', 99 Sqn, Newmarket, November 1940. From left: J. H. Parry (W/Op), J. R. Goodman (Capt), G. A. Masters (2/P), G. B. Cooper (Obs), R. Wickham (Front AG). *Grp Capt J. R. Goodman*

set some trucks on fire, while the HE had stopped the train. In seconds one of the trucks flared up, then an enormous explosion took place. Our Wimpy rocked as the blast hit her, so we scuttled away, undamaged, leaving behind a splendid firework display as what was clearly an ammunition train blew up.

'No pilot with any experience of Wellingtons would spin one intentionally, and no sane pilot would ever spin one at night. However, Nobby Clark and I found ourselves in the latter category soon after the ammunition train incident. We took off on the night of 5 October 1940 in our faithful T2508, ''T-Tommy'' and headed for the German barges crammed in the Rotterdam dock basins. We climbed steadily from Feltwell to 9,000ft and, after crossing the English coast at Southwold, tested all guns and headed for Holland. Eventually the front gunner uttered a laconic warning, ''Enemy coast ahead'' and we became especially watchful. The Hook of Holland loomed up out of the darkness and soon we could see Rotterdam and the target dock basins. The navigator now took his place in the nose and Nobby gently circled the town, then set ''T-Tommy'' straight at the docks. Meanwhile the Germans had not been idle; searchlights and flak were well in evidence. The heavy flak was something of a nuisance and from time to time there was a crump, crump as shells exploded

147

Above: R1333, the 'Broughton Bomber', which was initially delivered to 99 Sqn at Newmarket. Contrary to previous published statements this machine crashed, fully war-loaded, on take-off for an operational sortie on 18 December 1940, on the 'Devil's Dyke', and exploded in flames, killing the rear gunner.

Right: No 99 Sqn crew at Waterbeach, mid-1941. From left: L. B. 'Joe' Knight (F/AG), Bob Holden (2/P), Percy Hawkins (Wop/AG), F. G. 'Stan' Holloway (Capt), Jim Dermody (Obs, a New Zealander), and R. 'Bob' Butler (R/AG). All except Dermody were later to be killed on ops. *N. Didwell*

Below: Winter 1940-41 at Newmarket. A 99 Sqn Wimpy with appropriate protective covers in a snow landscape. *Planet News Ltd*

nearby. The bombing run continued and Nobby Clark concentrated on what was happening on the ground. I noticed our speed was dropping, then the bombs began to leave the racks as the navigator pressed the bomb release button. At this instant there was a loud bang as a shell exploded beneath us, and "T-Tommy" reared up like a startled horse, hovered momentarily, then fell over to starboard and rolled into a right-hand spin.

'When an aircraft spins the pilot is pressed hard into his seat by centrifugal force or reaction — call it what you will — and Nobby had his work cut out in applying left rudder and pushing the control column forward in his attempt to stop the spin. Nothing happened and the Wellington continued to flail downwards. I was pressed firmly against the metal former behind the pilots' cockpit and could barely move. Nobby now took emergency spin recovery action, blasting the throttles open and closed and moving the control column sharply back and forward in an attempt to shake the Wimpy out of its spin — "Tommy" merely continued to rotate. Nobby now called, "Jump, jump!", the order to abandon the aircraft. At this command I attempted to pull myself forward towards the nose in order to let the front gunner out of his turret, but I couldn't get forward. Looking again at the skipper, I could see that he was still trying to stop the spin, and I heaved myself across the bottom of the cockpit and grabbed the right rudder pedal and pulled like mad. To my astonishment — and joy — it moved and helped Nobby to hold a little more left rudder. He blasted the engines again and the spin suddenly stopped, leaving us in a steep dive with all the blind-flying instruments haywire.

'Luckily, the night was clear with a good horizon, so we were able to level out and settle on to a good course until the instruments behaved normally, then we turned for home at about 1,000ft and limped along, gaining a little height as we progressed towards East Anglia. Nobby found that he could move the rudder but the elevators were stiff, so he decided to use the latter as little as possible. Some two hours later we arrived at Feltwell and Nobby brought "T-Tommy" in for a skilful landing, avoiding the use of flaps because their operation would also require considerable forward movement of the control column to hold the nose down. After landing the full extent of the damage was revealed. Large areas of fabric had been torn from the fuselage, but the major horror was that the elevators had moved bodily sideways and the rollers on which they rotated were just touching their companion rollers on the tailplane. We had been literally a fraction of an inch away from complete disaster.

'The time now came for me to take over a crew of my own, and I climbed aboard 37 Squadron's dual Mk 1c Wellington, R2937, with Nobby Clark's crew at their usual stations, but with

Above: Remarkably clear view of interior of Wimpy T2888, 'R-Robert', 99 Sqn, Newmarket, November 1940 — taken with a box Brownie camera!
Grp Capt J. R. Goodman

Germany and they had not. However, we quickly became friends and conducted ourselves as a crew should, and soon began to operate over Germany in our own "Cloth Bomber" (as the Wimpy was also known).

'My third trip as skipper was to be Bremen and we bounced along the flare path on the night of 16 October in R3224 with everyone relaxed and the Pegasus engines roaring reassuringly. At 90mph I eased her gently into the air — then things began to go wrong. She absolutely refused to gain speed. I checked that the wheels were up and locked, then retracted the flaps which had been set at 15 degrees before take-off — the Wimpy accelerated to 95mph! I checked the cooling gills but they were correctly set. The second pilot and I went through everything with a fine toothcomb but found nothing to account for the aircraft's strange behaviour. Meanwhile I'd eased her gently upwards and levelled out at 800ft with the exhaust rings glowing red-hot. I throttled back slightly and she began to lose height, so back to full throttle we went. The most urgent need now was to land as soon as possible, but this could not be done at once because aircraft of 37 and 75 (NZ) Squadrons were still taking off. So round and round Feltwell we went until at last I could fly over the take-off point and flash my downward indentification light and receive a reassuring green from the airfield control pilot's Aldis lamp, giving permission to land. The circuit and approach to land were normal except that a great deal of power had to be used even though we were descending. At last we crossed the airfield boundary and levelled out above the grass — there were no runways then. I was a little too high so closed the throttles — which was a mistake because the Wimpy immediately sank and landed heavily, driving the undercarriage through the wings. She skidded along the ground quite gently and came to a stop parallel to the flare path. I switched off everything electrical, there being a grave fire risk, then the crew and I abandoned ship smartly.

'We were met by the CO of 75 Squadron, who was OC Flying that night, and I told him the strange story. He said nothing and we walked round the Wimpy together while he shone his torch on the aircraft. When we were at the trailing edge of the starboard wing

the squadron commander, Wg Cdr "Willie" Merton (later, Air Chief Marshal) in the right hand seat. I went through all the drills under the CO's eagle eye and put the Wimpy and its crew through flight procedures which were well-known and practised by us all. After just over an hour the CO pronounced himself satisfied and we landed. I reported to this officer shortly afterwards when he informed me that I was now an aircraft captain! I was just 19 years old, the youngest "skipper" on the squadron! My chest swelled with pride and I felt nine feet tall — but I was soon to be cut down to size. The thing I recall strongly about my new crew is that every one of them was older than me — two were even married. The only advantage I had over them was that I'd flown ops over

he suddenly stopped and said, "That's the trouble", pointing at the top of the wing at its deepest point. He was shining his torch at the petrol filler flaps, which I could see were down but not locked. These were metal hinged flaps covering the necks and caps of the main fuel tanks, and after refuelling these flaps had to be latched securely. Failure to do this would mean that on take-off these flaps would rise into the area of reduced air pressure above the wing and would become spoilers, destroying the smooth airflow over the wing and the precious lift it gave. This had happened to us — we might easily have been killed and no one would ever have known the cause. I should add that the airman responsible for not locking the filler flaps was given 28 days detention. No doubt he deserved this, but it was an object lesson to me and I became a positive misery about these flaps, particularly when I became an instructor at 15 OTU at the end of my ops tour; though I have little doubt that my insistence on checking they were locked saved other pilots' lives.

'Sadder and wiser now, in rapid succession I dropped visiting cards on Dusseldorf, Emden and Bremen, and then at the beginning of November No 37 Squadron become non-operational in order to prepare to fly out to the Middle East. We awaited the order to move, then quite suddenly I was struck down by a ghastly attack of 'flu and ended up in station sick quarters. Three days later the squadron flew off to Egypt, while I was eventually sent to another UK-based squadron in order to complete my tour; No 99 Squadron at Newmarket.

'My arrival at Newmarket could not have happened at a worse moment. The leading light on the squadron had failed to return from operations that night, and no one took much notice of the new arrival. Worse was to follow; I was allocated to B Flight and given the jinx aircraft, R-Robert, L7802. Every squadron had its jinx aircraft — one to which everything seemed to happen and which would go missing at the drop of a hat. In 99 Squadron there were two such kites — "B-Bertie" in A Flight, and "R-Robert" in B Flight. My arrival had coincided with the loss of the most experienced and popular captain in "B-Bertie". My new crew must have looked askance at me because they'd completed half a tour with "Ginger" Rothwell, a New Zea-

lander who had now gone on "rest" — if pounding a circuit at an OTU for up to 80 hours a month can be termed "rest". They did not relish the idea of changing skippers in mid-stream. Nor did I like the prospect of changing crews. In Bomber Command no one ever relished any change in crew; if, for example, a gunner was sick and was replaced by another for just one operation, the crew immediately become uneasy — in some odd way, they felt they had became more likely to get "the chop". However, the powers that be at HQ 3 Group had decided in their infinite wisdom that it made sense to post a Wellington skipper who'd completed half a tour to command a crew at another squadron who had also got through half a tour. In fact, it all worked out well and we

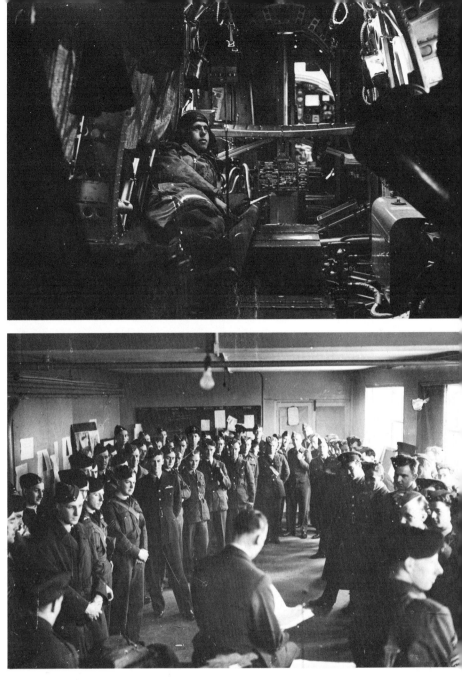

Top: Another 'inside' view of a Wellington, looking towards the nose. *IWM*

Above: Briefing, early 1941 style. *British Official*

Right: Putting on the clobber — a Wimpy crew dons flying clothing, circa April 1941. *British Official*

Below: No 75 (NZ) crew leaving the hangar at Feltwell, early 1941; an interesting view of contemporary flying clothing styles.

Bottom: Full crew complement of No 75 (NZ) Sqn posing for the Press at Feltwell, early 1941. *British Official*

finished our tour without too much bother — by contrast, my 37 Squadron crew ultimately perished in the Middle East.

'I lost no time in telling my new crew that I didn't believe in jinx aircraft, and that I had certainly no intention of going down in "R-Robert". Brave words, and oddly prophetic; we bore charmed lives in "R-Robert", but on the two occasions on which we went on leave "R-Robert" went down with other crews, so the jinx was preserved. Nor did "B-Bertie" fare any better. Aircraft workers at the Broughton factory at Chester "bought" a Wellington, R1333, and "presented" it to Bomber Command, where it was allocated to A Flight, 99 Squadron. It was given the code letter "B", possibly because it was named "The Broughton Bomber", and prepared for operations. The day came when this "B-Bertie" became operational and a delegation from the works came to watch the take-off. She got airborne and almost immediately crashed into the Devil's Dyke at Newmarket, catching fire and then exploding with the loss of all on board.

'The winter 1940-41 was as cold as charity and my faithful crew and I spent the best part of it living in the open grandstand at Newmarket Racecourse. Only when we'd become senior members of the squadron, ie we were well on towards completion of our tour, did we move into what was regarded as more salubrious accommodation at the Jockey Club in the town. Nevertheless, I recall with affection the spirit which prevailed on the squadron despite the wretched "domestic accommodation" — well did we deserve the appellation "The Mad Nines".

'Operations continued throughout the winter, though the weather was as great a hazard as the German defences. One night, on the way to Duisberg, we flew through heavy cloud and ice piled up on the wings; then suddenly the propellers turned blue and great sparks flew from one to the other — St Elmo's Fire, a manifestation I'd not seen before but was to encounter now and again thereafter. The ground staff too had their problems. There were no hangars at Newmarket, and the fitters, riggers, etc had to work in the open in all weathers. During that winter engine tents were placed over the Pegasus engines, with paraffin heaters inside, to stop the oil freezing. This was the only protection the fitters had, yet they survived. Places like Newmarket seemed to bring out the very best in everyone — life at the "permanent" stations didn't have the same zest.

'On 18 February 1941 something occurred which was quite outside the operational experience of the crew of "R-Robert". We were breaking in a new second pilot, doing circuits and landings at the Rowley Mile (our airfield). While taking off towards the town, with the new second dickey at the controls, I suddenly saw great gouts of smoke and debris ahead and realised that the town was being bombed. The bomb bursts were tracking towards us and I looked above them to see a German Dornier. He hadn't seen us and, after releasing his stick of HE, the pilot made a gentle turn to the left, presumably to check results. This gave me the chance to change seats with the second pilot and to close on the Dornier. We come up from underneath on his starboard side and as soon as we were close enough my front gunner, followed quickly by the rear gunner, opened fire. As we flew alongside him — for perhaps 10 to 15 seconds — he suddenly jerked and then hauled up into cloud. I pursued him but the murk was thick and I couldn't find him. After a few minutes I returned to base and reported the incident to the Flight commander, Sq Ldr J. B. Black, and there the matter might have ended. Later in the day, however, the Flight commander sent

Above: Climbing aboard. 75 (NZ) Sqn crew enter their Wimpy. Note AG carrying spare gun barrels.

for me and said a Dornier had crashed some 11 miles from Newmarket, and that the Army had reported it at low level and engaged it with light ack-ack fire. The Flight commander said no one could be positive that it was the Dornier which had bombed Newmarket, but it seemed very likely, and the thought I deserved half a "victory". Knowing how bloody awful the Army gunners were in those days, I think "R-Robert" deserved the whole victory — but who ever heard of a Wellington "fighter"? Within a day or two the incident was forgotten — we had something far more important to bother about; like surviving the rest or our ops tour. And a month later, on 17 March, my tour of duty with 99 Squadron ended, and I was told I was to go to 15 OTU, Harwell as a "screened captain" — the term then for Bomber Command skippers "resting" between operational tours.

'Before going to Harwell, however, I was to fly a reinforcement Wellington to the Middle East, so my crew and I duly reported to the Overseas Flight at Stradishall, where we took over a new Wimpy, T2614, and carried out a fuel consumption test in preparation for the trip. For some time reinforcement Wellingtons had been flown to Malta, thence to Egypt, but at Malta many had been destroyed on the ground by Ju88s operating from Sicily. The planners in Air Ministry got out their pieces of string and maps and discovered that a Wellington, carrying two overload tanks in the bomb bay, could fly

Right: Wimpy crew boarding at night, recalling Shakespeare's words. *Gentlemen of the shade, minions of the moon* (Henry IV Pt 1). *British Official*

Below right: Wg Cdr C. E. Kay, DFC (rt), OC 75 (NZ) Sqn and his second pilot at their stations. *IWM*

Left: Harwell OTU, May 1942, From left: Flt Lt P. A. Willatt, Plt Off J. R. Goodman, Flt Lt (later, Wg Cdr) P. E. Berry DFC. *Grp Capt J. R. Goodman*

nonstop from Stradishall to Dunkirk, thence to Marseilles, on to Algeria and ultimately to Benina airfield, near Benghazi — a trip of 11-12 hours. The 12 crews selected to make the initial trip were guinea pigs, though all had operational experience and we took-off just before dark on the night of 31 March. Eleven and a half hours later T2614 landed at Benina. In fact 11 out of the 12 landed safely at Benina; the 12th man having found himself over the sea at dawn decided to turn south and eventually motored in to Sirte airfield — where he and his crew were promptly made prisoners of war by occupying enemy troops!

'After a hurried breakfast, we flew on to Heliopolis, outside Cairo, and next day delivered T2614 to Abu Sueir, the MU near Ismailia. I was then instructed to report to HQ Middle East, where I was told that although I'd finished my tour of operations, the situation locally was serious, and for the time being I must rejoin a squadron. I elected to go to my old outfit, 37 Squadron, then based at Shallufa, at the southern end of the Suez Canal zone. I remained with 37, on desperate operations, until finally being told that my crew and I were ''on rest'' and would be going home to the UK.

'Thus, I only reached 15 OTU, Harwell at the end of November 1941 — some eight months after my initial posting notice. While on ''rest'' at Harwell, from November 1941 to August 1943, I flew three more Wimpy ops. Two of these were the ''thousand-bomber'' raids on Cologne and Essen in May-June 1942, while the third was a desperate business to Essen when we were almost literally shot down to ground level from 10,000ft by heavy flak. We were in Wimpy HD942 (which some idiot crashed a few days later and burnt up). However, I have one of the exhaust stubs in my possession still and treasure it; HD942 carried us gallantly to Essen and back that night and I have never forgotten her.'

Air Gunner

Steve Challen's first taste of 'action' was as an air gunner in Short Sunderlands with 201 Squadron, from August 1940. After three months of monotonous patrols and virtual inactivity, however, he volunteered for more lively employment:

'Sunderlands were a marvellous experience, but not my idea of action. My request for transfer from 201 was duly granted on 10 November 1940 I was posted to 40 Squadron, based at Wyton, Huntingdonshire. A few days after arriving at Wyton I was sent over to B Flight, which was detached at Alconbury. Here we were billetted in Alconbury House, not far from the airfield. The squadron's conversion from Blenheims to Wellingtons was proceeding quite rapidly, and in fact most of B Flight were near operational standard. The crew to which I was allocated were well through their tour on Blenheims, and were now in a hurry to become operational on Wimpys so that they could finish their tour and go on "rest duties". The captain was Fg Off Whithead. We did cross-countries, some low flying, air firing, and a height test. Then for some unknown reason I was posted to A Flight, which suited me because we were now billetted in the prewar barrack blocks of the Wyton station.

We did some ground and flying training from Wyton, which at that time was still a grass field.

'More local flying practice, a height test when we reached 15,000ft after a struggle, more practice, a load test, night flying, — we were deemed ready for operations. Each flying day then, over to Alconbury by bus unless one had one's own transport. I'd begged, then bought, an old New Imperial 250cc motor-bike from a pilot. Petrol was hard to come by, but it made me independent and able to go by the back roads to Alconbury most days. It was also useful in the evenings to get out to Huntingdon or St Ives, usually to the flicks (cinema), until one day at lunchtime when, doing a fast take-off from the front of the Mess, I met a car coming in! That ended motor-cycling until the forks were straightened.

'Sorting out of crews in A Flight went on until I was put with Plt Off "Tubby" Wills, a short, fat little man supposedly related to the Wills tobacco people. He was captain and first pilot. Fg Off "Mick" Spence, an Irishman, was the nav-bomb aimer, a peacetime RAF Observer with the appropriate "Flying Arse-Hole" O badge. The W/Op-AG was Don Pritchard. These were the Blenheim crew who were well on in their tour. The "new" boys

were Sgt Sargent, the second pilot, and the front gunner, Joe, was a peacetime wireless operator who had remustered to air crew. Joe had already completed a tour, but wished to continue at Wyton/Alconbury, because he was living with his WAAF girl-friend in the WAAF quarters (ex-married quarters) at Wyton.

'The crew, now ready for ops, continued with a few more training flights, one an oxygen test — the first time I'd experienced its use. Sgt Sargent did some circuits and bumps one day — and bumps there were. A wing dipped just enough to clip the Chance Light, carrying the top pot with us, careering down the runway with the remains perched on the wing. Wellington R1239 had to have a new outer section fitted — I didn't reckon much to our second dickey! Some leave followed in December, then more training until Christmas. Two days later — action.

'Our first novice operation was scheduled for 27 December. A night flying test (NFT) before lunch, briefing in the afternoon, all the crew. The target was Le Havre, the learner's initiation to ops. Take-off 1630hrs. Just before we made our way out to Wimpy T2515, we were issued with a flask and a bar of green foil-wrapped chocolate — the best thing ever issued. Flying clothing was just the stuff I'd been issued long ago at Manston — Sidcot, black, sheepskin-lined boots, silk gloves, leather gauntlets, helmet. We did have the parachute harness suit, known as the goon suit, which kept things a bit tidier. What a job to get into the turret, especially with the parachute pack clipped to the upper left-hand side. It was easier to get in, then lean back, bringing the 'chute forward over the top. All was not too bad once you were settled. Too much heavy breathing steamed up the perspex, which was very difficult to remove. No difficulty in locating the target, plenty of broken cloud to give a glimpse of the coast. The flak coming up was the biggest give-away. We didn't seem to spend much time identifying the aiming point before Mick Spence said "Bombs gone", whereupon Tubby made a steep turn away to sea, nose down for speed, towards home. An uneventful trip back to base and landing just after 9pm.

'De-briefing didn't mean much to me. I couldn't think of anything of importance to report. Should I describe the flak colours, the shape of the so-

called "flaming onions", the noise of near-bursts? No one ever explained why that noise sounded like marble dropping on to a drum. Most of the noise, I suspect, was the pressure vibration rattling the fabric on the stringers. There were a few small patches noticeable next time out to dispersal in daylight. Another thing I noticed was a helluva draught coming up the link chute which made my eyes water when looking through the reflector sight; I determined to remedy this as soon as I could.

'Apart from a few NFTs, then standdowns, for the next two weeks nothing happened. We were issued with

Top: Wellington Z8736, 'Q' at Luqa, Malta, and its crew. From left: Sgts G. S. W. Challen (R/AG), Harry F. J. Gibbons (W/Op), Charles W. Ingram (Wop/AG), Paul H. Morey (Nav), R. Gordon Murray (2/P), Flt Lt K. F. Vare, RNZAF (Captain). *G. S. W. Challen*

Above: Wellington crews of A and B Flights, 108 Sqn, gather for a Press photo. *G. S. W. Challen*

Right: Wellington at 105 Maintenance Unit (MU), April 1942, on arrival via Malta. *E. A. Sanders*

Above: Air Gunners sorting out ammo belts for the rear turret of Z8900 of 214 Sqn, Stradishall, 1942. This aircraft had previously served as 'C-Charlie' in No 9 Sqn in 1941.

sheepskin flying suits which had plugs for heated gloves and boots. I could only just get my goon suit over the top; the zips were very difficult to start. Wilhelmshaven on 16 January 1941 in R1239 was a tryout of these gloves and boots, which seemed to get too hot. The only way to control the heat was by unplugging for a time each extremity; not an easy thing to do, especially reaching your ankle where the boot connection was located. Another "extremity" was equally hard to reach when you wanted to pee in the empty bottle alway carried by most rear gunners. Apart from the sheepskin trousers and parachute harness straps in the way, the centre-piece of the goon suit, about three or four inches wide, came through your legs from the back, up the front under your chin where the zips connected, and you zipped downwards to make a tight fit around the legs. Removing gloves to use the "relief" bottle, your hands soon became cold enough not to know when you put them back in the heated gloves whether they were hot, warm or cold. I suffered blisters on occasion through not feeling how hot the gloves had become.

'The following day I explained to the rigger of our kite my idea for the turret bottom. The link chute came out and in its place we fitted a little hinged trapdoor made of aluminium with a felt seal. The catch was arranged so that I could operate it with my foot. All empty cartridge cases and links could then fall to the curved bottom of the turret, whereupon I could open the trap. It needed a kickabout with your feet to get rid of them all, push the trap shut and move the catch with your other foot. This trap also came in useful for usual bottle of pee and other "presents" I used to carry for Jerry, including half a dozen 4lb incendiary bombs. Mick Spence was always asking for drift sights, so I thought a pinpoint of light on the ground would be better than any glint of water or careless blackout to train my sight on. I used to chuck out the odd one through the hatch in the turret glazing by my right hand too; useful for taking photos with my little Zeiss Ikonta! Not much to identify on these photos except streaks of light from the searchlights, flak or fires on the ground, and very cold on the hand. What would have happened if a bit of flak had lodged in the incendiaries doesn't bear a lot of thought ...

'A few more visits to the "Happy Valley" (Ruhr) followed, then on 12 March 1941 the target was announced as Berlin. The briefing room, wasn't very large, mostly taken up with tables where the navigators had their maps spread out. All crew members gathered round these tables while briefing took place. The usual guff about route in and out, searchlight and flak concentrations, expected weather, cloud, moonlight etc, and any other intelligence. Not a word about time over target — we usually just took-off and got there as soon as we could. "Attention" was called, the Station Commander and other "scrambled egg" types crowded in, and then it was realised that Lord Trenchard, "Father of the RAF", was amongst them. A little pep talk from the old boy and good wishes for our success.

'Take-off at 2000hrs. A mixed bomb load, HE and incendiaries, with the weight reduced for maximum fuel. We had an uneventful crossing until well into Germany when flak and searchlights started together. We were as high as the old Wimpy could manage with a decent load — about 12/13,000ft, and only then after a struggle. Magdeburg en route put on a real show. We'd not seen anything like the amount of light and heavy stuff coming up, some of it at our height; I could see some black "puffs" at our level, and we must have passed through some as there was an acrid smell of burnt explosive. Tubby was changing height and direction to put off any accurate prediction, and it must have worked because there weren't any bursts near us to do any damage, though that rattle on the fuselage could be heard. Then a slight lull until well over Berlin Then several groups of searchlights came on together, making it impossible to see anything downwards, or upwards for that matter, except a layer of smoke or cloud. I suppose the idea was to silhouette us against this background. Mick Spence was already on the floor in the nose at his bomb sight. "Bomb doors open"... a bit of "Left, left, steady"... and it was "Bombs gone, close doors". We were coned by lights now, causing Tubby to get a wee bit rattled until Mick got back up and gave him some reassurance and directions to get out of the cone. The Wimpy had a good testing as we did steep diving turns, climbs and other gyrations. Tubby admitted later that he really didn't know what attitudes the aircraft was in, or how we escaped a complete loss of control! It says something for the Wellington that it survived structurally without permanent warpage.

'Once out of the lights tension eased somewhat, though there was so little flak to be seen that it put us on our guard for nightfighters. I found myself staring at points of light which turned out to be stars, exhaust sparks, or simply lights reflected in the perspex. Cold was eating into me after the sweat over the target. Coffee would be welcome, so off with the gloves whilst I fiddled with the flask. Frozen slush

poured into the cup, so I put the lot into the bottom of the turret, then struggled my gloves on again and connected them. I must have left the connection in too long because I found later that the back of my left hand was blistered. No other excitements before landing back at Alconbury at 0645hrs. Debriefing took a little longer, the Intelligence Officer asking all sorts of questions before we were allowed a bus-ride back to Wyton. There was an argument about the "ops breakfast" as we coincided with the ordinary breakfast and off-duty air crew types tried to get in on the bacon and egg, rather than dried egg on fried bread.

'We operated four more times in March — Bremen and Cologne — while in the following month it was Kiel's turn, four times. Tubby, Mick and Don were nearing the end of their tour, while Sgt Sargent was made up to captain with a crew of his own, so we had a new second dickey, Plt Off Whyte. Further trips to Merignac aerodrome, Bordeaux, Kiel twice more, then the finish of Tubby, Mick and Don's tour. A celebration was in order,

Above: Mighty Wurlitzer — the rear gunner's office in a Wellington from the inside; rear defence of Wimpy N2990, which served with 115 Sqn ('P'), 11 OTU, 24 Sqn ('NQ-D' & 'ZK-9'), before being struck off RAF charge on 19 March 1943. *IWM*

so all available went off to the Golden Lion St Ives. What a send-off — all those who could piled into the bangers which passed for cars, roaring off to the pub. I remember Tubby and Hugh Lynch-Blosse doing a fiendish dance on a table top, finally collapsing on to some locals (who didn't think too much of us rowdies!). After a hectic ride back, the party continued in the sergeants' mess until the SWO (Station Warrant Officer) closed the bar and persuaded the commissioned types to stagger off to their own quarters. I never heard again of Tubby, Mick and Don, or their subsequent adventures. Joe the front gunner, finally went to an OTU instructing, when his cushy number at Wyton was rumbled. I applied for a transfer to Boulton Paul Defiants — but I'm glad I didn't get it!

'Sergeant Sargent didn't seem to gather a new, permanent crew together, consequently I, as a spare gunner, flew with some of his new faces on three ops — Brest and Hamburg (twice). His next op, with a scratch crew, ended in disaster. On return he tried several approaches but each time decided to go round again. Visibility wasn't that bad, just ground haze. Suddenly there was a labouring of engines — then portentous silence. He had crashed in a field across the road from Alconbury House, killing all on board. I then left for a gunnery refresher course. On this, all classroom work was done at Stradishall along with some static turret firing into a sandpit close by. Then three days of air

firing, flying from the Newmarket Race Course, with Spitfires and Hurricanes doing simulated attacks from all angles.

'On return to Wyton/Alconbury it seemed I was still the 'spare' gunner; no one came eagerly after my services despite my refresher course! A pilot I'd flown with just before the course and his crew, however, were without a rear gunner, who was on the sick list with eye trouble. The captain, a New Zealander in the peacetime RAF, was Flt Lt K. F. Vare, an expert pilot. Second dickey was Gord Murray, RCAF; nav/bomb aimer was Sgt Paul Morey; plus Sgts Charles Ingram from London, and Harry Gibbons from Wales. We got on well together, and after a couple of NFTs and standbys on successive days, were off to Dusseldorf. Vare proved to be absolutely unflappable, insisting that the aiming point be absolutely identified, and going around twice before he would let 'em go.

'An AMO (Air Ministry Order) had appeared on the notice board calling for volunteers for the Middle East. My new crew thought it'd be a good idea, so our names went forward. A posting came through, to Harwell. After some leave, we reported to Harwell where a new Wellington awaited us. After two consumption tests — extra fuel tanks were fitted — we took off on 26 June 1941 for Gibraltar, reaching that short, dicey runway after 11 hours in the air. A quick look up and down the main street, some snatched sleep, and morning saw us gathering tropical KD (Khaki Drill) — one shirt, one pair of KD shorts and socks. Then off from that short strip, bound for Malta. Here we were soon bundled away from the aircraft down a deep shelter operations room, where we were told we'd be leaving again that night, though not in the kite we'd brought in. So, out into the heat to move our gear into a weary-looking Wimpy. ''Our'' kite had already been allocated to 148 Squadron who were trying to operate a detachment at Malta. We were to fly to Kabrit in the Suez Canal zone for major maintenance, this being 148's main base.

'We took off from Luqa at 2330hrs — they didn't want us around when dawn came as there was usually an air raid then. Take-off was to the west and the old kite didn't seem to rise at all; in fact, once clear of the island it sank lower. We crossed the Egyptian coast somewhere west of Alexandria, then

Below: Rear turret in Wellington TK-T of 149 Sqn. *IWM*

160

south for a view of the Pyramids south of Cairo, before landing at Kabrit. Here we found there was not going to be any action for some time, so spent our days making our quarters — tents — comfortable and getting generally acclimatised. Days were spent swimming in the Great Bitter Lake, evenings in Shafto's cinema or in the mess. Some more adventurous went off on leave by

hitching a lift in an aircraft which went to Tel Aviv, Palestine, once per week to collect oranges — or so they said. Suddenly, in August 1941, it was all go; pack up and move to Fayid, which the RAF was to share with the Fleet Air Arm. RAF accommodation at Fayid was unfinished, so it was tents again, and we spent some time digging in our tents, filling sandbags and building these around the tents. This latter precaution proved invaluable when one RCAF navigator used to wake in the early morning, after a night on the beer, firing his Colt 45 at rats — real or imaginary!

'On 24 September we were briefed for our first raid; the "milk run" to Benghazi. The practice was to air-test at base, then fly to an advanced landing ground, usually LG 09, top up the fuel, sometimes change the bomb load, then take-off for target later the same night. Vare was rather keen to make a good show of our first op in the Middle East, so we stooged straight over the target — supply ships against the harbour moles. There had been a few arrivals before us, so all kinds of flak was coming up and searchlights seemed to ring the town. The lights made it difficult to pinpoint anything, so round we went again. Vare decided to alter height and approach from a different direction in a shallow dive, hoping the increased speed and different height would baffle the predictors. No chance! The lights clamped on us and a coloured curtain of flak seemed to be draped around us. I'd

Above: Frazer-Nash (FN) 20A four-gun tail turret in Wellington III, X3763, KW-E, of No 425 ('Alouette') Sqn, RCAF, which failed to return from a sortie to Stuttgart on 14/15 April 1943.
Central Press

Right: Nose armament. The twin-gun turret gets a final polish of its perspex by a diligent sergeant.
Flight International

been firing short bursts on the first run, but this time I fired a longer, calculated squirt until my port gun jammed. Again, no "Bombs gone". I stripped the gun to see what the stoppage was, putting the bits with such funny names as "rear sear retainer keeper and pin" on the ledge where the sides and dome of the turret joined. Around again, lower down, and slower, from another direction. The chant began, "Left-left, right a little . . . steady". I never heard the "Bombs gone" because there was a bang, a rattle against the turret, and a smell. I put my hand out to feel where I had put my breech block bits, but only felt a breeze. Then a sensation in my throat. I wanted to cough but couldn't. I put my hand to my throat — it was sticky wet. I knew I'd been hit.

'Switching on the mike, I tried to report it but could tell there wasn't much coming from me. The crew knew something had happened, however, because Gord Murray said, "OK Steve, coming back". The turret wouldn't move by the hydraulics, so I engaged the hand gear. It needed two hands to turn the handle and move the turret central so that I could open the doors and climb out. There seemed to be a lot of lights shining on the port side — quite a hole where a lot of fabric had gone. I tried to find the stop valve for the hydraulics but it was too late; the pipes were punctured and oil was spraying all round the rear of the aircraft. I thought maybe the rudder or elevator controls were damaged, but couldn't see anything, so walked along the catwalk and met Gord on the way. I sat on the fold-down cot while Gord shone a torch on my damage. Not much to be done other than place a field dressing over the wound which I held in place by hand as I lay on the cot. The other crew members came back to have a look, though Vare seemed busy flying the Wimpy whose control wasn't quite right. With dawn coming it was light enough for me to write some questions in a diary, like

Above: 'Weary Willie' of 149 Sqn parked in moonlight at Mildenhall, May 1941. *British Official*

Left: Winter panorama. P9228, KX-Z of 311 (Czech) Sqn at dispersal, late 1942. This aircraft next went to the CGS and collided with Wellington P7530 on 13 August 1943, subsequently crashing near Lakenheath. *B. Rijnhout*

"How big is the hole in my f...... neck?", "Where are you dropping me?", and "Get my kit together — keys in the locker". We landed at Fuka Main at 7am, where an ambulance was waiting. I crawled out via the belly hatch which at one time in the design had been intended for a "dustbin" gun turret. Incidentally, this hatch came in useful at a later date, when plenty of light was needed over a target. I arranged for extra flares, placing them around the hatch opening clear of the door, with cords from the fuze pins tied to Barnes Wallis's geodetics. When the word came, it was hatch open, one, two, three etc, all gone in seconds, out and burning. Couldn't say these did much good, however; we seemed to stooge around for a long time still before dropping bombs.

'I was taken to 21 MRC (Medical Reception Centre), a tented hospital in the desert, where I was operated on by a Sqn Ldr Wallace. Then a hospital train to 15th Scottish, Cairo, from where, after many examinations, I was allowed out back to the squadron. Got to Heliopolis and was lucky to hitch a ride which dropped me off at Fayid. Back at the squadron I had to convince my skipper and the MO that ops were the "cure" for me, because shrapnel had severed my vocal chord and lodged in the larynx. They nicknamed me "Whispering Willie", but after an intercomm test, Vare was satisfied I was OK. We operated six times in November — Benghazi, Derna, Martuba, Barce railway etc — all in Wellington Z8763. Gord Murray was skipper on one op, but this was scrubbed when we reached the ALG; he did *not* like carrying our bombs back to base and having to land with a full load! This was our only activity in December, because Liberators began arriving direct from the USA, via Takoradi, and 108 Squadron commenced gradual conversion. In February 1942 I was back on Wimpys for four trips; two of which were completed to Martuba airfield and the Benina airfield near Banghazi. Both were difficult targets to find, despite my private brand of target-lighting. These were my last runs as Arse-End Charlie in Wimpys; no combats, no bale-outs, no crashes, no casualties (except my neck) — I was a survivor.'

163

Makee-Learn

Alan Butler was an Observer — the early-war equivalent of navigator-cum-bomb-aimer-cum-dogsbody in all RAF aircrews before more specifically delineated aircrew categories in bombers came into being. A prewar RAFVR member, Alan enlisted for aircrew training and, after instructional courses at Staverton, Prestwick and Bassingbourn — the latter supplying him with just eight hours night-flying experience — he was posted to No 9 Squadron at Honington in the autumn of 1940. His crew was skippered by a Canadian, Plt Off D. McIntosh (awarded a DFC in August 1941), a pilot who believed in close liaison with his aircraft's ground crew. On his promotion to Flying Officer for example, McIntosh took all his SNCO crew and the ground staff into a Bury St Edmunds pub for a celebration drink. On trooping into the pub's lounge bar with five sergeants, a corporal and several erks, he was told the bar was for 'Officers only'. He

promptly walked into the public bar — followed by every officer present in the lounge bar . . .!

Butler and his crew were allotted Wellington 'P-Peter' (or 'P-for-relief' as they privately dubbed it), and duly prepared for the start of their first full operational tour. Butler takes up the story at this point:

'It was the general practice in those days to give all new ops crews what was known as a 'Makee-Learn' trip, after the skipper had done about four or five sorties as a second dickey with another, experienced crew. My skipper, McIntosh, had done two trips and, having had an outstandingly good report from Fg Off Lamb, and being dead keen himself, he asked the squadron CO, Wg Cdr E. A Healey, whether he might take us on our air "makee-learn". Accordingly, we were briefed for Schiedam, an aerodrome in Holland, which was a favourite 'soft' target for our squadron. However, weather conditions interfered and the

Below: T2468, 'Y' of 9 Sqn at Honington in August 1940. After completing 13 sorties, it crashed on 4 December 1940. *R. D. Cooling*

trip was cancelled. Next evening we were briefed for Schiphol in Holland, but again the weather was against us. The next day was 12 October 1940 and 9 Squadron was going to Lorient that night. McIntosh went to the CO and pleaded so hard and so eloquently to be allowed to go that Wg Cdr Healey gave his permission for us to be a standby crew, although he would not allow us *definitely* to accompany the squadron. (Healey was relatively quite old and didn't fly on ops, but always waited up until all his crews were back, and was deeply upset when any went "missing".) "Standby" meant that if any aircraft became u/s (unserviceable), instead of sending an experienced crew in the spare aircraft, the CO would let us go and thus give the experienced crew a "stand-off".

'We were duly briefed but no aircraft was unserviceable. Luck was with us, however, because Group HQ wanted an extra aircraft put on by the squadron, so the Wingco gave us the "get set". Weather conditions were the same as on the previous two days — cloud and icing — over England and a big likelihood over the whole Continent, but it was expected that there would be fairly clear skies over the target area. The actual target was the nest of submarine bays in Lorient harbour, and we had 12 250lb eggs to lay. We decided to lay them in two sticks of six if possible.

'We were airborne at 2135 and climbed to 3,000ft before signing off the R/T and setting course. Right there and then trouble began! Within three minutes, and at a height of about 4,000ft, the wireless went west — frozen up. Ice was also forming on the wings, though the de-icing equipment seemed to be working fairly effectively. We continued to climb in spite of the ice. The W/Op was working hard to get his set going; meanwhile I found out what our drift was before we got into cloud, and had just got a new course on to which we set the aircraft. Five minutes later, with a complete sheet of cloud between us and the ground and another massive and solid-looking layer above us, the W/Op told the skipper that the wireless was definitely "kaput". Navigation in those early days was very different to now; astronomical navigation had yet to make its appearance as a general practice, and dead reckoning (DR) depended on the wireless, observations by the observer-navigator on the

Above: Two views of Alan Butler's Wellington after the fire was doused. *Bundesarchiv*

ground below, loop bearings, and drifts taken on the ground, usually by the rear gunner. There was no place we could use the loop on this raid, the ground was obscured, and the wireless dead — a nice problem for a brand-new observer!

'McIntosh told me to come up beside him for a moment. I knew what was coming and quickly reviewed the situation, not forgetting possible icing-up. The only thing I could do was to keep a very accurate air log and a DR position, but it *was* our first trip — turning back would only look as if we'd funked it. It came, "Can you still get us there?" I said, "I think so but there's nowhere to use the loop on. Personally I want to go, but there's a definite possibility we'll get lost". The skipper hadn't asked me this on the intercomm as he didn't want the rest of the crew to know we were in this mess yet. He thought for a while, then plugged in his intercomm and called up the crew, telling them that the wireless set was u/s, but that we were going on. Each man was to report everything he saw both to him and to me as it might help my navigation.

'I glanced along the wings at the ice and, touching Mac on the shoulder, pointed exultantly at them — they were now free of ice! Height 8,000ft and just entering a second belt of cloud. Would the moisture in them ice up or not? As we entered this second belt of cloud we both kept our eyes fixed on the wings... minutes passed... still we climbed, in spite of ice forming and weighting us heavily. At last good old "P-Peter" limped gamely out of cloud at 15,000ft and the de-icing gear soon began to free us. Time went by slowly... all I could do was my air plot... still solid cloud layers below us... at last we became due over Lorient. Nothing to report, nothing to be seen except cloud, cloud and cloud. Then the rear gunner spoke, "The cloud's thinner here... I think I can see the ground". I dived into the bomb-aimer's position for a look. At first I could see no difference, then as my eyes became accustomed I saw the blackness of ground below. I went and got my maps to try for a pinpoint... a few more seconds and I realised that in fact we were over the sea. I did some quick thinking and decided we must have overshot the target. I gave the skipper a reciprocal course and just after I'd plotted it the front gunner reported flak ahead and about three degrees port. I pulled my bombing switch down in readiness and asked the skipper to put the master switch down and open the bomb doors. A few minutes later we could see fires and explosions ahead and below — it was Lorient OK. I was about to drop my first bomb on enemy territory...

'We ran up at a speed of about 130mph at 10,000ft. They were firing at us now and the skipper was jinking away from the numerous searchlights. I was having great difficulty in keeping the target area in my sight, but picked out the submarine bays and directed the skipper to steady her for a second. He did so and I corrected the course over target with a quick "Left-left". He nosed the aircraft over and began to jink again. I kept my eyes glued to the target after making necessary adjustments to the bomb sight. Just before I was about to bomb I called the skipper to keep her steady, then reached for the bomb release tit.

' "Steady... steady... steady... bombs gone!" At the very second I pressed the tit, the kite seemed to jerk unsteadily; either we had been nearly hit or Mac had started to jink again. With a sinking heart I looked down for bomb bursts. I'd missed the target! There was a spit of land jutting out into the sea just to port of our objective, and the lurch of the aircraft had flung our

Below: Sgt Alan Millington, the second pilot. In background is the famous 'Marble Arch' — Mussolini's boasted 'gateway to Tripoli'. *Bundesarchiv*

bombs to port. But I'd got *something*. I watched the bomb bursts run across that strip of land and then a series of greenish flashes shot erratically over the whole area — they looked like electrical flashes. I resolved to complete the job I'd started. I had six more bombs to drop, and this time nothing disturbed my aim. The bombs fell squarely on that strip of land with the same result as before, and now fires were springing up most successfully.

'The crew were jubilant and, as we circled so that I could observe and note the fires and damage caused by my predecessors, they were all yelling congratulations at me over the intercomm. ''Can it'', I said, ''I missed the target''. ''Well chum, you sure hit something good'' was the reply from Mac, and I knew then he'd back me up for dropping the second stick where I'd laid the first. I gave him a course for home.

'Reaction set in soon after I got back to my nav table. I alone knew that it was purely good luck that we had got to the target — now we had to get back... somehow. I was far from happy — after all, I had only eight hours' night flying experience. However, we stuck grimly to our course, keeping a sharp lookout for the French coast... nothing... just those bloody clouds again... time for the English coast now... *is* that a coastline?... no, just a darker cloud... wishful thinking. I scanned my list of beacons, those friendly lights

which would tell me where I was, and picked out the most useful. I asked Mac to try to get under the clouds as we *should* be over England by now. We came out at 4,000ft this time... but no beacons.

'We had to turn on ETA and, sticking to my guns, I firmly gave a course on the intercomm in a confident voice — though inwardly I wondered where we were. Mac turned on to it without comment; he wasn't one to alarm the others, though he must have realised the mess I was in. Good old Mac, a blasted good skipper! ''Twenty minutes late'', I said, ''We should see our own beacon or one nearby within five minutes. All keep your eyes open '. A miracle occurred — the front gunner reported a beacon ahead. As we got nearer he gave me the letters it was flashing — it was Mildenhall, only 15 miles from our own 'drome. I told Mac to fly to it and when we got there I was ready with a new course. Meanwhile we switched over to R/T and contacted our own 'drome. After five hours and 50 minutes flying, we touched down — home again.

'We were interrogated and I explained that the first stick of bombs seemed to have caused so much trouble below that I'd deliberately dropped the second stick there. Squadron Leader Harrington nodded, and having consulted plans of the harbour said we must have hit a torpedo dump. I observed that the discharges were

Below: Sgt Steve Bevan, the rear gunner, under initial interrogation. *Bundesarchiv*

greenish and looked electrical, but he shrugged his shoulders and, pointing to the plans, said that there was nothing marked there but storehouses and shed. Late next day, however, he summoned our skipper and told him we'd destroyed the submarine wireless control station, and congratulated him. Mac was officially reprimanded for going on the trip without wireless — then privately congratulated for not turning back. I was reprimanded for the paucity of navigation notes in my log, which consisted mainly of meteorological information. I didn't care . . . we'd got there!'

From his first 'Blooding' until March 1941, Alan Butler continued on ops over Germany and France, and then volunteered for service in the Middle East zone. For this he was crewed with Sgt Alan Mackay (skipper), G. L. Millington (2nd pilot), Jim House (W/Op), Bill Ainsbury (front AG), and Steve Bevan (rear AG):

'On 19 March 1941 my crew were briefed for Malta, the first stage of our trip to the Middle East. We were airborne from Stradishall at 2150 and when no more than 100ft off the deck the air speed indicator (ASI) conked out. Our wireless was fitted up for the Middle East, as was our R/T, so we had no means of communication with the ground. Meanwhile, the aerodrome had already doused all flarepath lights. We fired off all our Very cartridges but received no answering signals from the ground. Then to make matters worse, we lost sight of the aerodrome.

'Now this was my first trip with Alan Mackay as skipper and I was curious to see how he would react. Landing an aircraft without an ASI is no joke even in daylight, when you can at least judge your speed, but landing at night in pitch blackness is a highly ticklish problem. Moreover, Mackay might be forced to put her down in any old field he could find. Would he cope as well as my old captain, McIntosh? As far as I could see, the rest of the crew — who had all done 12 ops already with him — had complete trust in him.

'Glancing at the met-forecast wind, I made a quick calculation on the CSC and told him roughly where the 'drome *should* be. We flew off and in a few minutes we managed to find the aerodrome again by means of the local church. Mackay was perfectly cool — at least, to all outward appearances —

and he told us he was about to land as best he could, and to brace ourselves for a crash. Should this occur we were to get out just as fast as possible because we were carrying 1,030 gallons of petrol and the kite was likely to catch fire. I rapidly finished off my log, then prepared for a bit of quick action.

'We were just coming up to the 'drome, and had just passed the perimeter hedge, when the lights came on for the flarepath. Mackay neatly lifted the Wimpy over a cement-mixer which might otherwise have got mixed up with our undercarriage, then made a perfect landing. I now *knew* there wasn't much wrong with my new skipper — he'd done better than finely and, though white with the strain, was quite calm. After all the explanations had been made, we trooped off to the mess to stand our skipper a few well-earned drinks, not to mention restore our own composure. Here we ran into more trouble— this time with the Station Warrant Officer (SWO), because we were in flying boots. I don't think that SWO knew just how near he was to getting thumped that night!

'Next afternoon we were briefed for Benina, near Benghazi, on the North African coast. This meant a trip of 1,920 miles, a distance only just within our flying range, leaving us no safety margin whatsoever. (It was, I believe, the first time such a trip had been attempted.) We became airborne at 1935 and set course for the English coast just near Clacton at 1940hrs. It was a very dark night and difficult to pick up landmarks. However, we were able to see where we crossed the coastline and then set course for La Carmagive, a small place near Marseilles.

'There was little to record about the actual flight. To our surprise, we were fired upon while flying over "Free France" but as we observed a large fire some 30-40 miles away to port, it's possible they had good reason for their dislike. The night was clear of cloud and, beyond temperatures etc, there was little to record in my met notes. I found we were approaching high mountains about 30 miles before we were due over our objective point and, taking a wireless bearing from Malta to check this, altered course direct for Tunisia. We duly crossed the French coast on an ETA correct to the minute and commenced the long sea-crossing. I checked all navigation for possible

errors, found nothing wrong, and got ready for the next stage. Again, our ETA was correct and we made landfall on the Tunisian coast to the minute, turned on ETA inland, all according to briefing instructions.

'After setting our easterly course we crossed the coast once more and, shortly after, passed close to the isle of Lampedusa; correct for track and time. It was now too cloudy for sea drifts — cloud appeared soon after we passed Lampedusa, and within an hour put a 10/10ths blanket of cloud between us and the sea. We saw the dawn, and a wonderful sight it was. The nose of our Wimpy was more or less pointed into it, so that in spite of our tiredness we had to look at it in any case. We were at 10,000ft with complete cloud below and a little cloud above us. When our ETA arrived I had a good look below for possible cloudbreaks, and told the W/Op to get his QDM. We'd been trying to contact Benina for the last hour, but apparently there was some sort of trouble with the wireless — something broken or lost — and he (the W/Op) had been unable to make contact; unfortunate, because we only needed a solitary bearing. Therefore, there was only one thing to do — go down through cloud and find out whether we were over land or sea. So, some five minutes after our scheduled time, we broke cloud at 1,000ft — only to find we were still over sea.

'I was not, as yet, unduly worried. It was a long trip from Tunisia to Benina, and it would be quite possible to be 20 minutes or so incorrect with a bad Met wind and no navigational data — which was the position we were in. Meanwhile, for the past three hours Mackay had been having considerable troubles. The starboard wing was "heavy", and to keep the aircraft anywhere near level he was having to put his full weight on the stick. For the whole trip our second pilot had been of no practical use; he was feeling far from well and spent most of the trip on the bed. He had not actually been airsick — had he been so he might have recovered and been able to help the skipper — but he seemed unable to remain at the controls for more than a few minutes. So I contacted the rear gunner and told him we must get a drift if at all possible, in spite of the very choppy sea. I put every kind of sea marker over but, in spite of Steve's very keen eyesight, he was unable to get a very imperative drift.

'I turned back to the wireless again and asked Jim House to get a bearing from Malta, and while he tried this I discussed the situation with the skipper. There were now two possibilities. One, which I favoured, placed us down in the Bay of Syrte, while the second meant that we had passed the huge hump on the north coast of Africa and were blissfully flying on down the Mediterranean. (I think Mac thought this was the case at the time). The W/Op gave us a QDM at the same time, telling us he thought it was "fishy". After I'd asked him what he meant, he said he thought it might be a "twisted" or false bearing put out by the Germans. I didn't know what to think! Twisted bearings, second pilot ill, unable to obtain drifts, petrol running out, and dog-tired after 12 hours' flying; I was in a quandary. Anxiously I pressed the petrol gauge knobs... they *said* 60 gallons, about 50 minutes' flying... IF the petrol came through from the "heavy" wing... which I didn't think it would.

'Then Sgt Millington pointed to star-board and said, "I believe that's a coastline". Steve Bevan said he too had been watching it and thought it was coast, so I had a look through binoculars and thought so myself. We decided to edge in closer and see. It was undoubtedly land; a blessed sight since we were certain it must be in British hands as the latest news placed British positions at El Agheila, which we should have already passed. Confidently we turned in to the coast at 900ft and at about 100mph. I collected my maps ready to try to get a pinpoint, and a few minutes later we turned to port and flew parallel with the coast, about a mile out to sea, and I fixed our position at 0805hrs. Then we got it!...

'I heard a ripping sound... fabric tearing off... the starboard engine stopped... there were clouds of black smoke all around us. "Can you turn out to sea?" I asked "I'll try" answered the skipper. He presented our tail to the enemy guns and Steve, in the rear turret, took this golden opportunity to pour bullets into the range of low hills in which the enemy guns must have been situated. It was no good. We were losing height so fast there was nothing for Mac to do but make for the coast. This he did, telling us all to prepare ourselves. I went forward and let Bill Ainsbury out of his front turret, then hurried back to destroy my maps etc.

The rest of the crew were doing various things in preparation for abandoning an aircraft in enemy territory; the W/Op destroying his log, his set and any other vital instruments.

'Mac did a wonderful job. With perfect coolness, he put the undercart down and scraped on to the hardest-looking patch of sand in sight as neatly as if he'd been landing on a proper aerodrome. Personally, I feel I owe him an everlasting debt; twice in 36hrs he'd displayed coolness, courage and a quiet determination.

'We set about destroying the air-craft. The German were still firing at us; as I got out of the astro-dome a shell burst directly over my head — I jumped down rather quickly! That kite was the very devil to set on fire. We wasted a whole box of matches trying to set fire to some spare maps and papers, then eventually tried the more general method of using a Very cartridge. It was only by this last means that the Wimpy took fire. We hurriedly removed ourselves from the immediate vicinity to watch the blaze.

'We hadn't been any too soon. We could see Germans approaching from the east, while within moments it became apparent we were also being approached from the south and the west. When they got closer we realised they'd inadvertently paid us a high compliment — a great semi-circle of infantry, light tanks, armed motor-cycle units, armoured cars, and several types of light machine gun carriers; I would not have been particularly sur-prised to have seen a U-boat pop up! They certainly seemed to have expected six British airmen — all unarmed — to cause a lot of trouble! Somewhat puffed up with pride, we stood up.'

Alan Butler and his fellow crew members were taken by truck to HQ, Afrika Korps and interrogated separately, then flown next morning by Junkers Ju52 to Tripoli. Another Ju52 took them on to Reggio, Italy, and next day onward, via Bari, crossing the Alps, and eventually landing at Munich. From here to Frankfurt, then by car to Oberursel and the Dulag-Luft. For the next four years, Butler remained a 'Kriegie' in — successively — Stalag-Luft II, Sagan, Heydkrug, Thorn, and Fallingbostel, before ultimately being liberated on the morning of 16 April 1945 by the British 7th Army Division.

Below: A more formal POW view. Standing from left: Sutherland, Alan Mackay, Steve Bevan, Bill Ainsbury, Greager. Seated; Jim House, Alan Butler, Alan Millington. *A. Butler*

By Day, by Night

John — 'Jo' — Lancaster joined the RAF with no particular desire to fly bombers, though he was eventually to fly intensive operations in the classic aircraft bearing his name. Nevertheless, his individual wishes were ignored with the delicacy of decision long associated with the RAF Record Office hierarchy of those years, and his lengthy wartime flying career proved to be wholly associated with 'heavies': 'I didn't want to be a bomber boy. In 1940, with the Battle of Britain and all that, I distinctly fancied myself as a glamorous fighter boy, and even made it as far as a fighter FTS, on Miles Masters at 5 FTS, Sealand and Tern Hill. However, I was a member of the only Flight on our course who completed the night-flying part of the syllabus, and we were all posted to bomber OTUs; in my own case to 20 OTU, Lossiemouth on Wellington 1cs. Having resigned myself to becoming a bomber type, it seemed reasonable to me that, having recently served an engineering apprenticeship with Armstrong Whitworths, helping to build Whitleys, I should transfer to the Whitley OTU at Kinloss, some 12 miles further along the Scottish coast. I gained an audience with my CO, Group Captain Smyth-Piggott, and told him so, but he wasn't very convinced. So, Wimpys it had to be — and I never regretted it from that day on.

'I joined 40 Squadron at Alconbury, and looking back on my time with that squadron it comes through as a very happy, easy-going period, which was due, I believe, mostly to the fact that our cosmopolitan crew teamed up together at OTU and quickly developed a very close bond of friendship. We all had total loyalty and confidence in each other. We were, of course, periodically scared stiff together, but at the very earliest opportunity thereafter we celebrated our 'reprieve' together in pretty good style! My tour on 40 Squadron covered the period May to October 1941. For the most part the nights were short, and quite often it was getting quite light as we crossed the enemy coast on the way home. One morning the sun was almost up as we hurried across Belgium, and we passed a Dornier going the opposite way, only about 500 yards away — presumably on his way home too.

'In retrospect it all now seems to have been very casual. By mid-morning each day we would know if ops were on or off. It was commonly said that if one visited the bar of the George Hotel in Huntingdon at lunchtime, the senior Intelligence Officer, Sqn Ldr C........., was certain to be there, and could be relied upon to disclose the "target for tonight". I never personally tested this out, but I believe it to be true. We'd carry out an NFT which usually included most of the ground as well as air crew, and invariably consisted of a beat-up at

nought feet up one side of the Bedford Canals and back down the other side. These are a pair of dead straight parallel canals which run between Chatteris and Kings Lynn. We gleefully terrorised the Land Army girls and others working in the fields, and sometimes landed at neighbouring airfields to pay social calls on friends and perhaps join them for lunch. There was no specified or mandatory route to or from any target, and no specified take-off time or time over target.

'Each crew was allotted its own aircraft and the luxury of its own individual ground crew; one Fitter IIE to each engine, and two Fitter IIAs for the airframe. Here again, a tremendous team spirit, pride, loyalty and mutual confidence was engendered. On one occasion on run-up prior to an op, there was a massive mag drop on the port engine. The fitter who 'owned' that engine, Cyril Bell, fell upon it in an absolute frenzy. This was high summer and the nights were short, so when the time came it was too late to start, we scrubbed. By that time Cyril was literally in tears. He ignored ''Chiefy's'' order to pack it in, and continued his frantic efforts to rectify the defect — which was in no way due to faulty maintenance — through the night.

'A few characteristics of the Wimpy 1c should be mentioned here. The

Left: Sprog. Jo Lancaster as a newly-commissioned Pilot Officer. *J. O. Lancaster*

Above: T2701, 'S-Sugar' of 40 Sqn at Alconbury 1941. On 24 July 1942, while serving with 25 OTU, this aircraft collided with DV476 and crashed. *J. O. Lancaster*

Right: Finals. Pilot's view of the final approach to Alconbury, 1941. *J. O. Lancaster*

cabin heater was a liquid heat transfer system from an exhaust pipe muff to a radiator which heated air before it was fed into the cabin. Even when it was working properly it was very ineffective, but it was so unreliable, due to a tendency to boil dry, that it was generally given up as a hopeless job. Instead, we wore most marvellous wool/silk mixture "Long John" underpants and long-sleeved vests, silk gloves, and full inner and outer Sidcot-type flying suits. The gunners wore electrically-heated Irvin suits. Even so, we were often extremely cold for many long hours.

'The Pegasus 18 engine was, thankfully, very reliable. This was just as well because at 925hp each, and having non-feathering props, it was really under-powered and could only manage a protracted descent on one engine — even if the Pilots' Notes said otherwise! A fairly regular event was for a valve rocker box on one of the cylinders to come adrift, which effectively put that cylinder out and resulted in quite unpleasant vibration.

Top: Embryo Wimpy crews at Lossiemouth OTU, prior to the award of wings etc. *W. Toop*

Above: OTUs did ops too. Wellington DV439, PP-D of 25 OTU which crashed in Holland on 1 August 1942, nr Loon op Zand. *G. Zylstva Collection*

Right: Crews and Wimpys of 149 Squadron prior to a raid over Germany on 10 May 1941, at Mildenhall. Nearest aircraft's insigne is a kangaroo, probably denoting an Australian skipper. *British Official*

Below right: Crew of 'H-Harry' of 419 Sqn, RCAF at Mildenhall on 9 February 1942. From left: Sqn Ldr F. W. S. Turner, Plt Off K. E. Hobson, Flt Sgts G. P. Fowler, C. A. Robson, N. G. Arthur, and H. T. Dell — all Canadians. *Public Archives of Canada*

The flap lever was undoubtedly responsible for a number of crashes from the overshoot condition. This lever was next to, and resembled, the undercarriage lever. It was very light in operation, and unless extreme care and finesse were exercised to make very small and momentary ''up'' selections, the flaps were liable to retract almost instantaneously, with probable catastrophic results. Eventually, a restrictor device was introduced on the flap lever to at least partially remedy this. The pilot's seat I recall as being very comfortable. One particularly good feature, never to be repeated, was a large adjustable support pad which supported each knee. Although our aircraft were fitted with an early form of auto-pilot, like the cabin heater this never worked for long, and we had to ''pole'' the aircraft manually for long weary hours, so a comfortable seat position was most welcome.

'On 24 July 1941 the *Scharnhorst*, *Gneisenau* and *Prinz Eugen* were lying in Brest and La Pallice. A small force of Halifaxes and Stirlings was despatched in daylight to La Pallice, whilst a small force of Wellingtons was simultaneously to attack the ships in Brest. 40 Squadron contributed six aircraft, including our Wimpy, T2701, ''S'', flying in two ''independent'' vics of three. The day was hot and cloudless, with thick smoke haze over southern England. The route to the target in this case was laid down, via the Scilly Isles. We went in at 10,000ft, and the sky over Brest was thick with black flak smoke. We stuck very close together, held our heads down, gritted our teeth, and pressed on in. One stray Wimpy passed from right to left underneath us with an Me 109 on its tail. Our rear gunner, Keith ''Kiwi'' Coleman, turned his turret to the port beam, and as the 109 broke off his attack on the other Wimpy in a vertical climb, Keith plastered him and the pilot was seen to bale out. On the way home we saw what was probably the same Wimpy, with its starboard engine on fire, ditch some miles off the Brittany coast. As his dinghy was stowed in the starboard engine nacelle, it was obvious that this would have been burned. I thought of dropping them our dinghy, but decided this wasn't practicable because it would almost certainly have finished up wrapped around our tailplane. Instead, we sent a radio report, though we never heard whether our valiant air-sea rescue chaps were able to snatch them back. Short of fuel, we made for St Eval in Cornwall, as did a number of other aircraft, mostly well shot up and carrying dead and wounded. It was a fair shambles, and we all had to muck in together to help as best we could. Our little trio came through without casualty, though the aircraft were in a bit of a mess. Mine, in addition to being well perforated, had a hole through the windscreen and the hydraulic system out of action. The other Vic from our squadron broke formation and one was lost, while another suffered fatal casualties among the crew from an Me 109 attack. Having been told at briefing that there was to be a fighter escort of Spitfires, we were naturally somewhat indignant that none of us had set eyes on any Spitfire. In all fairness, however, I'm sure that we had our ''unseen'' Spits to thank for the fact that the sky had not been full of enemy fighters.

'Ice protection on the Wimpy 1c consisted of alcohol sprays for the props and engine air intakes, and alternate hot air for the carburettors. The wing leading edges were smeared with a substance popularly known as ''snowdrop grease'', which looked like marzipan, and which, of course, frequently got knocked about by refuelling hoses. I've no idea of the effectiveness of this treatment but it was never used later in the war. On the night of 30 July 1941, while on the way home from Cologne in Wimpy R1168, ''B'', I handed over control to my second pilot, Gordon Byrne, and took up station in the astro-dome. We flew into cloud and, when it became clear from the turbulence and St Elmo's Fire that we'd entered a lusty cu-nimb electrical storm, I instructed Gordon to select carb hot air and to turn 180-degrees to get out of it. When the starboard engine began to surge I decided to go forward

Below: Wimpy 'G-George' of 432 Sqn, RCAF over the unit base at Skipton-on-Swale, Yorkshire in mid-1943. *Public Archives of Canada*

Above: Wellingtons of 214 Sqn at Stradishall in 1940. Nearest aircraft is BU-V, W5442, *SRI GUROH*; a Wimpy which had previously flown three ops with 12 Sqn as PH-B. *IWM*

Above: R1448, 'L' of 218 Sqn, *AKYEM ABUAKWA*, later re-coded as HA-N. Eventually transferred to 20 OTU, it crashed on 6 August 1942. *IWM*

Right: W5361, 'C-Charlie' of 12 Sqn refuelling at Binbrook, 1942. After 18 completed sorties, it failed to return from ops on 31 May 1941. *T. Mason*

and resume control. As I passed the wireless operator, he was out of his seat, recoiling from his equipment which was all aglow. Having changed places with Gordon again, I found he had *not* selected carb hot air, and had *not* turned through 180-degrees. This totally uncharacteristic stupidity was undoubtedly the result of not having a serviceable oxygen tube, even though we were only at about 10-11,000ft. Things then started happening very quickly. The whole aircraft was aglow, it was extremely turbulent, lightning was lighting up the inside of the cloud, and after wild surging the starboard

engine died — shortly followed by the port engine. The aircraft was difficult to control and must have been badly iced up. Then there was a colossal bang and a blinding flash — obviously a lightning strike. I had to turn the lights up full and even then it seemed a long time before I could see the instruments clearly.

'As we rapidly lost height we heard the unmistakable sound of flak, too close for comfort, and could see signs of searchlights playing on the cloud base not far below. By this time — naturally — the crew had taken up their bale-out positions. We were all waiting, putting off the evil moment until the last possible second, when, having lost height down to about 3,000ft, the starboard engine suddenly showed signs of interest again. As I nursed it back to full chat, hey presto, the port engine recovered its senses too, and we were soon able to start gaining height. The jubilations which erupted were soon flattened, however, when there was no reply from Keith in the rear turret. We thought he must have baled out. Then, as I sent Gordon down to the rear to have a look, Keith came back on the intercomm. He explained that as he prepared to abandon ship, parachute pack clipped on his chest and turret turned to port beam ready to fall out backwards, he could see the altimeter which formed part of the oxygen regulator. As all was silence on the intercomm, he deduced that the rest of us had departed, but as there was still three or four thousand feet showing and the kite was quite steady — or at least, right side up — he decided to stay put until the last moment too. Then he heard one engine going again, then two, and his altimeter started to show a profit. Checking further, he discovered that in putting on his parachute pack he'd inadvertently pulled out his intercomm plug just as Gordon banged on his turret from inside the fuselage.

'About one in ten of 40 Squadron's 1cs had their normal bomb doors removed and the bomb bay faired-in, leaving a recess deep enough to accommodate a 4,000lb "Cookie". Normal max bomb load was nine 500lb, or nine SBCs (Small Bomb Containers) each housing 81×4lb incendiary bombs. The maximum standard fuel load was 750 gallons, though on some occasions we were fitted with two 140-gallon over-

load tanks in the bomb bay. We could not carry full internal fuel with a full bomb load, so a balance was decided according to the distance to target. In each wing were six fuel cells and a tank in the nacelle. The pilot's fuel control consisted of an on/off cock for each wing tank group, and a cross-feed cock. There was a panel with (I think) 12 contents' gauges — one for each cell — and all hopelessly inaccurate anyway. It was quite impossible to judge the fuel situation, so a system was evolved whereby the cock on one of the nacelle tanks could be turned on or off from the fuselage by manipulating two wires which emerged from the wing root. This tank could then be turned off during flight until, hopefully well on the way home, one engine cut, whereupon the pilot opened the cross-feed, whilst the second pilot hastily turned on the nacelle tank; we then knew we had 40 minutes in which to get down.

'Periodically we had a new second pilot, and to each one I gave a very careful briefing and demonstration of this nacelle tank operation. One of them, a rather timid, sensitive type whom I personally considered totally

Above: 149 Sqn Wellington awaiting its bomb load at Mildenhall.

Below left: R1006, 'H' of 301 (Polish) Sqn, about to be bombed up at Swinderby, November 1940. It had an ill-starred career, flying just one sortie from Bremen on 1/2 January 1941 and crashing on return. Transferred to 18 OTU, Bramcote, it then caught fire on the ground on 2 February 1942. *Central Press*

Below: Wimpy skipper. Pilot Officer J. H. Cameron from Warialda, Australia, at the controls of his 466 Sqn RAAF Wellington at Leconfield on 26 September 1943. *RAAF*

unsuited for the job was George B......... . On the very first occasion when I yelled for him to turn the tank on, after a long interval, he said he couldn't find the wires! I had to hastily get the W/Op back there to do it. Naturally, I was somewhat displeased and later gave him another thorough demonstration. The next op was to Hanover on 12 August in Wimpy X3174, "X", and when this time I called for him to turn on the tank , George said "It is on — it's been on all the time". When I asked why he hadn't told me, he said, "I was afraid you'd be cross" . . . ! With finger nails bitten down to the wrists, we thankfully slid into Wyton. We found that the tank, in fact, was *not* turned on, and next day there was not enough fuel left in the main tanks to even taxy. George did more than the normal eight ops with me, and eventually — very much against my advice — was given his own crew. Taxying out for his first op as a skipper, he put his wingtip through our front turret — thereby grounding us — and did not return.

'On 25 August, in T2701, "S", we suffered our only true engine failure. With a full bomb load we had just taken off from Alconbury and were climbing away at about 750ft, when I noticed that we'd lost all oil pressure on the port engine. Oil was streaming from the engine and it shortly seized up. Fortunately, we were able to just make it to neighbouring Wyton, where we landed out of the twilight, unannounced and unscathed; a main oil pipe had fractured.

'On 7 September we went to Berlin — the "Big City" — in Wimpy Z8859, "S". Weather was clear over the target and, by the standards of those days, the attack was successful. On the way home, however, together with a number of our other aircraft, due to a big change in the forecast winds, we drifted too far north over ten-tenths cloud, and flew back over Hamburg, Bremen, Emden, Wilhelmshaven *et al.* This route suffered almost continuous flak and eventually, down on our port side, we could see the causeway which crosses the entrance to the Zuider Zee. Just as we were all distracted by this sudden glimpse, a great shower of red tracer shot just over the top of us, followed by an Me 110. We quickly went into a tight defensive left-hand turn. The Me 110 went round in a wide left-hand turn and tried another attack. We went into a steep spiral

dive, and in attempting to follow us the 110 presented a view of its belly to Keith, who raked it from end to end. It disappeared vertically into cloud at about 4,000ft. Now, the limit in speed of a Wimpy 1c was 266mph — officially. In the recovery from our dive, our airspeed was indicated as 330mph! We sustained no damage, either from the 110's efforts or by having exceeded our "limiting speed" by 25%, and arrived back at Alconbury after eight and a quarter hours in the air without overload tanks.

'The longest op we did was in Wimpy Z8859, "S" on 29 September, to Stettin. This time we had overload

178

tanks and were airborne for nine hours and five minutes. There was little opposition over the target, and we made four "practice bombing range" type run-ups before Glenn, our navigator-cum-bomb aimer, was satisfied that he had got it all exactly right. Speaking of bomb-aiming, incidentally, during this late 1941 period we had to negotiate a wide belt of very efficient searchlights — the "Kammhuber Line" — which stretched down through Holland and Belgium. This caused us considerable disquiet. For our revenge, when the target was in the Ruhr area, we often retained one of our 500lb HE bombs and, on the return leg, made a careful run-up on one of the searchlights. They must have been able to hear it coming, because invariably the light went out before we saw the bomb burst. We normally carried a few empty bottles which the second pilot would drop down the flare chute, and when I'd been a second pilot I'd taken great satisfaction in dropping bricks, marked "London Brick Company", taken from a pile adjacent to our dispersal pan.

'Having completed 31 ops with 40 Squadron, I was posted for the statutory year of OTU instructing to 22 OTU, Wellesbourne Mountford. In May 1942, still a screened instructor and still on Wimpy 1cs, I was roped in for the first of "Butch" Harris's "Thousand-bomber" ops, target Cologne. I was given a screened navigator and wireless operator, plus two pupil air gunners, while the aircraft, X9932, "X", was one normally engaged on dual circuits and bumps

training. It still had its dual controls fitted, which made entry and exit rather difficult — particularly if one was in a hurry. We took off in very grotty weather but on the return trip the weather was fine as, with dawn breaking, we cruised back towards Wellsbourne Mountford at about 1,000ft. The W/Op, Flight Sergeant Harrison, came up forward to sit beside me and we were enjoying a cigarette when — I think almost simultaneously — we saw the starboard engine oil pressure gauge drop abruptly to zero. Fortunately, Harrison was a very experienced Wimpy man and knew exactly what to do. He dashed aft and started to transfer oil from the 14-gallon reserve oil tank by hand-pump, and the oil pressure quickly recovered. The engine had drunk its normal oil capacity of 17 gallons in less than five hours' flying. Two nights later we took the same aircraft to Essen, but this time we didn't wait for the starboard engine to consume all its oil before replenishment.

'In October 1942 I returned to the operational scene proper by joining 12 Squadron at Wickenby, where I did three more ops in Wimpy IIIs before we converted to Lancasters. These Wellingtons had Hercules XI engines with feathering props, which transformed the Wimpy into quite a "hot ship". After 12 Squadron, I went back on to Wellingtons for a short period with No 1 Group's 1481 Gunnery Training Flight at Binbrook, where we flew Wimpy IIIs and Xs. With these I discovered that at low airspeeds there was a slight overbalance on the rudder, so I made a habit of very steep power-off sideslip approaches using full rudder deflection — quite spectacular when seen from the ground, I was told. However, the Wimpy really had no aerodynamic vices. From Binbrook I finally achieved my ambition of a posting to the A&AEE where, incidentally, I did some flying on the big sister Warwick aircraft, but my association with the dear old Wimpy was not completely over because early in 1946 I was seconded to Boulton Paul's at Wolverhampton for a few months. There, amongst other jobs, I did some production testing of a small number of Wimpys, modified from Mark Xs and 19s as flying classrooms — virtually the forerunner of the later Varsity, I suppose.'

Webfoot Wimpys

The contribution of the Wellington to the unceasing maritime war against marauding enemy submarines received minimal publicity during — or for that matter, since — World War 2. Yet 'salty' Wimpys played a significant part in the eventual defeat of the ocean wolves, destroying or at least seriously damaging a minimum of 51 submarines during 1942-45, and doubtless — if unconsciously — preventing or dissuading unknown numbers of possible attacks on merchant shipping convoys merely by their ever-vigilant presence. As with all Coastal Command operations, irrespective of aircraft type, anti-submarine patrol work was an accumulation of endless hours of 'watching water'; monotonous flying which rarely produced even a sniff of a U-boat, let alone any form of visible success. It was a task requiring stoic patience and physical endurance, combined with a talent for instant reaction on those rare occasions when a submarine was spotted.

One vital ingredient of success was the Leigh Light; a moveable swivelling searchlight remote from the cockpit — usually, in a Wellington, in the mid-belly position — for night illumination of any detected, surfaced U-boat. No 1417 Flight RAF was formed at RAF Chivenor, Devon, to develop the Leigh Light Wellington and to form the nucleus of No 172 Squadron as the first Leigh Light unit for maritime operations. Among the first air crews posted in was Donald Fraser, whose account of those embryo days follows:
'I was an RCAF Warrant Officer 1st Class pilot with No 150 (Wimpy) Squadron in RAF Bomber Command when I was posted in early February 1942 to 1417 Flight of Coastal Command Development Unit. I was not enamoured with the Wellington aircraft, and was looking forward to a new challenge. My arrival at Chivenor, late Sunday night, 8 February 1942,

was not very auspicious. I learned immediately that in the Chivenor Beaufort OTU there had been three fatal crashes during the past two nights. Therefore, I was relieved somewhat when I was told, next morning, that 1417 Flight was *not* connected with the OTU, but was a "hush-hush" unit located in a far hangar. Imagine my reaction when I first saw the plane, a white Wellington with porcupine-like vertical and horizontal aerials sticking out of the fuselage, and two forward-pointing Yagi aerials under the wings. There was no nose turret, but the front was covered with perspex to give a greenhouse appearance — Leigh's invention was ready for practical testing.

'I soon realised that most Coastal Command pilots had trained on other types of aircraft and that the unit was anxious to have somebody with flying experience on Wellingtons. An outline of problems involved in U-boat detection and destruction was presented by the commanding officer, Wing Commander Jeff Greswell. U-boats in early 1942 were crossing the Bay of Biscay at night with impunity on the surface on their way to their second "Happy Time" where they could attack undefended shipping off the coast of the United States of America. Airborne radar (ASV) had already been installed in the Wellington and had permitted homing-in on surfaced U-boats, with a maximum detection range of about seven miles. But frequently, with a sea running, in the last mile contact was lost due to sea return on the radar screen. Hence the Leigh Light, which was installed in the mid-under turret position.

'The next four months were devoted to intensive training. The effective operation of the searchlight had to be co-ordinated with its controls mounted in the nose of the aircraft. The Light was to be lowered below the fuselage when ASV contact was made, and

Top: Leigh Light Mk XIV
Wellington of Coastal
Command, with underwing
rockets. *via S. Howe*

Above: Mk XIV Wellingtons of
Coastal Command about to
start a submarine patrol.
IWM

swung back and forth, up and down, until the object of the ASV blips was detected. The Helwick Light Vessel in the Bristol Channel served for practice detection at night. Practice bombing was done against a floating target off the steep cliffs of North Devon; the aircraft would approach from the land, dive towards the floating target to simulate an attack on a surfaced U-boat from 1,000ft altitude and one mile distance. This training was not without its casualties. One Wellington, with the squadron's gunnery and navigation officers, a Flight commander, and a full crew, homed in on a blip which they thought was the Helwick Light Vessel. Unfortunately, the blip was an American tanker steaming up the Bristol Channel. Its

alert crew opened fire — the burning Wellington fell into the sea. There were no survivors.

'Originally there was only one Wellington with Leigh Light available for training purposes. Greswell sent a signal to Group HQ ''Request some operationally-tired Wimpys from Bomber Command to familiarise our pilots flying the Wimpy and to perfect their low-level bombing techniques''. Gradually more Leigh Light Wellingtons became available, but slowly, ever so slowly. Their assignment priority seemed obvious; the first to the Wing Commander, the next two to the Flight commanders, the fourth to Pilot Officer Blackmore, an experienced CCDU pilot. Warrant Officer Fraser was, naturally, further down the list. Another

Above: Stickleback. Mk VIII Wellington, W5674 with ASV Mk II antennae and aerial masts, believed to have served with 331 Squadron. *MOD (Air)*

Right: Mk XIVs (NB895, 'G', nearest) of 38 Squadron. *P. H. T. Green*

Bottom right: Wellington GRXIV, LB129/G at the TRE.

Canadian, Plt Off Russ, arrived, and he was assigned to fly as second pilot and searchlight operator with Plt Off Blackmore's crew. Russ was first on a short ferry flight to St Eval in Cornwall. It was a misty day, his plane disappeared. The following week the wreck was found on the cliffs behind Hartland Point, near Chivenor. I had by then my own crew but no aeroplane, so I immediately volunteered to fly with Blackmore in Russ's place until I got my own aircraft.

'Training went on. Squadron Leader Leigh periodically showed up on the station to oversee developments. The three-tiered bomb bay held the four Torpex-filled depth charges, the long case of batteries for the searchlight, and an overload fuel tank. The Wellington flew tail down even with trim. Blackmore and I worked on an obvious solution, moving the batteries into the nose of the machine. A wooden case for the 14 batteries was built under the searchlight operator's seat in front of the pilot. The aeroplane now flew better. With an all-up weight of 33,000lb, the two 980hp Bristol Pegasus engines were severely tested. Even in Bomber Command the same aircraft had an all up weight of only 29,500lb. The unfavourable power/weight ratio affected the single-engine flying characteristics of the aircraft, but this was later rectified when 1,425hp Hercules engines replaced the old Pegasus plants. It had taken four months — perhaps not really very long under the circumstances — but by early June 1942 the Leigh Light Wellingtons were ready to be tested in battle.

'The first operational sorties of 172 Squadron were flown by four aircraft on the night of 3/4 June 1942, and Greswell was the first to draw blood, flying aircraft "F". As he homed in on an ASV blip near the coast of Spain, he lowered his searchlight and illuminated a submarine dead ahead. He overshot it because his altimeter had given a wrong altitude, due to changing barometric pressures this many hundreds of miles from base. (It was some months later before a radio-altimeter corrected this problem.) On his second run-in the submarine fired recognition signals into the air. Was it a British sub? Then Greswell recalled that British submarines never shot up recognition signals, but burned flares on the surface. He attacked, dropping a stick of Torpex depth charges across the submarine's bows.

'The effect of Greswell's attack is best described directly from the log of the Italian submarine, the *Luigi Torelli*, of the 1,200-ton Marconi class. On the night of 3/4 June 1942, on a true course of 264 degrees and at a speed of nine knots, latitude 44° 43' N, longitude 06° 46' W, it was surprised by the first Leigh Light Wellington at 0227hrs. The captain of the *Luigi Torelli* [Lt-Cdr Augusto Migliorini] reported a sudden appearance of a huge searchlight on a low-flying plane. It illuminated an area about 300m to the right of his bow, then centred upon him. Immediately the navigation officer on duty gave orders to steam full speed ahead and turn to the left. However, the aircraft kept overhead with its light on the submarine. Finally, it was switched off. The night was very dark with no moon, but much phosphorescence on the sea. Now the captain reduced his speed to a minimum, believing that the aeroplane was detecting him by his phosphorescent wake. As he prepared to dive the searchlight of the aeroplane lit up again his stern from the right side, approximately 300m away, then centred on the conning tower of the submarine. The captain turned to the right and gave orders to open fire with the anti-aircraft guns. The plane passed over him low (250ft height) also firing, then turned off its searchlight again. When the captain thought that the aircraft had lost him because of his small wake he gave orders for a rapid dive.

'But all was not over. While the captain still had his head stuck out of the hatch, the submarine was again illuminated from a very close range. The bosun had signalled with the hooter to dive, when the captain gave orders to turn to port. Only seconds later the ship was bracketed by a stick of 250lb depth charges that exploded under its hull. The *Luigi Torelli*, covered by columns of water, jerked violently and went down by the bow. As a result of the explosion the catch freed itself from the hook and the hatch closed by itself over the captain's head while the diesel motors were still running. This created a very strong decompression before the motor could be stopped. The captain therefore introduced air into the chambers with the watertight doors near the bow to equalise the air pressure. Although out of the immediate line of fire, the *Luigi Torelli's* troubles were still not over. In some three minutes the conning tower hatch cover opened again and the

bosun's mate, who was still *out*side, told the captain that the aeroplane was still near; it had passed over twice, firing its machine guns.

'The captain's Log gives the damages resulting from Greswell's attack:
* Breakage of a considerable number of battery elements that resulted in leakage of acid.
* Fire in the chambers of two batteries, accompanied by smoke in the chambers over the batteries.
* Complete loss of power.
* Damage to compass and steering apparatus.
* Some development of chlorine.
* Breakage of shelves and fixtures.
He considered the condition of the

Left: Dropping a flame float for checking drift over the North Sea. *British Official*

Above: Sound & fury. NB773, RW-O of 36 Sqn taking off from a snow-bounded runway at Chivenor, February 1944, piloted by Flt Lt Look. *G. Jones*

interior of the *Luigi Torelli* and decided to steer to a French port (St Jean-de-Luz). The battery fire was not extinguished or even diminished, and strong smoke was produced mainly in the wireless cabin and the officers' and NCOs' quarters. Repeated attempts to enter the front chambers with extinguishers failed. The captain ordered flooding of the ammunition store in the bow after retrieval of the cannon shells, and at length the fire was extinguished.

'In the meantime Greswell and his crew spotted a second submarine nearby. He is now of the opinion that it may have never seen him because it was submerging when spotted with ASV and searchlight. What saved both these submarines was the failure of the pursuer to get a signal of the attack to the other three Wellingtons on patrol in the area, and home them to the place of the attacks. I was second pilot and searchlight operator on the nearest Wellington, and can testify that no message of this attack was received. Undoubtedly the coded signal "472" ("Sighted sub. Am attacking") had been sent to base at Chivenor, though it may not have reached there immediately because of the low level at which the aircraft was flying when the signal was sent or because of atmospheric disruptions. This weakness in communication was later rectified, when attacking aircraft remained in the vicinity of the attack as long at their petrol supply would permit in order to home other aircraft into the area.

'In any case, the *Luigi Torelli* escaped. Other submarines later attacked by Leigh Light-equipped anti-submarine aircraft were not that lucky. Shortly after, my own connection with 172 Squadron ended when, in mid-August, I was commissioned and posted to Wick, where another Leigh Light Wellington squadron, No 179, was then forming.'

The *Luigi Torelli* was to have a long and chequered career after this first encounter with 172 Squadron. On 5 June 1942 she was hastily repaired in a Spanish harbour, left this haven on 6 June, only to be attacked twice by Sunderlands of No 10 RAAF Squadron and further damaged. Putting in to the Spanish port of Santander, the submarine was officially interned; yet a month later made a dash to freedom. In 1943 it went to the Far East, was taken over by the Germans after Italy's surrender and retitled UIT-25; then when Germany surrendered in May 1945, was retaken-over by the Japanese who titled her RO-504. Four months later she fell into American hands, but was finally scuttled by her ultimate (sixth) captain in 1946. 172 Squadron's first true kill was to come just four weeks after Greswell's blooding attack, on 6 July 1942, when an American pilot in the unit, Pilot Officer W. Howell in Wellington "H" sunk the U-502.

The successes of the Leigh Light Wellingtons were to continue until the final victory in Europe in May 1945; with the final confirmed U-boat sinking by a Wimpy occurring on 2 April 1945 when Wellington 'Y-Yorker' of No 304

(Polish) Squadron sank the U-321 at the location 50°N, 12° 57′ W. Indeed, as merely one example of the sustained effort made by the maritime Wellington squadrons, the record of No 304 Squadron shows that during its three years' sojourn with Coastal Command its crews had flown 2,451 sorties, accumulating therein 21,331 operational flying hours. During these they attacked 34 U-boats and sighted nine others, had 31 combats with German fighters, and lost 106 aircrew men killed or missing. In balance the Poles of 304 Squadron could claim just two U-boats destroyed and a third seriously damaged. The first confirmed sinking came on 18 June 1944, when Flt Lt J. Antoniewicz, skippering Wellington 'A-Able', destroyed the U-441, killing its captain Kapitanleutnant Klaus Hartmann and his entire crew.

U-441 was nearing the end of a two-weeks patrol, and some 50 miles from its intended haven at Brest when it had the misfortune to cross the path of Antoniewicz's Wellington; the aircraft having had a complete breakdown in its radar-search equipment, and merely relying on the 'Eyeball Mk 1' for the completion of its patrol in the bright moonlight. What followed was contained in the prosaic terms of the Wellington skipper's official report of 20 June:

'Wellington A/304 on A-U patrol ''V'' was flying on course 324deg(T) when at 2254hrs (on 18 June) Captain sighted 050deg, red, four miles, a tin trail of vaporous grey smoke on the sea. Weather was fine, visibility four-five miles, sea calm, 9/10ths cloud at 2000ft. Captain was just about to alter course to investigate when he sighted 045deg, green, three miles, black object which he identified almost immediately as the conning tower of a surfacing U-boat. He turned to port to get on an attacking course. At the same time he lost height. He approached U-boat on a course between 060 and 090(T). When one mile away 2nd pilot and radar operator, in the astrodome, sighted another U-boat which had apparently just surfaced 10deg, green, 1½ miles away. Captain kept on his course to attack first U-boat, which then started to submerge slowly. At 2257hrs six DCs were dropped from 100ft, spaced 60ft, and set to 14-18ft, 155deg, green to U-boat heading. Rear gunner distinctly saw positions of entry, the first two hitting the water to

186

Above left: Leigh Light Mk XII of 172 Sqn (?). *J. Rounce*

Left: Wellington GRXIV of 14 Sqn at St Merryn on 28 April 1945. *FAA Museum*

Below left: Wimpy Mk VIII with ASV Mk II aerial array

Above: Directional Wireless Installation (DWI) Wimpy, L4356 of No 1 GRU, a unit later integrated with 162 Sqn in March 1944, in Egypt. It had previously served with 214 and 419 Sqns, and was SOC on 27 July 1944. *F. Spelman*

starboard quarter of UB (No 2 about 10 yards away from hull) and the remainder across the UB and on its port bow. Then he saw them explode, and the explosions and plumes completely obscured UB. He also saw a long black pipe-like object blown about 100ft into the air with the DC explosion. When the explosion plumes subsided there was no sign of the UB, and the conning tower was only just visible when the DCs were dropped. Aircraft then returned to port. Almost immediately after the attack the second UB was seen to submerge. One minute later the aircraft tracked over the scene of the attack and saw:

'(1) Two flame floats burning about 500ft apart
'(2) Between the flame floats a spreading bubbling patch of oil
'(3) Close to the second flame float two dark cylindrical-looking objects about 30ft long
'(4) A considerable quantity of smaller pieces of wreckage between the flame floats

Regarding the bubbling oil patch, this was first seen by radar operator in the astrodome as soon as DC explosion had subsided. Aircraft made three more runs over the scene, and during the second run ($1\frac{1}{2}$mins after the first) the oil seemed to be gushing to the surface and spreading outwards into a circle fringed with iridescence. At the third run (about $2\frac{1}{2}$mins after the second) the bubbles and gushing had ceased, and the oil patch exceeded in size the area of 500ft between the flame floats. During the fourth run the oil patch was still spreading, and the wreckage described above was still evident.

Having dropped marine markers, the aircraft then set course on patrol at 2312hrs.'

If Wellingtons were prominent in the unending campaign against the U-boat in European and Atlantic waters, they were not the only active or successful Wimpys in this role. One example of Wimpy labours in the 'side-show' zones of operations was No 621 Squadron. Formed initially at Port Reitz, Kenya, in September 1943 and equipped with Wellingtons for general reconnaissance of the approaches to the Red Sea et al, 621 was based at Aden by early 1944 with various detachments in the area. Their operational area was vast, including the Persian Gulf, while enemy activity was by no means minimal; in January 1944 alone, 16 sightings of U-boats were reported.

On the morning of 2 May 1944, Wellington 'T-Tommy' of 621 Squadron was carrying out an anti-submarine patrol just south of the Gulf of Aden. Skippered by Flt R. H. Mitchell, its other crew members were Warrant Officer Harvey Riddell, the Canadian second pilot, Flt Sgt O. Gomersal (Nav), and two W/Op AGs, Sgts W. R. Stevenson and S. Philips. They could hardly believe their eyes when they suddenly came upon a U-boat, fully surfaced and steaming along at about 12 knots. Swinging immediately into an attack run, Mitchell bore in for the kill. The U-boat was U-852, commanded by Heinz Eck, which had been active in the area for several weeks, and on spotting the incoming Wimpy, Eck gave immediate orders for a crash-dive — too late. At 800 yards range the Wellington's front

Above: DWI Wellingtons on patrol in the Middle East. Nearest, L4374 originally flew with 149 Sqn in the UK, and was ultimately lost over the Mediterranean on 31 January 1942. *F. Spelman*

guns opened up, slashing a hail of bullets round the conning tower, and at 50ft a stick of six depth charges was placed with deadly accuracy up-track, two of these at least falling within lethal range of the sub's hull. The damage caused was severe enough to prevent the U-boat submerging, and she wallowed helplessly on the surface.

Signals were sent from Wimpy 'T-Tommy' for assistance in finally 'nailing' the sitting duck, and six further attacks by aircraft from Nos 621 and 8 Squadrons were made during daylight hours; each attack being fiercely contested by the crippled U-boat's gunners. Meanwhile HMS *Falmouth,* at the time of 'T-Tommy's' initial attack escorting a convoy from Mombasa to Aden, was ordered to leave the convoy and proceed to the scene. Early next morning, the U-boat was sighted and before *Falmouth* could reach her, Eck ordered the submarine to be scuttled and set on fire, while surviving crew members made for the nearby shore. Here they later surrendered to a naval landing party.

The aftermath was the award of a DFC to Flt Lt Mitchell and a DFM to Sgt Stevenson; while the U-boat commander and two of his senior officers were eventually sentenced to death by a military court in Hamburg after the war for the murder of British and Allied seamen from the steamer *Peleus* which U-852 had encountered only weeks before its ultimate action.

Peter Brewster was a Wop/AG with No 612 (County of Aberdeenshire) Squadron, AAF from March 1944 to February 1945:

'My crew was John Saul (skipper), Jack Church (2nd pilot), Jack Royans (Nav), Bill Bates, Fred Floyer and myself, all Wop/AGs, and we crewed up at No 6 (C) OTU, Silloth, near Carlisle in November 1943, where we flew many of the earlier marks of Wimpy. On posting to 612 Squadron we began flying Leigh Light Wimpys fitted with Mk 3a radar, initially operating from Chivenor over the English Channel and the Bay of Biscay, covering the D-Day operations. The radar was quite unique in those days, being a radial time-base with aerial situated in the nose of the aircraft; the front turret having been removed and replaced with a single 0.50 Browning machine gun on a free mounting.

'The Leigh Light was hydraulically operated and lowered from the dorsal turret position about halfway along the fuselage — usually by the wireless operator. The operator, being the second pilot, when operating the Light, lay in the bomb-aimer's position, on top of the Light's batteries. The Wimpy was also fitted with a radio altimeter in order that an attack on any U-boat could be carried out accurately from a mere 50ft altitude.

'After D-Day, because of our sensitive radar, we were posted in September 1944 to Limavady, Northern Ireland, to combat the *Schnorchel* being used by U-boats in the North-West Approaches. Our radar was capable of picking up an echo from what amounted to a drain-pipe sticking-out of the sea. Soon after, however, we moved again, this time on 18 December 1944 to Langham, Norfolk, where we adopted an anti-shipping role, operating from the Hook of Holland to the German coast, and attacking convoys which were apparently supplying German forces in their attempt to break through the Allied lines in the "Battle of the Bulge". Again, the radar played an important role because not only was it accurate, but also released the bombs on to target automatically. The only problem was that the aircraft had to be flown at a maximum height of 1,250ft for the accuracy to be maintained. In this job we were supported by Beaufighters and Mosquitos with rockets and cannons of New Zealand squadrons when we carried out attacks known as "Percolating". In short, after bombing a convoy we called up the New Zealanders and, after laying an artificial moonpath, they would attack with their RP and cannons.'

Also based at Langham, from November 1944 to May 1945, was Andrew Hendrie, a Wop/AG with No 524 Squadron:

'I flew Wellington XIVs with 524 Squadron as a W/AG, with Fg Off Lister as captain for most trips. Operations were against E-boats, which would attempt at night-time, and at an esimated 50 knots, to come over from the Dutch coast to the Humber estuary or off Harwich to attack our shipping. Our patrols were off Dan Helder, Ijmuiden, Rotterdam and Frisians. At briefings, therefore, areas of flak concentrations were usually stressed. We lost a lot of crews through aircraft going in too close to the coast. The first comment made to me by the squadron adjutant on joining 524 was, "Have you a car? There are so many here, and the former owners are now unknown". We had a Wellington detachment at Dallachy, home of a Beaufighter strike wing, whose role was to act as pathfinders by circling an enemy convoy, dropping a series of flares, to light the way for the Beau boys. At least, this was the proposal towards a three-squadron Beaufighter strike, escorted by Mustangs, which went to Norway. The Mustang "escort" circled the wrong enemy fighter aerodrome — thankfully, the Wimpys' part was called off!

'I recorded only one successful attack against E-boats. This was on 6 April 1945 in Wimpy NB772, skipper Flt Lt Meggison, with take-off from Langham at 0045hrs. The wake of E-boats could be seen easily in bright moonlight, giving an indication of their speed. We found three of them. We gained height to about 6,000ft, the minimum specified altitude, otherwise we'd blow ourselves up too. If memory serves me, we dropped a stick of six 250lb bombs, intended to explode in mid-air and provide a wide "shrapnel" effect. The E-boats would almost certainly have seen us, despite our black camouflage, in the bright moonlight, and they opened up with their single cannons fitted in the stern of each craft. We were hit only once when there was a brilliant flash near the rear turret. The gunner hadn't fired — he wanted to keep our position secret — and we thought we'd lost him. On return to base, we found quite a neat hole in the tail plane, which had missed the elevator mechanism by merely an inch or so.

'One experience of purely personal interest was the night of 7/8 March 1945, when we spotted V2 rockets being launched from the enemy coast area. That night one landed near my home at Hornchurch and brought half of it down — meaning there was a good chance I'd seen the launch of the actual V2 which blasted my own home!

'Regarding the Wellington, frankly, I didn't like it; especially after flying Lockheed Hudsons with two previous squadrons. I rather think my reasons were that it was night work instead of day, meaning the crew members were away from each other, giving a feeling of isolation. They were also fitted with Marconi radio, whereas most of the Hudsons I'd flown in had had Bendix radio which was much easier and more precise in tuning. In Hudsons all could and did take an actual part in flying the aircraft; this we could never do in Wellingtons. Another thing, at that time over the North Sea, we experienced on occasions quite severe icing on props and leading edges, whereas Hudsons, even over Norway, seemed to keep relatively free of such troubles.'

Below: Flt Sgt W. R. Stevenson (left) and Flt Lt R. H. Mitchell, DFC of 621 Sqn, Aden, 1944. *W. R. Stevenson*

Bottom: Awards of DFC and DFM respectively to Flt Lt R. H. Mitchell (shaking hands) and Flt Sgt W. R. Stevenson (4th from right), 621 Sqn, Aden, 1944. *W. R. Stevenson*

Above: GRXIVs of 304 (Polish) Sqn on 25 April 1945. *IWM*

Below: A GRXIV and its crew of 304 (Polish) Sqn, 1945. *IWM*

Fishes and Photos

Having been designed as a bomber, the Wellington is most usually remembered or regarded in such a prime role. Yet the versatile Wimpy's distinguished Service career was to include many equally important roles imposed upon it during 1939-45. Just two such operational facets were torpedo-bomber and photographic reconnaissance. Group Captain M. J. A. Shaw, DSO — 'Mike' — joined the RAF initially in April 1938, and from 1941-45 was to be associated with the Wimpy in both of these specialised operational uses for the Wellington. His introduction to the design came in August 1941, when he was posted to No 1 Torpedo Training Unit at Abbotsinch:

'My first Wellington was a Mk VIII, and my first impression was that it was much bigger and heavier than the Beaufort I had been used to up to then. I soon found, though, that the Wimpy could be thrown about pretty well and the brief trials we carried out indicated that the tactics used for Beauforts were applicable to the Wellington as far as training for torpedo operations were concerned. It was, to me, a very comfortable aircraft to fly, and the only minor vice was the change of trim when the flaps were put down. However, one soon got used to the need to ensure that the tail trimmer was adjusted before selecting flaps.

'Moving the following month to Limavady, and later Turnberry, in the six months that I commanded the Torpedo Training Squadron of No 7 (Coastal) OTU, we found the Wimpy an excellent aircraft for the job, bearing in mind that we were training crews primarily for *night* torpedo operations. I remember noticing quite a difference the first time I flew a Wellington with a full load of two torpedoes. The extra weight certainly made itself felt, both on take-off and in general handling, but they were splendid aircraft for low flying over the sea — very stable, with

adequate, though not superlative, visibility from the cockpit.

'I was next posted to command 221 Squadron at Luqa, Malta, and arrived in Malta in June 1943, after the fiercest part of the war in the Mediterranean was over. We had a few torpedo trips — all at night or at dawn — but enemy targets by then were few and far between. After the Allies invaded Italy in September 1943 we came to be used more and more for

Above: Fish Porters. Lining up the two-torpedo load for a ship-hunter Wellington in the Middle East.

Left: Group Captain Mike Shaw, DSO
Grp Capt M. Shaw

anti-submarine work, at night, and my main recollection of that tour is of doing long trips on convoy escort, starting at dusk and going right through until after dawn — sometimes as long as 12 hours. A member of the crew had to pump oil through to each engine from a tank in the fuselage every hour — a tedious business. We carried a second pilot whose main function was to take the controls for an hour or so to enable the captain to have a rest on the camp bed rigged up halfway down the fuselage. Some of those second pilots had not been taught to fly Wellingtons — they might have had a bit of a problem landing the aircraft if anything happened to the captain!

'These aircraft were, of course, the Hercules-engined Mk XI, XII and XIV Wellingtons — much more powerful than the old Pegasus versions I'd flown back in the UK. Their single-engine performance was much better too, which was a considerable consolation. I found the Wimpy quite unpleasant when flying in the bumpy conditions sometimes met in electrical storms at certain times of the year in the Mediterranean, and remember having to return early from patrol on two occasions due to extremely bad weather conditions. Overall, though, my memories of the Wellington during my 221 Squadron tour are pleasureable. Although a fairly sedate old lady, it had a fair turn of speed and was very easy to fly. We were also used for occasional bombing missions at night, using flares to illuminate targets, which were confined to roads, railways and bridges near the coast of Italy. These were mostly carried out from fairly low altitudes — below 1,000ft — doubtless because we did not carry oxygen!

'My final tour of operations in

Top: Wellington XIII, JA416, 'L' of 221 Sqn over Malta on 3 January 1944. *Grp Capt M. Shaw*

Above: 221 Sqn Wimpy doing a 'runner attack' on a British destroyer off Malta, December 1943. *Grp Capt M. Shaw*

Left: Yet one more victim of Malta's 'runways' . . . *R. Slater*

Wellingtons, from June 1944 to August 1945, was with No 69 Squadron of the 2nd Tactical Air Force (TAF). The squadron was reformed at Northolt in May 1944 to provide night visual tactical reconnaissance in support of the ground forces during the invasions of France, Belgium, Holland and Germany. Specially modified Mk XIII Wellingtons were used and these had clear perspex noses fitted to facilitate visual observation, together with a moving film camera, and a pistol discharger for letting off photo-flashes, so that photographic confirmation of visual sightings could be provided, and finally a flare chute for launching the load of 54 flares.

'One of the bonuses stemming from the selection of the Mk XIII Wimpy was the relative quietness of the aircraft, from the ground observer's point of view. I'm certain that this characteristic enabled us to achieve a modicum of surprise, particularly when operating on moonlight nights where flares were not required. Which was just as well because we were operating at pretty low level — below 3,000ft — and often ran into heavy ground fire from the German flak gunners. The Wimpy turned out to be an excellent aircraft for the job, and I certainly enjoyed that tour very much. We normally flew with a crew of five, giving several pairs of eyes to carry out the recce task. We were part of No 34 Recce Wing — along with No 16 Squadron (Spitfires) and 140 (Mosquitos) — and while the rest of the Wing provided plenty of recce by day, the gap. as far as the army was concerned, was what happened at night. There was little tactical recce by night — and by tactical I mean right on the front line and just behind it — so the Wimpy filled this gap. We were usually given a length of roadway or canal or railway within 20 miles of the front line, and had to go and survey this more or less all night to see if there was any enemy movement, transport, troops, etc.

'We did this normally from very low level, dropping flares at about 3,000ft and then circling down below these to see what was revealed. If anything interesting was seen we were supposed to take photographs with the special camera; an open shutter type with a moving film linked to the pistol discharger, which was a sort of "Mickey Mouse" box with (I think) 12 photo-flash cartridges (same size as the Very

Cartridge). These latter were small and did not give great illumination, but enabled photos to be taken providing they were taken at low level — you couldn't take them above 1,000ft with any certainty of success. It turned out to be a hairy business, flying straight and level under 1,000ft, and we got a lot of flak directed our way and lost quite a lot of aeroplanes. Nevertheless, it did a good job, and the army was always pleased with the information we obtained.

'The versatility of the aircraft — and their crews — was demonstrated in several ways. For example, towards the end of the war we were a bit fed up with not being offensive, and got permission to carry bombs instead of flares when we had a moonlight night, when we could see the ground without the use of flares. On these occasions we carried a load of 250lb HE bombs and dropped these on anything which looked interesting — which added a bit to the excitement. They were very short trips, being purely tactical, with the average being about one hour and 20 minutes, but each crew would often fly two or three such trips each night. Being tactical meant, or course, that we moved forward with the army from Normandy to Amiens, Brussels, Melsbroek, and finally Eindhoven in Holland, so it was easy to carry out up to three sorties each night, being so close to the front line at all times.

'Then, early in 1945, a threat from German midget submarines presented itself off the Belgian and Dutch coasts, and yet again the Wellington demon-

strated its ubiquity. One flight of the squadron had their aircraft modified to carry depth charges, and were deployed to the small airfield at Knokke on the Belgian coast. Here they carried out anti-submarine patrols — just like old times in the Mediterranean!

'The Wellington's ability to absorb punishment in terms of enemy fire was most welcome, and confirmed over and over again. Many Wimpys came back quite badly shot up but still flying — though I must add that losses were fairly high. But even the tough old Wimpy couldn't stand up to the concentrated punishment we received on the ground at Melsbroek on 1 January 1945, when the Luftwaffe had its final fling. They burned beautifully! However, we were fully re-equipped within 48 hours with new aircraft — a quite remarkable achievement. To the best of my belief, No 69 Squadron was the only squadron to be operating Wellingtons right up to VE-Day (in Europe), so I suppose it can be said that the Wimpy, along with the Spitfire, was one of very few British aircraft to operate right throughout the war.'

Left: Quarry-hunting on Malta
— literally! *G. S. Leslie*

Centre left: On a sandy beach
in Egypt . . .

Bottom left: Wimpy XIII of 69
Sqn over English countryside,
June 1944.
Grp Capt M. Shaw

Right: Mike Shaw with his
adjutant, flight commanders
and gunnery Leader, 69 Sqn,
Melsbroek, early 1945.
Grp Capt M. Shaw

Below: Wellington victims of
the Luftwaffe's *Bodenplatte*
strafe on Melsbroek, 69 Sqn,
1 January 1945.
Grp Capt M. Shaw

Ginger's Tale

'Ginger' — Jim Ware, DFM — was a rear gunner in Wellingtons, who flew more than 80 operational sorties before his ultimate, near-fatal trip. A born Cockney, he was 25 years old on the morning that Neville Chamberlain told the British population that '... this country is now at war with Germany' and, still recovering from the previous night's celebrations — or in his own phrase, 'Pissed and patriotic' — he immediately went to the nearest recruiting centre and volunteered for RAF aircrew duties. He was accepted for 'straight AG' — air gunner without the normal accompanying wireless training — and after initial training joined No 99 Squadron at Rowley Mile Racecourse, Newmarket, in March 1940:

'It was there that I was crewed up and my skipper was Sgt Jack Hatton who spent some weeks knocking us into shape. He was a grand chap and by the time I met him he'd already done a few ops. By the time we were ready as a crew for ops I'd realised what a wonderful aircraft the Wellington was. I suppose it was underpowered, but it was tough, strong, and somehow I always felt safe in it. I learned later in my career as an AG that it could stand a hell of a lot of punishment and, providing you still had one engine going, it would get you home. In a way I fell in love with the Wimpy, if it is at all possible for a man to love a machine — I guess other Wimpy men might understand what I mean.

'My first real op was on 10 May 1940 when we were detailed to attack an aerodrome in Holland. It was a short trip and uneventful, though I can remember on the way back seeing the huge fires in Rotterdam; a sight which made me realise that all this was no game, but the real thing. We were kept very busy during this period, and on 29 May we were detailed to bomb a target in France. That day our regular skipper was ill, and we had a young pilot officer take us over. All was well, and we'd bombed the target despite a fair amount of flak, and had no troubles until we got back to England. Here we found the whole country covered with fog. We went from 'drome to 'drome but couldn't land anywhere, and eventually ran out of fuel. We had no alternative but to bale out — I was never so frightened in my life before. I remember after I'd gone out that I looked *down* and saw our Wimpy, and only then realised I was falling upside down. I pulled the ripcord and — to my great relief — the 'chute opened and all seemed so quiet. I heard the Wimpy crash on my way down, but was feeling great because I'd got away with it. What I didn't know at that time was that three other aircraft from our squadron were in the same predicament, and all their crews had to bale out. I'd no idea where I was when I hit the deck — I'd landed

Below: 'Ginger' Ware (left) and another 99 Sqn AG at Newmarket, Sgt Gardiner, 1941. *N. Didwell*

in a field, but couldn't see a thing. After a cigarette, I started to walk, and after what seemed ages I heard voices and was then picked up by some chaps in army uniform (probably LDV blokes).

'At that period everybody was thinking about invasion and these chaps thought I was a German parachutist — I don't know who was more frightened, them or me! The officer in charge asked for my identity card, and when I told him I had nothing on me to prove who I was, I was promptly locked up in a hut until early morning, when I was rescued by a squadron leader who told them he'd been looking for us all night. It was then I learned that four crews had baled out that night, and also learned that my pilot had stayed in the Wimpy and crash-landed it at Honington. Twenty-three chaps from 99 Squadron baled out, but only 22 made it; one pilot was killed by jumping too low. It had been my seventh trip — the war was getting dangerous.

'I did 17 trips with Jack Hatton, after which he was posted to an OTU and our second pilot took over. Trips were getting longer now — Berlin, Munich, Hamburg, Kiel, Wilhelmshaven, etc — but our dear old Wimpy, despite taking a beating at times, always got us back. By September 1940 I'd finished my first tour of ops and the crew split up, mostly going to OTUs as instructors. I didn't want to be an instructor so, after a spot of leave, stayed with the squadron as a ''spare'' AG for ops. On getting back from leave I hardly knew any of the chaps; during my three weeks' absence many of my mates had been shot down or posted elsewhere, so I didn't have a regular crew, but flew with any crew needing a rear gunner.

'It was on one such trip, on 16 January 1941, that I was asked to stand in for a gunner who'd gone sick. I didn't know the crew, while they assumed I was new to the squadron and therefore promised to look after me — they'd only been with 99 for about three weeks! The target was Wilhelmshaven and off we went — a long trip over the sea, with little for me to do except to keep a lookout for fighters. We received the usual attentions of the flak boys, dropped our bombs on target, and away home. I was cold and looking forward to my ops' bacon and beans when we got back, when I heard the navigator and pilot arguing as to where we were. The nav said we were over Lincolnshire, but the pilot thought somewhere else. I was thinking to myself ''Make up your bloody minds!'' . . . I then realised we really were lost, and suddenly saw some balloons. I immediately thought. ''We're over London'', then told the pilot about the barrage balloons below. There followed real panic! To cut a long story short, the pilot spotted an

Below: Aircrew billets for 99 Sqn — the race-stand at Newmarket, 1940. From left: Bill Shankland (rear AG in Jack Hatton's crew), Jim 'Ginger' Ware, and Quibell. *J. Ware*

aerodrome shortly after, a small one, made a couple of attempts at landing, and finally made it, running off the 'drome and finishing up in some trees, minus a wing, but collecting bruises all round.

'The aerodrome was Kenley, a tiny fighter station near Croydon. Once again I'd got away with it, but my troubles on this trip were not quite over. Next morning we collected our gear from the wreck, and we were taken to London, to Liverpool Street Station for a train back to Newmarket. Just as we were offloading our stuff at the station from the lorry, something whacked me on the back of the head, and a voice screamed, ''German bastard!'' It was some dotty old girl clouting me with her umbrella! We were still in flying gear, so she thought we must be Germans.

'By then I felt I must get myself a regular crew; I was fed up with being reserve man for other crews, so I managed to join up with Pilot Officer H. ''Robin'' Grant as a regular gunner. A few weeks later the squadron left Newmarket and moved to Water-beach; a new aerodrome where we had proper rooms, baths, showers, a decent Mess, and what's more WAAFs (which made life more interesting . . .). It was like changing from a doss house to a first-class hotel for 99's boys.'

In January 1942, No 99 Squadron left the UK for India. Grant and Ware organised a scratch crew and proceeded to fly out with the squadron to the Middle East, but were 'tumbled' there and attached to Shallufa, where they kicked their heels for a while, 'organised' themselves on to No 40 Squadron (Wellingtons), and got back on ops again with this unit. Flying against such targets as Benghazi, Tobruk and Derna, Ginger ran up a further 17 or 18 sorties. Then, on 7 August 1942, his luck finally ran out. The target was Tobruk, and the crew of Wimpy 'O-Orange' comprised Flt Lt Robin Grant (pilot), Sgt H. 'Jock' Whyte (second pilot), Plt Off John Hull (observer-nav), Sgt A. 'Arfer' Dunn (W/Op), Sgt 'Chuck' Dauphin (front AG), and Ginger Ware in his customary rear gun turret:

'I woke up that morning with a funny (peculiar) feeling that something was going to happen that day, and that things weren't quite right. I had a cup of tea with my crew and was very quiet, which was not my usual style.

Some mail arrived from the UK that morning. The rest or the crew got letters, but none for me, which didn't help the mood I was in. I went out to the aircraft, checked my guns and turret; everything was OK. I began to think what a bloody fool I was. My skipper asked me if I was OK. I was rather short with him, saying I was, so he left me to get on with it. We were on that night and the target Tobruk, which we'd been to before and therefore knew what to expect.

'Our journey to the target was uneventful until we reached the target area where we got the usual hot reception with plenty of flak, and for a while were coned in searchlights. The skipper, with a lot of evasive action, managed to get away from the searchlights, we bombed the target area, and set course for home. By then I was feeling ashamed of myself for the mood I'd been in all day, and was beginning to feel like my old self again. We had been on our way back for about three-quarters of an hour or so when Johnny asked me to take a drift for him. He threw out a marker and I got my gun sight on to it and took the drift for him — I'll always remember it read five degrees starboard. I looked up from reading it, to tell him the figure, when to my horror I saw another Wimpy right on top of us, coming from the port quarter! There was no time even to shout to the pilot before he hit us, there was a terrible crash, and I saw him go down in flames.

'I was stunned — I think I must have banged my head — and just sat there unable to move. The warning light on my turret flashed, telling me to bale out. I pulled myself together and became conscious of a horrible silence — I could hear no engines. I put my manual handle into gear to turn the turret to the beam but it would only go part-way round, so I got out into the fuselage to escape by the rear escape hatch. Though all this seemed like ages to me, it could only have been a matter of a few seconds. I kicked out the escape hatch with my left leg and was just about to go out when we hit the ground. As we careered along the deck I knew I was hitting my leg but for the moment it didn't hurt. We finally stopped and, somehow, I was outside the aircraft. I've still no idea how this came about, but I'd alway been frightened of fire and possibly it was that fear that got me clear. I noticed the landing lights were on and gave a shout. Robin answered me and found me, and I realised he'd stayed in the aircraft and made a pretty good crash-landing.

'I knew I'd hurt my leg pretty badly, so Robin got the first aid kit and I injected myself in the thigh with a dose of morphine, then, after a cigarette, dozed off. Next morning we had a good look at my leg — and it frightened the life out of me! There wasn't much of my foot left, and the lower part was smashed right up; all we could see were pieces of bone. There was little we could do about it except rip a parachute up and put a rough bandage round it. At least this hid the grisly mess from us. Some time later Jock

199

Above: 149 Sqn crews walking out to their Wellingtons at Mildenhall, 1941.

found us and told us that he'd found "Arfer", who had broken a leg and had his face burnt, being unable to see properly. Both of them left me and fetched "Arfer" back to where I was. They later found Johnny's body — his 'chute hadn't opened properly because he'd jumped too low. We never saw Chuck again.* After Robin and Jock had made "Arfer" and myself as comfortable as possible in the circumstances, it was decided that both pilots would go and seek help for both of us. Jock was a damned good navigator and had worked out our position roughly. They both decided to go because they felt that then at least one of them would get to the German lines — we were too far from our own lines. We agreed on this plan, and about mid-day on the Saturday (8th) they set off. I watched them as far as I could and when they disappeared I felt very miserable and alone.

'By that time my leg was beginning to hurt like hell, and I knew poor "Arfer" was in great pain too. I felt helpless as there was literally nothing either of us could do except wait and hope for the best. As the day wore on I began thinking all sorts of things; wondering how Robin and Jack were getting on — of my parents — then it dawned on me that we'd crashed on my young sister's birthday. I could imagine them all at home being over

*Jock told me after the war that Chuck wandered about for quite a time before being picked up by some Italians.

the local, supping it up and enjoying themselves, unaware of what was happening to me. Then I pulled myself together smartly — thinking of such things would only send me starkers. Sunday came and went, and by Monday morning — 10 August — "Arfer" and I were both in a pretty bad way. I knew that if help didn't arrive soon we'd both die, yet strangely, I was not frightened about this; in fact I think I'd have welcomed death at this stage as I was in terrible pain. Then I thought of Robin and Jock walking miles across the desert to try and save us both — it wouldn't be fair to them to just give it up now.

'Around noon on the Monday I heard what I thought was the sound of aircraft engines, but felt I must be imagining them. As I searched the sky I saw them, two of them, Fieseler Storch light aircraft. They landed near us and I could see they were German Red Cross planes. A doctor was with them, and they told us that this was their third search for us that day — and would have been the last. Robin and Jock had got through — we owed them our lives. We then learned that they'd been picked up the evening before by an aeroplane, and I was also told later by a German officer that Robin and Jock, at one time, walked through two German minefields and never knew it! The Germans tried to bury Johnny, then put "Arfer" in one aircraft and me in the other. They took us first to Mersa Matruh, but kept us apart, then after a few days I was flown to Athens, where I had my leg amputated.'

200

Prangs

Right: Wellington burning in Crete, 1941, *via S. Howe*

Below: Wellington shot down by flak during a 'Nickel' paper-raid on 23 March 1940, near Eifel.

Right: Remains of Wellington T2963 of 115 Sqn which ran out of fuel and crashed into some council houses at Debach, Norfolk in the early morning of 24 June 1941. Two crew members were seriously injured, two slightly injured, and one was unhurt. *S. Evans*

Left: General Sikorski inspecting Wimpy R1697, '*Sonia*' of 304 (Polish) Sqn at Syerston, 1941. *W. Baguley*

Below left: R3295, SR-P, of 101 Sqn shot down at Schienmonnihoog, Holland on 30 November 1941, killing four crew members. *via B. Rijnhout*

Below: Wellington T2990, KX-T, of 311 (Czech) Sqn going down in flames to the guns of the German nightfighter ace, Major Prinz zur Lippe Weissenfeld on the night of 22 June 1941. *B. Rijnhout*

Above: Bent Wimpy at LG 09, North Africa, 1942

Right: Wellington graveyard in Libya, 1942.

Below: R1804 after a collision with a steam roller at East Wretham on 19 July 1941; a 311 (Czech) Sqn aircraft.
B. Rijnhout

Above: K-Kitty, R1090, ED-K of 21 OTU Moreton-in-the-Marsh.

Right: A-Apple (T2703) of 15 Sqn, shot down on the night of 31 March/1 April 1941 in Holland. *G. Zylstva Collection*

Below: Another 115 Sqn victim, X9873, KO-P, brought down near Schiermonnihoog, Holland. *B. Rijnhout*

Right: The *Werkhalle* at Rechlin, with its collection of shot down Allied aircraft. Visible aircraft include L7788, KX-E of 311 Sqn and T2703, LS-A of 15 Sqn.   *B. Rijnhout*

Centre right: A 205 Group Wellington, possibly a 150 Sqn machine (?), from Foggia, Italy, which raided the Manfried Weiss factory in Budapest on 3 April 1944. This aircraft, piloted by an Australian, Flt Sgt Gordon Pemberton, who was severely wounded, was ditched in the Keszthely Bay of Lake Balaton. By staying at his controls Pemberton saved the lives of his crew, but died himself, being buried in the nearby cemetery.   *L. Tabori*

Below: A Wellington T10 after a fiery crash-landing.

Sun, Sand and Stars

Although the Wellington acquired a doughty reputation on operations over Europe, from the first day of the war, by mid-1943 its bomber role against Germany had been taken over by the newer, four-engined heavies, such as the Lancaster and Halifiax, and the ultimate (officially) bombing sorties were flown by Wimpys of No 300 (Polish) Squadron against Hanover on the night of 8 October 1943; the close of four year's sustained operations by the Wimpy in this context. However, in September 1940, No 70 Squadron — based then at Kabrit, Egypt with Vickers Valentia biplane bombers — began re-equipment with Wimpys, and on 18/19 September the first Wimpy operations were flown; including a raid on Benghazi harbour which inaugurated the famed 'Mail Run' to that priority target by all subsequent Wimpy units. In November 1940, Nos 37 and 38 Squadrons arrived in Egypt to complement 70's Wimpys, and further Wellington units were formed or re-equipped in the Middle East zone over the following two years. And despite the later provision of long-range designs such as the Liberator, Middle East Wellingtons were to continue on firstline operations until early 1945.

N. E. McIntyre was a sergeant observer when he first joined 37 Squadron at Feltwell in August 1940, and was to remain with the squadron until September 1941 when, having completed his tour of ops, he returned to the UK:

'My initial crew — captain, Sgt D. Beddow — did 12 ops over France and Germany, ranging from "makee-learners" on the ports holding barges for the intended German invasion to targets in the Ruhr, Leipzig and Kiel. Navigational aids were conspicuous by their absence, and it was DR (Dead Reckoning) coupled with pinpoints when visibility was good which brought us on to target areas.

Incidentally, "Willy" Merton (Wg Cdr W. Merton, OC, later ACM Sir Walter) impressed upon us at each briefing the necessity of doing a three-course wind-check over target areas for a correct wind-setting on the bomb sight. This meant flying three straight-and-level courses for a few minutes, usually with plentiful flak to contend with — it can be left to imagination what captains and navigators thought of such a scheme!

'Sergeant Beddow completed his first tour in November 1940, and I joined another crew, with Sgt R. T. Spiller as captain, and the squadron was posted to Middle East Command, some aircraft stopping over at Malta to boost the efforts against the Italians. The squadron flew individually at intervals to Malta, via Worthing, Marseilles and Bizerta to Luqa. We made a landfall at Bizerta at about 9,000ft at approximately 0700hrs, to be greeted by a fair amount of friendly French flak thrown at us, and as we scuttled away an Italian Macchi 200 jumped us. We dived to sea level and eventually shook him off, with the assistance of our phlegmatic New Zealander rear gunner and his Brownings, but not before collecting a few hits, one of them peppering the backside of an unfortunate armourer travelling with us. We made Luqa at 0900hrs and the armourer survived after a few days in sick bay, despite initial bleeding. Whilst at Malta we flew sorties against Brindisi and Valona, Albania. This latter I particularly remember because of the severe thunderstorms we met over the Balkan coast, preventing location of both primary and secondary targets, and with the DR plot ending up like a spider's web due to the numerous changes of course we had to make.

'We left Malta on 20 December and flew to Shallufa in the Suez Canal zone, which became our main base for the remainder of our Middle East tour.

Targets from there included Benghazi, Tobruk, Derna along the northern coast, and Rhodes and Karpathos in the Dodecanese. From Shallufa we enjoyed two detachments to Greece and one to Iraq. Operating from Menidi, near Athens and Paramythia, a landing ground in from the west coast towards Corfu, I recall two sorties from Paramythia ("Valley of the Fairies"). On 20 February 1941, in company with another Wimpy (Flt Lt M. Baird-Smith), we dropped bales of bread and bully-beef to the Greek Army at Kelcyre inside the Albanian border. We made it as low-level as possible, and could almost see the joy on the faces of the men below as they scampered through the snow to the drops. On 16 March Intelligence learned that Mussolini was due in Tirana, the Albanian capital; we hoped that our bombs more than shook him in the royal palace.

'The Boche was by then coming down through the Balkans and we finished our stay in Greece with a raid on the Sofia railway yards, Calatos aerodrome on Rhodes, and German transport concentrations coming south through Ptolemais, Kozene and Florina. I well remember that last op. The CO (Wg Cdr R. M. Collard) decided to skipper the aircraft and, after bombing and strafing the German transports on the road through the three locations, the weather closed in on us and, with Mount Olympus (9,500ft) quite handy, we climbed in as tight a spiral as we dared, eventually breaking cloud, heading east, and (with a sigh of relief) pinpointed the three-fingered peninsula south-east from Salonika. This was on 16 April, and three days later we packed our bags and bade farewell to Greece, now being invaded by the Germans. Just after leaving Athens Ken Bevan, our Kiwi rear gunner, reported a fighter chasing us. We dropped to sea-level and, with his customary cool commentary and marksmanship, he persuaded the Messerschmitt to break off.

'A detachment to Iraq from 1-12 May gave us our first opportunity to be angry during daylight. Based at Shaibah, we flew "security patrols" over Habbaniyah and bombed "Raschid aerodrome" and the military installations and 'drome at Mosul. In addition to bombs we dropped "meaningful" messages to one Raschid Ali, the villain of the piece. On return to Shallufa, Vic Slater and myself volunteered for ACP duties in the "Blue" at Fuka satellite aerodrome, where we spent just over three weeks gradually becoming proficient in dousing goose-neck flares before the Boche came over, and relighting them in time for our aircraft to land. Then on 26 August we returned to Shallufa, and three weeks later left the Middle East for the UK by sea, via Durban and the Cape.'

Chas Hughes was a Wop/AG, trained at No 1 Signals School, Cranwell, and the gunnery school at Evanton. He next went to 15 OTU, Harwell but was 'detached' to Harwell's satellite at Hampstead Norris in early 1942, at the time of the famous Harris 'Thousand-bomber' raids, where he was commissioned as a Pilot Officer:

'The 1,000-raids produced lots of panic, with all hands to the wheel to spread that horrid brown de-icing paste over wing leading edges, spinners, etc. Then to the briefing where we were told that everybody must bomb from 14,000ft — a joke! It should perhaps be well recorded that Wellington III, HX876, "O-Orange" actually bombed Bremen from 6,500ft — and was hanging on its props at that! My skipper then was Plt Off Brian Hunter, a bank clerk from Hull who was later to lose a leg when he hit a bowser landing at Malta in early 1943; while my second pilot was Plt Off Clem

Below: In the shadow of Gibraltar's famous Rock, X9889 of 40 Sqn, in late 1941. *IWM*

Fowler, a London lad who later flew Beaufighters.

'After the OTU "sessions" we were off to Portreath in Cornwall to collect a brand-new Wimpy III fitted with torpedo-dropping gear, "P-Peter", then off to Gibraltar. Our call-sign was "Tablet, P-Peter" and Gibraltar was "Sermon", and I'd been calling and calling on the R/T to no avail, when Brian overshot after touching down and we nearly ended up in the sea. As we climbed hurriedly away a voice from below finally piped up saying, "Hello Tablet P-Peter. Are you in trouble?". My retort was, "No, nothing that a bit of finger-extraction on the deck can't solve!" We stayed at Gib until the following evening when, with two wing-tanks on the rest bed and cylinder tanks in the bomb bay, we took off with instructions to fly to LG224, 26km from Cairo, and to be sure to be east of 30-degrees east by daylight because of a German fighter base at Pontalaria — we were! Fourteen hours and 35 minutes later we arrived at LG224 near Cairo, where I removed my jacket and hung it on the tent pole, only to find when retrieving the jacket a few minutes later that my wallet had been stolen. Though formally charged with "losing my paybook in an active theatre of operations", the bit that really hurt was the loss of £20 in cash, which I couldn't report because we were officially only allowed to take £5 out of the UK!

'On to Almaza, and then to 148 Squadron at Kabrit on the Great Bitter Lake, where we left "P-Peter" and never saw her again. All we had on the

squadron were clapped-out Mk 1as. Using the same airfield at that time were Nos 40, 70, 104 and 108 Squadrons. Owing to the lack of space in the accommodation, my navigator, Sgt John Chandler, and I slept under a verandah in the open on charpoy-type beds, with each of the four legs standing in basins of creosote to stop bugs and "beasties" crawling up the legs into the beds. We weren't placed on the battle order on the first night, but a crew with a sick navigator borrowed ours. I turned in before the scheduled 10pm take-off, and when I woke next morning I turned to look at my nav's bed but it was empty. On enquiry, a corporal simply pointed to Wimpy "V-Victory" in the lake with its tail in the air. It had gone straight in on take-off and my nav was killed. We buried him at Geneifa.

'We moved from Kabrit and went up "into the Blue" to a strip known as Kilo 40 on the Cairo-Alexandria road, and on 23 October when El Alamein broke we moved up to LG 106 at El Daba to give the Eighth Army support. One morning at LG 106 I woke to find a Wimpy barely 50 yards from my tent, shot up on its belly. It had arrived during the night, yet I hadn't heard a thing. The next few weeks were hectic when we flew close support sorties against enemy transports etc to help the army move faster. Each op took about 2½-3hrs, and we had to do two ops each night to make them count as one operation. Just prior to El Alamein we did nearly all our sorties to Tobruk or Benghazi, bombing shipping, with occasional odd trips to targets like

Mersa Matruh. With us then was a pilot called Charlie Klimkie, who had a delayed take-off one night and was therefore told to stooge around the desert for something to bomb. He spotted a light below and decided to hit it with four 1,000lb bombs. It was a German ammo train outside Mersa Matruh station and Charlie hit it from about 1,000ft — and very nearly went up with it.

'We next moved to LG 67 on top of an escarpment 30 miles south of Bardia. Whoever chose this site must have been around the twist, because it was one hell of a job for the lads to get petrol and water bowsers up to us. My last raid in the desert was an easy one. Having rendered Heraklion airfield on Crete unserviceable, we used El Adem as an advance base for a raid on Crete's other airfield, known as Casteli Peliadi. On landing at El Adem we burst a tail wheel, and toil as they might the ground crew couldn't remove the wheel. Came darkness and they gave up, and we slept under the wing. Next morning the erks tried again and Geronimo! — it came off at the first turn of the spanner. After much bad language we set off to take the bombs back to base. Shortly after we handed over our few remaining Wimpys to 40 Squadron and went back to Cairo by road, and from there, by

devious forms of transport, sea, road and air, I returned to the UK.'

Jim Sterrett was a bomb-aimer, initially trained in South Africa, whose introduction to Wellingtons came in July 1944, at 77 OTU, Qastina in Palestine, and who subsequently flew the type on operations with No 104 Squadron:

'We had crewed-up en route to the OTU except for a "Drivers, airframe" and when the posting of pilots arrived we all agreed that we didn't want any gong-hunting sprog pilot officer, but rather a mature type who looked as though he had a wife and family he'd wish to see again. Thus, our eventual choice, Doug Skinner, was snapped up because he then had prematurely iron-grey hair! Our first confirmation that the Wimpy was a good, tough aeroplane came on 18 July 1944 on our first cross-country exercise. Over Baltim the starboard engine blew a cylinder head and lost some of its cowling. We were ordered to standby for a bale-out. As the bomb-aimer I would have been the first to go and, looking down through the open hatch waiting for the dreaded order "Go", I remember I thought "Why now? We haven't even been on ops yet". After some colourful language over the inter-comm, the two drivers thought they

Below: Wimpys of 205 Group awaiting their bomb-loads, Egypt, circa 1942. *IWM*

might be able to feather the engine and hold the kite steady for a while, so we set course for El Ballah, a gunnery school, were we landed safely with one very overheated engine. We all got out, went on our knees in the sand, and gave heartfelt thanks to Allah . . .

'Eight days later we set out on a cross-country to Cyprus, where we carried out the usual exercises — photography, bombing, gunnery, etc. On the way back Charlie Williams, our rear gunner, noticed that the bomb doors were still open. A certain amount of hand-pumping followed, but we were forced to make a flapless approach. The undercarriage collapsed and bits of propellers flew off. The runway burst through the hatch and belly and the inside of the aircraft was full of dust and debris; yet Doug managed to hold her steady. Following the normal drill, I exited through the top hatch on to the wing and, very conscious of a sizzling sound from the hot engines, completed my first-ever 100 yards in even time! Charlie had banged his head against his Brownings and was dazed. He got out of his turret, dripping blood, and not realising it was so high in the air due to the posture of the aircraft . . . it again proved to us how robust the Wimpy was. Doug was torn off a strip next day by the CFI, but then a fault in the hydraulic system was discovered. The kite was a write-off.

'My first op with 104 Squadron, from Foggia, Italy, was on 17 October 1944 as bomb-aimer to Sgt Parks' crew, his usual bomb-aimer being "unserviceable". We flew in Wellington X, LP549 and the target was Vinkovci's marshalling yards. Enemy aircraft were sighted but the TIs (target indicators) were late, so we had

Above: 'The Jeep', 'W' of 70 Sqn, which was eventually shot down in flames over Derna, North Africa on 11 November 1942.
G. E. Wilson

Left: Mail-Run pioneers. A trio of 37 Sqn's Wimpys, May 1941. Nearest is T2875.

Right: Landing victim at LG 09, Middle East.

to go round again; NOT a popular decision, particularly coming from a sprog bomb-aimer! We had a good run-up and dropped nine 500lb and nine 250lb GPs. On 21 October I again flew with Sgt Park in "R-Robert" to bomb Maribor marshalling yards with six SBCs of incendiaries and three 500lb GPs. There was the usual flak and a sight of the ground battle, while enemy aircraft were reported, and weather was bad over the target. Checking the bomb bay on the way back I noticed that two or three 500lb GPs were still with us; the news was not well received. After going through all the normal drills without any success, it was decided that I chop up the floor so that I could effect manual release. One bomb we did, the other(s) landed with us . . . Park greased the Wimpy in VERY gently . . ! The ground crew were very annoyed about the state of the floor, but at least I'd missed the hydraulic pipes due to careful axe-work.

'Our first op as a complete crew came on 17 November 1944 in Wimpy 515 "Y" — a raid against troop concentrations and transport at South Jenica/Novi Pazar, but we were recalled to base after sighting the enemy coastline, and jettisoned 18 × 250lb bombs in the Adriatic. We went back again next day in daylight and dropped three sticks of 250-pounders on some MT. Subsequent sorties included attacks on a bridge and troops at Podgorica, more troop concentrations at Rogatica, a supply drop to Predgrad — this one on 2 December when the DZ was covered in 10-10ths cloud and we had to bring our goodies back — and a similar drop next day to Berane, where the DZ was again obscured by cloud, but we released the load on a Gee fix. On 15 December we were in "P-Peter" but were told to stand down. We were all ready to dive off to Foggia when we were told that ops were "on" again. Our original wireless operator suddenly went "special sick" — he was eventually graded LMF — and we flew with a spare bod. We took off with a load of 18 × 250lb GPs to bomb MT and troops north of the town of Klopot, and it turned out to be a decidedly uncomfortable trip because soon after take-off the escape hatch above the cockpit blew open. We spent much of the time and energy trying to close it, even with the aid of sideslipping, but with no success. Charlie was brought forward from his rear turret to help — being the strong one — and he was nearly sucked out of his flying boots. However, because it was the skipper's birthday, we had to press on. We had no flying goggles with us and eyes became very sore after hours in the howling draught. We met some light flak, but we got some MT fires going and stoked up others a bit. Next day was spent just bathing our sore eyes.

'More sorties against troop concentrations and transports followed, then on Christmas Eve a general stand-down was declared, except for crews who drew straws for ops on Christmas Day — our crew drawing one straw. That evening I won a bottle of White Label in the mess draw, together with a chicken, cigarettes, chocolate, etc; all of which were shared out in a tent party which ended early — at 0100hrs! Next day — Christmas Day — we took off at mid-day for a supply drop to Crnomelj, near Predgrad; a straightforward trip with a good drop,

and coming home on a wireless homing to a belated Christmas dinner which we were too clapped out to enjoy. Yet more supply and bombing trips followed. The weather was bloody cold; indeed, a supply drop to Circhina on 8 January in "V" had to be aborted because of icing up to 11,000ft which built up on the wing leading edge faster than I'd ever seen. As our skipper said of this trip later, "It was the most frightening experience of instrument flying, instruments at loggerheads, speed falling off when the altimeter was unwinding in descent off the clock, then speed shooting up again when the altimeter was winding up".

'On 20 January 1945, in "W", we dropped our first 4,000lb Cookie, from 8,500ft over Odine marshalling yards. We'd arrived a little early and got some flak before finally dropping. Then came a spot of leave in Sorrento — running water and sheets on the bed — sheer luxury! *La Boheme* from Box 22 in the San Carlo and other touches of a forgotten civilised way of life, followed — back at Foggia a few days later — by the Anglo-Polish Ballet company performing *Les Sylphides* etc. Then back to work on 8 February when we bombed Verona; a good trip against the usual opposition, but a long wait on the circuit afterwards for the "green", and an overshoot after first touchdown. Fiume in daylight followed on the 15th where we dropped our load on the oil refinery and harbour installations; a trip where I was distinctly put off by the box barrage being clearly seen into which we'd have to go during our approach — it had never seemed so bad at night. On 20 February we

dropped our second Cookie, on Udine marshalling yards; then on 24 February 1945 came my last trip in a Wimpy. We went to Brescia to drop two 2,000lb HC bombs on the marshalling yards there. It was a good trip, though the flak was accurate and we brought some back with us, and plenty of fighter activity. The grapevine said that Mussolini was giving the locals a pep talk at the time, so we liked the idea of setting off the Eyetie air raid sirens. After de-briefing the CO informed us we were tour-expired.'

Art Wahlroth, a Canadian, was trained on Whitleys on his OTU, then promptly posted to Wellington IIs with No 405 Squadron RCAF at Driffield and Pocklington for operations. He next instructed on Wimpy Ics at Wellesborne Mountford and Moreton-in-the-Marsh, before returning to ops with No 37 Squadron, 1943-44 on

EXTRACT :- D.R.O's DATED 14.5
R.A.F. STATION, TA-KALI, MA

A GIBBET HAS BEEN ERECT
ON THE CORNER OF THE ROAD
LEADING TO THE CAVES. ANY
MAN, WOMAN OR CHILD, CIVILI
OR SERVICE PERSONNEL, FOUN
GUILTY OF SABOTAGE, THEF
OR IN ANY OTHER WAY IMPED
THE WAR EFFORT AND SUB—
SEQUENTLY SHOT, WILL BE
HUNG FROM THIS GIBBET A
A WARNING TO ALL OTHER

Top: Z8345 comes to grief in North Africa, 1942; 'S-Sugar' of 104 Sqn
V. Cashmore via D. Vincent

Above: A notice board at Ta Kali, Malta in May 1942 which hardly needs amplification... *L. Jordan*

Wellington Xs. His memories of his Middle East tour are not simply of operations, but of incidents and individuals (no names, no pack-drill!) 'I'll always remember . . .

'The officious MO giving us yellow fever shots. We moved to the head of the line, feigning fainting and pain, with loud noises . . . resulting in a jittery line-up.

'The non-dressy chamois gloves issued for the Middle East. We looked at them with disdain . . . until we got there and tried to pick up anything with bare hands.

'The smell of eucalyptus trees in Gibraltar.

' "Pass the oranges" — always heard when a new crew arrived. A tin of ascorbic acid tablets would be passed down the table.

'The ever present sand — one had to blow a channel when writing a letter, for the pen to travel in.

'The ever-blowing desert wind . . . and the tail gunner who left his turret on landing and walked forward, not realising that the engines were still running until he was decapitated (I very nearly caught his head like a football . . .).

'The hung-over rigger who each morning would kick the tyres, sign his DI, and go back to bed. When I first saw this I hit the roof, but was assured that later in the day he would go over the machine thoroughly, and that I'd never have any trouble. They were right; I tried to catch him out for a month by odd tricks like reversing battery terminals, wires, gas cocks etc — and I never had any trouble.

'The squadron MO who gleefully and sadistically painted men blue who were found to have lice. Aircrews escaped this treatment, which wouldn't have helped in any escape situation.

'The obese armament Warrant Officer who *led* the parade of those running away from an unexploded 4,000lb bomb in a crashed aircraft.

'Travelling Arabs, father riding the donkey, mother and kids walking behind. If the area was suspected of having land mines, however, mother and kids walked in front.

'The Group Captain ("Teddy" Beare of 231 Wing) who would scrounge Canadian cigarettes from me . . . and enjoyed the Vees he got in the darkness of the flare-path, thinking they were Sweet Caps.

'The entire crew losing their break-fast when, after several years of RAF rations, we had a wonderful meal at an American hospital, for whom we were doing some ferry work.

'The Scottish dancing in the Mess, to the tune of two chanters, as a means of keeping warm. Visits to the bar between sets increased the tempo . . . and small men were periodically hurled right over the wall.

'The no-face patients at Heliopolis hospital in Cairo, mostly pilots of burnt-out P-40s which stretched in never-ending line across Africa.

'The police in downtown Cairo; one in a white suit on either side of the street in each block, and on each intersection two, in black suits, with shotguns . . . this protection was mainly for us.

'The rains, which turned our airfield into a salt lake. We had to use mudboards in order to move at all over the resulting gumbo.

'Stripping equipment and draining petrol from aircraft, and moving them from a small, unflooded taxi-strip, flaps down, brakes set, and full bore, to a nearby strip on stony, high ground.

'Yank fighter pilots taxying their P-38s at about 40mph, complete with long peaked caps, sunglasses, and chomping the inevitable cigar.

'The Thunderbolt that rammed one of our Wellingtons at Foggia. It was condemned and in a week was stripped down for spares. Our aircraft, broken in two, was resurrected and flying again in a matter of weeks . . .

'Seeing the tents blow away in a 5am gale, and the semi-clad refugees ultimately gathering into aircraft, which they started up in order to keep warm.

'The Yank officer in Italy, abjectly apologising to his crew chief for the damage to the aeroplane, when he belly-landed his B-17.

'Coming down the Adriatic near dawn, holding height to just brush over the 3,000ft mountain that forms a spur on the boot of Italy, then letting down to the airfield, feeling that we were going down into a hole.

'The crew who let their intercomm go out over the air and, on hearing me report in after a trip, commented loud and clear, "There's that bastard Wahlroth back again". Being the Flight Commander, I ripped off the pilot, one of my former students — for laxity in radio procedure. . .

'The intense activity of Russians, Americans and English alike to shift

masonry in an attempt to get my tail gunner out from under a collapsed building. . . and the subsequent funeral.

'The ENSA shows in the Opera House in Foggia, where troops in the balconies would blow up condoms, letting them float down to where the American nurses sat. . . at which point one of the nurses would reach up with a lighted cigarette and puncture one; this bringing the house down.

'The San Carlo Opera company in Naples, the opera *Lucia di Lammermoor* with the cast in Highland kilts . . . and all with baggy-kneed underwear.

'Crossing Italy from Naples to Foggia, across three ranges of mountain peaks, in and out of cloud. Searchlights ringed Foggia, coning at 15,000ft, we let down in a left-hand circuit around and through the reappearing and disappearing beams of light until we broke out, hopefully, in the clear below . . . a cold sweat was the order of the day.

'The constant relief from tension once we were off and climbing on course in the night sky . . .'

The Middle East Wimpys' saga of bombing operations was heavily complemented by the aircraft's role as a torpedo-strike vehicle in the unceasing struggle to deprive Rommel's Afrika Korps of essential fuel and other supplies. E. A. Sanders, after training at 15 OTU, Harwell, completed a tour of 35 ops with No 38 Squadron in the Middle East in 1942, was then screened as an instructor on Wimpys back in the UK, and eventually undertook his second ops tour on Halifaxes with 78 Squadron:
'No 38 Squadron co-operated with 221 Squadron, whose Wimpys were fitted with ASV equipment. 221 located any convoy and dropped flares, and we homed in on them and attacked either into the flares or along the moonpath. We had a sort of Heath Robinsonish bomb sight (home-made, I believe) mounted just outside the pilot's windscreen, but it was not often used. Our method was to fly as low on the water as we could, aiming the nose of the aircraft about half the ship-length ahead, and drop the torpedo as near as possible to the target. The best "way out" afterwards used to be over the ship, down on the water again, then a steep turn away. The torpedoes could be released singly or together by the pilot. Incidentally, our practice

torpedo-dropping exercises were carried out on the Great Bitter Lake, and one target I recall was King Farouk's yacht moored at Ismailia!

'No 221 Squadron's Wimpys had a massive array of aerials along the fuselage and were known as "Sticklebacks", and in addition to their ASV equipment they carried a considerable number of parachute flares which they dropped on our request. 221 was usually airborne about an hour before 38 Squadron, to enable them to search for any target convoy. Although we in 38 were based at Shallufa on the Canal, we usually operated from Gianaclis (LG 226) just over an hour's flying from base to the west of Cairo, and torpedoes were flown up there and stocked for operations. Opposition was always intense. For example, on 25 October 1942 we attacked a convoy between Malta and Tobruk consisting of two motor vessels, four destroyers and one escort vessel. We were attacked for some 15 minutes by three Junkers Ju88s escorting the convoy, but our low speed with undercarriages and flaps down enabled us to get away. I remember when our aircraft went up to Palestine (Aqir, if I remember correctly) for modifications, we understood they were coming back with front turrets removed and armour plating installed. In reality they were only replaced with fabric and plywood!

'As for the aircraft itself, I always found the Wimpy a wonderful aeroplane, and I eventually completed some 1,200hrs in the type. At first sight, when standing looking out of the astro-dome, it frightened me to see how the wings moved up and down in flight! I can still recall too the tiring effort of having to pump oil every two hours or so from the reserve tanks. The pump handle was a short affair on the port side on the floor, and it required quite an effort in winter, at height, when the oil was cold.'

In late August 1942, Rommel decided upon his final bid to defeat the Eighth Army in North Africa and thus capture the Egyptian Delta zone, and therefore asked for supplies to be shipped to Tobruk; a decision fraught with risk as it meant bringing Axis supply convoys well within range of the Wimpy torpedo-strike aircraft from their Egyptian bases. One such convoy was spotted on 28 August, steaming west of Crete, with a heavy destroyer escort.

Right: Crew from 104 Sqn, Foggia, Italy on 25 February 1945. From left: Sgts Wilf Eardley (Nav) & Charlie 'Ice-Cool' Williams (R/AG), Flt Sgt Jack Gray (W/Op), Sgt Doug Skinner (Capt), Sgt Jim Sterrett (B/A). Taken in front of Wimpy *'Flak-Happy Harry'* on the day after the crew's last sortie of their tour of ops. *S. J. Sterrett*

Centre right: Wellington *'Flak-Happy Harry'* of 104 Sqn, Foggia, Italy in February 1945. *S. J. Sterrett*

Bottom right: Sgt Doug Skinner, skipper of *'Flak-Happy Harry'* of 104 Sqn at Foggia, Italy in February 1945. This and the previous two views were deliberately taken *after* the end of the crew's ops' tour, due to a superstition about any photos being taken *during* the tour. . . *S. J. Sterrett*

That evening Wellingtons and Liberators set out and attacked the convoy due north of Derna, blowing up one of the two main fuel-carrying store-ships. In the early hours of 29 August a second wave of Wimpy torpedo aircraft took up the assault; one pilot being Flt Lt M. Foulis, DFC of 221 Squadron whose official description of his individual attack reads:

'We sighted the ships at 0015hrs in the moonpath. There was no cloud and a bright moon. We could see the ship clearly, a vessel of about 8,000 tons or perhaps a little less. There was one destroyer about two miles ahead of her, another about a mile on her port bow, and a third close in to her starboard quarter. I spent about 20 minutes flying across the moonpath on the west side to work out my line of attack. Eventually I made up my mind on the best approach and we commenced a long run-up on the ship's starboard bow. She was not fully in the moonpath but she was clearly visible. I could see no white wake astern of her, but the track in the sea along which she travelled could be seen. I dropped my first torpedo at a range of 700yd, and the second at 400yd. We flew ahead of one destroyer but were not fired upon until after the torpedoes had been released. As soon as the second torpedo was gone, I pulled the aircraft up and we passed over between the centre and the stern of the ship.

'The torpedoes were on their way but had not yet reached her. The destroyer close in and the ship herself both opened fire, the latter at point blank range. My rear gunner could not fire at the ship because he could not depress his guns sufficiently. I took violent evasive action and we escaped damage. The navigator, who was in the astrodome, reported two bright orange flashes on the vessel, astern and amidships. I swung the aircraft round and we could all see two great columns of water going up above her masts. It was clear that both torpedoes had hit.

'We ran up and down on the west side watching developments. Very quickly thick grey smoke began to come out of the ship. The destroyers closed in to her, and within five minutes a heavy smoke pall lay over all the ships. We could plainly smell this smoke in the aircraft; it smelt oily and acrid. We sent our first target report: "Two hits on tanker, stationary, smoking". After about ten minutes the smoke cleared and a large oil patch

was all that remained of the merchant ship. The destroyers were there but nothing else. We sent another signal ''Tanker believed sunk, large oil patch seen''.'

Acting Squadron Leader M. Foulis, DFC failed to return from a torpedo-strike sortie in Wellington HX487 on 18 April 1943.

If operations predominate the story of any wartime aircraft's career, it should be remembered that the quantitative bulk of any air force's personnel were not engaged solely in flying at the 'sharp end'. Behind the operational crews stretched a long line of men and women whose tasks and unceasing labours supported the firstline efforts. In the context of the Wellington, this theme was especially true for the Wimpy's service outside the UK. Take the wartime career of Peter Powell for merely one example. Awarded his wings and sergeant's chevrons in November 1941, he was eventually commissioned in February 1944, and reached the rank of Flight Lieutenant by late 1945. From July 1942 to August 1945 he served with Nos 1 and 3 Aircraft Delivery Units, and from October 1943 to May 1945 ferried no less than 42 Wimpys to various Middle East units:

'Towards the end of 1943, No 3 ADU (later, No 3 Ferry Unit) was based at Oujda in Morocco, and I had my first flight in what was to become my favourite kite, the Wimpy. At that time Wellingtons were being flown out from Cornish airfields to Rabat, and we were responsible for taking them on from there to Cairo and Italy. On taking over a Wimpy at Sale (the Rabat airfield), the first thing I did was to check the tyre pressures, and found that these were invariably about 20psi too high; a natural consequence of the difference in temperature between North Africa and the UK. I soon grew to love the Wimpy because one couldn't find a better aircraft for ferrying purposes. It had only one vice — a predictable swing to starboard on take-off which was counter-acted by opening the starboard throttle first and following this with port throttle when it started to drift to port.

'The ploy for a successful trip to Cairo was to organise a night stop not too far away — El Adem was favourite. An early start next morning ensured the disposal of the aircraft at Cairo West in time to be at the bar of the pub we ferry types used by opening time; necessary because we well knew that there were only ever two barrels of Stella beer available! One of the things we had to watch on a night stop, however, was the guarding of valuable equipment ie the sextant and navigation watches, though the things most likely to vanish unless we took action were thermos flasks.

Above left: Medicine in the field. A 38 Sqn Wimpy crew member with a broken back from a landing crash is treated surgically on the spot by the 'Quack', with the help of a Coles crane . . . *L. Jordan*

Above: Navigator in a Middle East Wellington in his office. *Bippa*

Right: Wellington XIII with ASV II radar stickleback array, possibly a machine from 221 Sqn (?). *IWM.*

'After 30-odd years one tends to mainly remember the good times, and I can still recall one beautiful morning in October 1944 in Wimpy HZ929 when we were making for Gibraltar for Oujda at a height of 5,000ft, when I told my navigator that he could go back to sleep — I could see the Rock when we were still 100 miles away from it. The bad times were invariably connected with bad weather, because in some 400 hours flying in Wimpys I never once had the slightest trouble from the Hercules engines. In lousy weather we became expert in coast-crawling, hundreds of miles following the north and west African coasts with cloud base down to well below 1,000ft. On one occasion in January 1945, in MF298, flying from Sale to Takoradi, we were flying at about 2,000ft — in winter we never went higher than this as it was too cold. My wireless operator, Ted Julian, was keen on flying, so I installed him in the cockpit and then got down to a game of chess with the navigator, Alan Tait. All three of us became so engrossed in what we were doing that we forgot we were running on an overload tank. This soon ran out and both engines cut. Alan and I looked at each other, then simultaneously shot out of our seats like startled rabbits. I heaved up a wing that poor Ted had dropped, while Alan went back to switch tanks.

'One winter trip which was very popular was to ferry Mk XIIIs and XIVs down from Rabat to the coastal squadrons based on the Gold Coast (Ghana). As the major part of this route was over Spanish and Vichy French territories it involved a gigantic coast-crawl, but it was very pleasant to get into KD (Khaki Drill) for a day or two, and get away from the North African winter. On one trip we ran into a line squall after taking off from Freetown, and had no alternative but to fly down the beach, as the base was down at about 100ft and visibility no more than 100yds. We did this for an hour — our only worry being whether any other aircraft was doing the same thing and coming in the opposite direction!

'Our last jobs, early in 1945, were re-equipping the Wimpy squadrons then based in Italy with Liberators. It became quite common to try out two or even three Liberators at Maison Blanche before finding a serviceable kite; yet on landing at Foggia we were presented with fly-back Wellingtons which literally went like sewing machines — a tribute to the Wimpy, and no less a measure of the high quality of maintenance on the squadrons.'

A Lament of Erks

Unpublicised, usually unhonoured, even occasionally unwanted, the Erks — the RAF's universal nickname for all non-commissioned airmen of the ground servicing crews — were (and for that matter, still are) the unshakeable rock foundation of the Service. Steely-eyed fighter and bomber crews may well have cornered the 'market' on glittering awards and lavish public acclaim, yet without loyalty, stoic endurance and unceasing toils of the ground crews, all aircrew would be redundant. Whatever the miracles of the micro-chip and computer, no machine of whatever complexity could (or can) wholly replace the ingrained skills and know-how of the experienced human fitter when aeroplanes are concerned. An Erk's daily life during World War 2 was never a sinecure. Pay was minimal, living conditions varied from the comparative luxury of a peacetime station barrack block to a pup tent, charpoy, and hole in the sand, and an overseas posting could often mean three or four years' separation from families and other loved ones. Working circumstances also varied widely. A hangar shelter from the elements, a dispersal hut improvised from spare wood planks, corrugated iron sheets, or whatever scrounged materials were available, a storm-swept open dispersal subject to the extremes of heat, cold or rain, depending on location.

Working hours — the fetish of the modern trades union shop steward or hierarchy — seldom existed in finite form; the job was top priority, 'keeping 'em flying', no matter *how* long it took. A seven-days' working week was the norm, with a 36- or 48-hours' leave pass a rarity, and actual leave a luxury. A bicycle, however ancient was a prized possession for transportation — cars were luxuries for officers only — while off-duty entertainment often depended solely upon self-improvisation. Indeed, improvisation was the key to much of an Erk's

Below: Winter landscape at the Lossiemouth OTU, 1944. *E. A. Saunders*

existence, whether at work or at play; adhering to the book, particularly in technical matters, was too often impossible due to lack of the proper tools or parts. Such omissions were never permitted to delay essential maintenance; the ubiquitous Erk always managed to find a solution, however crude or temporary the available material might be. The universal motto was *Ubendum, Wemendum*.

The following selected reminiscences by various ex-Erks, in differing circumstances, represent a vast population of the unsung airmen and airwomen whose labours and sacrifices provided the essential springboard for eventual victory in the air war of 1939-45. For every anecdote or experience quoted here, a thousand other Erks could tell a parallel tale.

Bob Watson was a prewar Halton Aircraft Apprentice — a 'Trenchard Brat' — one of that vast army of regular-serving Erks who had committed body and soul to the RAF by 'signing-on' at the tender age of 16 years or slightly younger, and undergoing a three-years' 'sentence' of engineering apprenticeship training at the RAF's No 1 School of Technical Training, Halton, Buckinghamshire, before passing out into the ranks of the Service to complete at least 12 years' 'Man's service':

'I joined as a Fitter II and spent the first year training on engines etc, and then the compound trade was split into Fitter IIE (engines) and IIA (airframes)

— so I became a IIA with no arguments! After leaving Halton as a fully-fledged Fitter IIA, my first posting was to a Mechanical Transport (MT) Maintenance Unit! The Records Office eventually discovered (or admitted) their error and posted me to Henlow which, by January 1940 when I arrived, was slowly organising itself into a Hurricane MU. While there I had my introduction to the Wimpy — as a security guard preventing the local populace from helping themselves to souvenirs from a pranged Wellington. I don't recall the cause of the crash — only that it was in the middle of nowhere, on a wet day, wetter evening to follow, and little protection from the elements all night except inadequate shelter from a leaky tarpaulin rigged up against a hedge, and mud, mud, mud everywhere. The following day was dry and we could then assess this strange aircraft in a more benevolent frame of mind; a frontline bomber, full of forbidden and secret things to our untutored eyes. It had belly-landed and the crew had escaped via the astrodome and cockpit roof hatch, and I had to climb over the wing, drop into the fuselage, replace the astro hatch and exit through the cockpit roof. Later, when Henlow sent out an armourer to remove the guns and ammo etc, I had to assist again and learned a little more about Barnes Wallis's brainchild; especially the contortionist method of entering the rear gun turret.

Below: Refuelling Wimpy R1598, KX-C of 311 (Czech) Sqn at East Wretham.
B. Rijnhout

'When business at Henlow slackened I was promoted from LAC to Corporal and posted to 57 Squadron — "somewhere in England". My movement order specified a particular RAF station, so I dutifully toted all my kit and caboodle there — only to be informed 57 had moved elsewhere! This process was repeated on two more stations, and I finally caught up with the squadron at Feltwell — only to be asked by the Orderly Room where the hell I'd been! No 57 Squadron had only recently converted from Blenheims to Wimpys when I joined them, and were sharing Feltwell with No 75 (NZ) Squadron. Life here was fairly typical of any bomber station then. On duty it was a case of work, work and work, while off-duty hours meant the Corporal's Club or down to the village for a pint, a game of darts, and — if lucky — a visit to the "Caff", a private house with two front rooms converted to a restaurant were we could sample standard fare of double-egg and chips — a scarcity in those days of rations for all.

'In 1940 the country as a whole was only just beginning to realise that it really had a war on its plate, and the authorities were still working to peacetime scales of issue for equipment and clothing; the £5 toolkit comprising King Dick adjustable, pliers, an 8-inch screwdriver, worn-out double-ended O/J spanners, and a 16-ounce "Brummagem Screwdriver" (hammer . . .) to service aircraft vastly more complicated than peacetime Harts, Demons, Audax, etc. Wet weather clothing was virtually unheard of, few "ferking jerkins", gumboots were scarcer than hen's teeth, and even a change of blue overalls was hard to come by. Yet the troops (a generic term for airmen beloved of officers but deeply resented by Erks . . .) seemed to accept it all, taking such things in their stride and almost happy to be roughing it in the circumstances. Two aspects of Halton character-training never mentioned on the official syllabi — ie self-reliance and ingenuity — came to the fore under such conditions. It was no problem to splice-up a new towing bridle when Stores had none in stock, or file up a spanner to fit any awkwardly-placed nut — it was a perfectly normal, accepted approach to the job in those days.

'No 57 was gradually working up to full operational standard, and, though a few night ops were carried out, most of the bombing effort was done by 75 Squadron at that time, some crews of which took perverse delight in heralding their return — until stopped by the CO — by turning on the air-driven siren as they joined the circuit; talk about noisy neighbours! Another nuisance occurred one lunchtime when a Junkers Ju88 appeared and proceeded to bomb us. Chaos reigned supreme, windows shattered, but no other damage in our hangar; though a Wimpy in the civvy contractors' hangar, sporting newly repaired and re-covered mainplanes needed further repairs after the raid. Not content, the Ju88 made a second circuit at even lower level to give his gunnner a crack, just as our duty crew was emerging from the hangar heading for the shelter. I bit the dust smartish (or rather, snow) under the nearest cover, and though I saw snow flicking nearby where bullets struck, his aim was slightly off — fortunately, because as I discovered afterwards my improvised cover was a 500-gallon petrol bowser!

'One merry morning I was calmly notified by the Orderly Room that I was posted to Persia! This turned out to be Pershore on the movement order, an equally mysterious place, because no one could tell me anything about it other than it was in Worcestershire. After a cross-country rail safari, changing from train to train to train, I eventually arrived to find that the camp was still very much under construction, and mud everywhere. Such was Records Office organisation that there were no aircraft to service for over three weeks, until concrete runways had been completed. Then we had a comedy of errors farce to remind us that the war was still on. The station was far from completed — just runways laid but no perimeter track, and few dispersal pans or roads — so "They" sent us a couple of Wimpys to be getting on with. The 'drome was still a sea of mud, and there was no place to park them other than on one of the runways not in use. That night was a fine one, with nearly a full moon, and Jerry decided to have a go at the Midlands. I can imagine that from 15,000ft or so those triangulated runways, virgin uncamouflaged concrete, must have stood out like neon signs in the moonlight. Some lynx-eyed Jerry evidently thought so and accordingly at about 2-3am carefully, nay leisurely, circled two or three times and then planted a trio of bombs. A

petrol bowser went up in flames, and the kites became Cat 3 with splinter damage — it was helluva way to start an OCU.

'As the OCU empire grew bigger, the satellite 'drome at Defford was opened, and again I was selected as a pioneer; making do and mending for a couple of months before "civilisation" in the form of SHQ was established. We commuted daily from Pershore by 3-ton truck or the clapped-out Mk I "Annie" — which was a damned sight noisier and almost as bumpy as the consumptive truck; then hutted accommodation became available. No particular Wimpy incidents there come to mind; just the inevitable burst tyres in heavy landings or brake failures, and the odd forced landings in impossibly small local fields etc. From Pershore/Defford I moved yet again, this time to Chipping Warden near Banbury, where another Wimpy OCU was formed. By the time I arrived there it was a going concern, and most erks were Wimpy-experienced.

'Life at "Chippy" was perhaps mundane, but had its moments. Jobs were tackled out on dispersal which in later years would be hangar work only; wing off, fuel tank out, self-sealing replaced after patch repairs. One item of human interest comes to mind. There was a blonde nymphomaniac WAAF on the Flight-line, whose world revolved around her crotch. It was tempting fate to send her on a DI (Daily Inspection) of a kite if airmen were also working on it, and you wanted the Form 700 signed up in a hurry. In an attempt to shame, or at least embarrass her, we constructed an extra large facsimilé of the male organ from remnants of self-sealing outer

Top: Carrying a spare 12-volt battery into a 142 Sqn Wimpy at Binbrook, December 1940. *via R. Bonser*

Above: Air and ground crew of a 412 Sqn Wellington, January 1943. Air crew members were Alan Gill (second from left), 'Mo' Moore (3rd from left), Phil Bond (3rd from right), Jock Sloan (2nd from right), and Norman L. Child (far right). *N. L. Child*

Right: Snow-clearance, a monotonous and regular morning chore in winter. Here erks of 142 Sqn at Binbrook, December 1940, cleaning 'D-Dog's' wings. *via R. Bonser*

Left: Hoisting a 1,000lb MC bomb into a Wimpy's belly, by means of the hand-crank winch at right

Below: Fixing the hoist hook to a 250lb GP bomb

Right: Kiwi. T2835, 'C-Charlie' of 75(NZ) Sqn, ready to go.

cover rubber sheet, a ball of Bostik properly "cured", cord and realistic paint finish. The work of art was carefully parcelled, stamped, and addressed to her, and artfully delivered with the rest of the day's mail to the Chiefy's office, who innocently handed it to her in the Flight stores — a daily routine then — in front of a crowd of erks already in the know. She opened it — and was delighted! "Just what we need in the billet" . . .

'There were too several tragic incidents. One Wimpy which was bogged down on damp grass couldn't be budged by the Fordson tractor alone, so the cry "Two-Six" went out and all spare bods lent a hand. One new member of the Flight, straight out of training school, was pushing on the tailplane along with others, and as the Wimpy began to shift this kid had his titfer (hat) knocked off by the IFF aerial wire strung from fuselage to tailplane-tip. He bent down, picked it up, fumbled, then straightened up as the rear cone of the nacelle hit him. He fell and the starboard mainwheel went right over him — ever seen an imprint of a human head in soft earth? Not a pretty sight . . . "Chippy" seemed to have more aircraft crashes than either Pershore or Defford. A pupil crew on a "loaded cross-country" exercise swung on take-off and finished up a blazing wreck against the ATC (Air

Traffic Control) building, trapping two fire-engines in the adjacent fire-house The "bomb load" was dummy — but it didn't do the crew a lot of good. Another prang — inexplicably with a staff crew of seasoned Bomber Command veterans sprinkled with DFCs, DFMs, etc — occurred when a railway marshalling yard was mistaken for the flarepath; or so the Chief Instructor decided.

'There were also occasions when Wimpys returned worse for wear after pupils had been "blooded" on short-range ops against coastal targets; shot-up controls, no hydraulics, or "continental" timber jammed through the nose just below the front gun position (I never could tell the difference between English and French oak or beech . . . !) One crew discovered it impossible to break the glass contents sight of the header tank with the escape axe, so punctured the metal tank itself to pour in coffee/tea/urine — only to find that the hydraulic loss wasn't a lack of fluid, just a duff EDP (engine-driven pump).

'Good relations with some of the staff crews meant a few opportunities at slack moments to get a few flying hours in, even as a second dickey in the dual-control Wimpys if on airtest for other reasons. And, of course, when "Butch" Harris was scraping the barrel for his "Thousand-bomber raids", "Chippy" was well and truly involved, and there was an air of increased excitement and dedication all round, even though the OCU Wimpys only went along to make up the numbers. Then, in 1944, I was on the move yet again, this time to SEAC (South-East Asia Command) and Wimpys passed out of my life.'

W. E. Wilkinson was an LAC (Leading Aircraftman) fitter when he first worked on Wellingtons with 142 Squadron at Binbrook in 1940:

'The squadron was equipped with Wellington Mk IIs with Rolls-Royce Merlin engines fitted with DH hydromatic airscrews, and during the working-up period — the unit began converting from Fairey Battles to Wimpy IIs in November 1940 — I became a fitter for Wimpy W5359, QT-B, of A Flight. By the time we were declared operational I'd been promoted to Corporal and was NCO in charge of three aircraft on one dispersal, including W5359.

'Possibly the biggest snag with the Mk II was its tendency to drop its nose in a dive, caused by the thrust-line of the Merlin being higher and the airscrew being further forward of the CG than on the Pegasus and Mercury engines of the Mk 1s. This meant a pilot had to trim the elevator back to fly straight and level. Unfortunately, the trim tabs were interconnected with the flaps in such a way that when flaps were lowered the elevators were also lowered to keep the aircraft on an even keel. No harm was done until the flaps were fully lowered after touch-down. If the pilot hadn't centralised the trim tabs before using the flaps he had quite an appreciable amount of trim on, so that when the flaps were fully lowered the hydraulic pressure of the flaps ripped the whole trimming box off the fuselage; even experienced crews were guilty of this, especially after a long op.

'Anybody who ever worked with Merlin engines will remember how easily they started, and the Mk II was, in my opinion, the easiest-started Wellington of them all; indeed, I think

Above: Z1091, 'A-Apple' of 419 ('Moose') Sqn, RCAF gets an early morning DI (Daily Inspection), 1942.
Public Archives of Canada

it was the only one which could be started by just one man. During 1941, however, we were re-equipped with Mk IVs with Pratt & Whitney Twin Wasp engines, and after our easy life with Merlins we were rudely awakened with the Wasps. The first snag encountered was a tendency for the bottom cylinders to fill with oil. We had to hand-turn the propeller four complete revolutions before attempting to start, to be sure we had not got an hydraulic lock in the cylinders. All too often we had, which meant removing cowlings and plugs to drain the bottom cylinders and then changing the plugs. Once this was accomplished, starting was not too bad until damp and cold weather started. As the Twin Wasp had petrol injection, we needed a crew member on the wobble pump to give us petrol pressure. As soon as the engine fired on engagement of the starter, the mixture control was moved from cut-out to auto-rich. This caused a jet of petrol at 5lb/sq in to be injected into the centre of the supercharger. However, if the engine didn't catch first time, it became so hopelessly flooded that there was no hope of starting.

'This bad starting business was such a problem that both Nos 12 and 142 Squadrons were equipped with special Commer vans. These had a large petrol blowpipe in the van which led, via flame traps, to four large-diameter flexible pipes. These pipes were wrapped around the engine and the blowpipe lit. Once it had been warmed up to normal running temperature, it would start up. By the time 142 was equipped with Mk IV Wimpys it had moved to Waltham, leaving 12 Squadron at Binbrook; Waltham being Binbrook's satellite, just outside Grimsby. One very bad mistake made with the Mk IVs was to underestimate their fuel consumption; so badly that on the first IV operations Nos 12 and 142 Squadrons had only 25% of their Wimpys get back to Binbrook. Several landed in the North Sea, some at North Coates. Flight Lieutenant Campling belly-landed at North Coates, having run out of petrol before he could get the undercart down. One landed on married quarters at Binbrook, while two others landed at Binbrook with dead engines. Where Merlins had consumed about 85 gallons per hour, the Twin Wasps were gulping down some 145 gallons per hour.

'Two other big snags we experienced with Twin Wasps were sludge in the oil preventing the two-stage supercharger changing speed, and the secondary windings in the magnetos breaking at the soldered joint due to the soldering flux not being removed during manufacture. Despite all my foregoing apparent "prejudice" against the Wasp, I would like to emphasise

that the Twin Wasp was in fact a very good engine, but it was certainly not designed to operate in English winter conditions.

'Incidents in the squadron life included several distinctly hairy occasions. When the *Scharnhorst* and *Gneisenau* were running from Brest, one of our Flight commanders flew directly over the *Scharnhorst* and jettisoned his complete bomb load. The Wimpy got badly shot up, but he couldn't believe that he hadn't caused a lot of damage. The bomb-aimer had sworn he had jettisoned, but unfortunately the pilot had not opened the bomb doors, so the master switch was "off" and they brought all the bombs back. Then we had one squadron commander, Wing Commander Gibson (not Guy Gibson, VC of 617 fame) who returned one night with damaged hydraulics. He managed to get the undercarriage down but not the flaps, and made a very hairy flapless landing in the dark. Next day he told his aircrews to practise flapless landings in daylight, just in case they met a similar situation. I was helping out on an engine at dispersal that day and, on looking up, saw a Wimpy charging down the runway at about 60kts, and already three-quarters of the runway behind him. I remarked to the fitter that if he doesn't lift off soon he won't make it. The fitter answered

"He isn't going up, he's coming down", which indeed he did — straight over the road and into a ploughed field! Then there was the new fitter who snatched a quick nap on the bunk of Wimpy "Q" instead of "O" — and went to Hamburg in just his overalls, instead of the expected circuit and bumps around Waltham . . .'

Reg Humphries completed his trade training as an electrician (Group I tradesman) at Credenhill in 1941, and on passing out was posted to Holme upon Spalding Moor:
'On arrival at Holme I found the construction workers still putting the finishing touches to the 'drome; one hangar being still without a concrete floor. We were to be part of an Australian squadron on its way to England, No 458, which finally arrived in August 1941 and eventually commenced ops in late October. The Wellington IVs we were to use had been arriving in ones and two, all brand new, all fitted with Pratt & Whitney Twin Wasp engines.

'As an electrician I was one of the section of eight to ten men. We had a flight sergeant, a prewar airman recalled for war service, one Corporal, and the rest of us AC1s or AC2s. As a Group 1 tradesman I found myself in charge of B Flight's aircraft, as well as the regular servicing inspections in the

Above: Wellington 1c, T2508, LF-O, of 37 Sqn is the centre of a hive of erk activities in January 1941 at Shallufa, Egypt. This aircraft was the usual mount of Flt Lt 'Cheese' Lemon, DFC, and carried an elaborate coat of arms insigne, with a motto 'Defaecamus Luces Purpuras'. *IWM*

225

Above: One for the squadron album — the ground crews of 38 Sqn in 1942. *L. Jordan*

hangars. Our day was usually the same routine throughout the week. Mornings would be taken up with repairs and servicing inside the hangars, carrying out normal 40-hours', 80-hours' and 120-hours inspections, keeping an eye on the battery charging rooms; though these latter were later manned (if that's the right word . . . !) by WAAFs with a separate trade of Battery Charger, thus relieving us of this duty. As soon as operations were known, the kites had to be given DIs, which meant a trip to each aircraft in turn to check all electrics were functioning correctly. The Wimpy had a distinct wiring system known as "loom" wiring which was quite advanced in those days. It enabled sections of wiring to be changed without stripping the whole system.

'It was a 24-volts' powered system and amongst the items which had to be checked were navigation, formation, landing, interior and call lights. Undercarriage indicators and bombing gear were also checked for correct operation, propeller feathering motors, gun turrets and bomb sights, even the pitot head was included. The ground crew needed to run the starboard engine so we could check that the generator was

charging correctly, and another essential item included in our inspection was the trolley accumulator and its portable batteries, used for starting the engines. If all was well on the first aircraft, it was on to the next and right through the procedure again. Any necessary repairs were done as soon as possible — if not before!

'Once all aircraft had been checked out and declared serviceable, the night-flying equipment had to be checked. First, the "Glim Lamps", small lights placed alongside each side of the runway, powered by a two-volts' wet battery with a six-watt bulb fitted under a reflector so that they could only be seen from the sides. These were backed up by the forerunner of FIDO — Goose-necked flares, or "Duck Lamps" as they were often called. These were similar to metal watering cans, filled with paraffin with a piece of cloth pushed down the single spout, and were lit when it was misty to help get returning aircraft into the aerodrome. The other flare path equipment was the Chance Light — switched on to illuminate landing areas and switched off immediately the kite landed — and the "Angle of Glide Indicator"; a small illuminated coloured glass panel which showed red for ''Too low'', amber for ''Too high'', and green for ''OK''. A field telephone had to be laid from the control tower to the controller's cabin at the end of the runway in use, but often the wind changed just as one had tested the line and we'd have to set it all up again on runway Two. As well as equipment on the 'drome, we also had to check the marker beacon, a neon-tubed tower, moved every night, which flashed the code letters of the airfield.'

Selwyn Barrett joined No 37 Squadron at Feltwell in October 1940, when the unit was equipped with Wellington Ics, and remained with the squadron until October 1942:
'The squadron did not stay much longer at Feltwell, moving lock stock and barrel to Egypt a month after I arrived. The journey out there was not without incident. The sea party, travelling through the Mediterranean aboard HMS *Manchester*, joined in a naval battle off Cape Spartivento! The *Manchester* was slightly damaged but several Italian ships were even more so, and we eventually reached Egypt and rejoined our air party (who had flown out via Malta) at Fayid in the Suez Canal zone. A couple of weeks later, along with 38 Squadron, we moved further south to Shallufa, which was to be our main base for more than a year. Then, early in 1941, the main party of the squadron set off by road to Alexandria, then by boat in HMT *Dumana*, to go to Greece. We only made it as far as Crete and later had rather a hairy trip back to Shallufa — we didn't even see our Wellingtons for a couple of weeks!
'During the two years I spent with 37 in the Middle East we also — at various times — sent detachments to Malta and Iraq (this for the Raschid Ali business), but our main targets throughout this time were Benghazi and, later, Tobruk — the famous ''Milk Runs''. For these the normal drill, when bombing Benghazi for instance, was to make a refuelling stop at one of the advanced landing grounds (ALGs), usually LG 09, an airstrip about 20 miles inland from El Daba and the coast road. In January 1942, in fact, the two operational flights moved en bloc to LG 09, leaving the maintenance flight, etc back at Shallufa. From 09 we operated successfully until the retreat back to El Alamein in June 1942.
'To alleviate the strain of operating

from a desert strip, where water was always short, beer not exactly plentiful, and the food pretty awful, crews were given five days leave in Tel Aviv occasionally. These were most enjoyable breaks with the added bonus of a few bags of oranges for the messes. To enable people to wash off the layer of sand which built up whilst at LG 09, a truck would take parties to the beach a couple of times a week when everything for the night's work was ready. The journey was terrible — over 20 miles of rough desert track when one didn't know whether to stand or sit; the bouncing was equally bad and painful. Swimming in the sea was a joy, and salt-water soap produced a reasonable lather to clean off the layers of sand. Ten minutes after start-

Below: 'Dress will be informal' — the armourers of 38 Sqn, Libya, 1942. *L. Jordan*

Bottom: Repair gang at No 5 METS, Shallufa with a Wellington which had been shot down by a German nightfighter. They had it back on ops within a week . . .

Right: Sand-boys. Erks of 70 Sqn at LG 237.   *G. F. Wilson*

Below: Scruffs! 70 Sqn erks in Libya, 1941.   *G. F. Wilson*

ing back, however, we'd have a fresh fine coating of sand, and by the time we reached the ALG all we were fit for was sleep.

'Being away from civilisation we were a bit out of touch with news, and it was the travelling padre who told us that Tobruk had fallen — which we found hard to believe, and it was only his dog collar which convinced us that it wasn't enemy propaganda! There followed hectic days and nights, and second sorties were flown from an even remoter ALG, from where when I left on the last Wimpy the corporal in charge with one assistant were about to destroy hundreds of 50-gallon barrels of fuel then drive east themselves. Landing back at 09 that morning we found everything packed and ready for moving out. Some of our ground transport had already left, and army units were streaming down the edge of the landing strip as the Wimpys were overloaded for the flight back to the Canal zone. After a couple of nights and operations from what is now Cairo airport, the squadron moved to Abu Sueir and operated regularly from there until the Allied advance in October 1942.

'The joy of Abu Sueir was running water, having spent six months out "in the blue" on a water-bottle full per day! Once we were organised the squadron operated smoothly again. It was during this period that the Wimpy was used in a tactical role against the Afrika Korps, with Fleet Air Arm Albacores dropping flares, and Wimpys dropping anti-personnel bombs and strafing enemy positions. The anti-personnel bombs used were either canisters of 40lb bombs or 250lb GPs with an 18-inch mushroom rod screwed into noses. The 40-pounders cost us several lives and a couple of aircraft in bombing-up accidents, falling to the ground while being fitted into canisters.

'Tobruk became the "Mail Run" and the AA defences were said to be the heaviest in the Middle East. Navigation aids were few and far between, but the stars were often bright and QDRs were obtainable on the way home. Low stratus over the Delta sometimes created problems; one of our Wimpys crashed into a plateau at the top of the Attaqa mountains early one morning, when letting down, killing the second pilot who was lying in the bomb-aimer's position looking for pinpoints. Other unforgettable incidents include the night one Wimpy taxied across the runway as another was taking off; both were fully bombed up. Then the evening that a visiting Boston crashed into the second of a line of ten Wimpys which were all fuelled and bombed-up ready for take-off. Four Wimpys were written off, two more badly damaged, and it might have been worse had not Flight Sergeant Robinson, B Flight SNCO, started and taxied away one which was already burning, thus enabling the fire tenders to get in close.'

G. F. Wilson was an LAC serving in the Sudan with No 223 Squadron (Vickers Wellesleys) in late 1940, when he was posted to Egypt and Wellingtons:
'In November 1940 I was posted from 223 to 70 Squadron at Kabrit, Egypt, in the Suez Canal zone, and two months later went to Greece with a squadron detachment to an airfield not far from Athens. For some months we waited while the Greek authorities tried to make up their minds whether or not the Wimpys should be allowed to bomb the Italians — they never did — and while the aircraft were idle the ground crews improved their expertise in crawling under the coils of barbed wire round the perimeter every time enemy fighters were spotted over Athens! Sometime in April 1941 the aircraft returned to Egypt, while the ground crews were flown back in a

Sunderland; a trip enlivened by one of the air gunners telling us that Ju88s were active in the area, and that our hope of survival in the event of an attack was to open the portholes and blaze away with our rifles!

'We arrived safely at Kabrit and I was posted to 148 Squadron on the same station, remaining with 148 from April 1941 until re-posted to Malta HQ in December 1942. We were quite busy during 1941-42, spending much of our time on various desert landing grounds. On one occasion, travelling into the desert, we passed our army going in the opposite direction. My first taste (literally . . .) of desert existence came when we were miles off the desert track, in a marquee erected by the advance party where we ate. For dinner we had what was to become staple desert fare — meat and vegetables, followed by rice pudding. I asked another erk sitting opposite to me why he was picking currants out of his rice and putting them on the side of

Below: Just another job for the metal-bashers . . . a Wimpy which got back from Benghazi — just.

Top: Major inspection and repair job at Aqir, 1943.

Above: Bones. Scrapheap of busted Wimpys — a treasure trove of much-needed spares for the erks.

his plate. When he told me that they were flies, I felt distinctly queasy, having almost finished my rice, flies and all . . .

'There was always a scarcity of water at ALGs. Each tent held eight men, and occasionally a lorry would bring water in 50-gallon drums that had once contained oil. Each tent received five gallons of oily water, in which we were supposed to wash; needless to say there wasn't a lot of washing among the erks. Each day we received one pint of drinking water, and considerable self-control was

needed to make it last until the next day's ration. I used to shampoo my hair in paraffin, and my clothes in petrol — the latter being a sure way of keeping free of body lice.'

Jim 'Curly' Gardner was a prewar regular armourer stationed at Abu Sueir when the war came to the Middle East. He remained in North Africa, Egypt, Libya, et al until the end of the North African campaigns before finally returning to the UK. Serving with a variety of units during his four years' sojourn in the sun, his memories of his

'Butlin's Tour' (his expression) are probably similar in character to a majority of erks in that theatre:

'Whatever the snags and uncivilised conditions of service in the Middle East, these were mainly outweighed in my mind by the climate — hot days, cool nights, and the knowledge that the sun would always rise tomorrow — and, especially, the terrific camaraderie of all ranks; at least, when we were at the operational sharp end. If you were with a firstline squadron, life revolved around the kites and the job you were all there to do. Parades, bullshit, proper uniform, proper channels, etc were for the gabardine-clothed penguins back in Cairo — out in the bundoo such items were disregarded. Cairo and Alex (*Alexandria*) were OK for a spot of leave, IF you could get leave, but even there any ranker was looked upon as a second-class citizen; it was a case of "officers only" in most decent hotels or restaurants, hence I often promoted myself by slipping Flight Lieutenant's double-rings on my shirt epaulettes when in town — nobody bothered you if you were wearing zobbitt's rank. I was only rumbled once, when one of our Flight commanders came into the same bar I was in — another officers-only joint — and sat on the stool next to me. His reaction was simply, "What are you having, Curly?" — and bought me a Stella! (He was killed over Tobruk three weeks later — an ex-Cranwell gentleman in every sense of that word.)

'Life on a forward airstrip was simply summed up — work. Everything boiled down to one priority, to keep the aircraft flying, no matter what it took. We were always suffering shortages — food, water, spares, etc — but improvisation was the order of the day. Though every tradesman had his distinct responsibilities, there were no demarcation lines on jobs — when it came to bombing up a line of Wimpys, for example, everyone pitched in; cooks, clerks and air crews if necessary. Accommodation was equally simple — a spade to dig a square hole in the desert, two planks of wood covered in a sack for your bed, and a pup tent rigged over the hole for a home; tents being varied in size and state of repair according to availability. On some occasions even these luxuries were absent, and sleeping was a question of making a hole comfortable enough to accommodate your hip bone. Food was monotonous,

yet apparently adequate, because I cannot remember ever being really hungry — only perpetually thirsty.

'Working dress on a forward airstrip was a joke. The variety of styles — worn by officers or erks — resembled a circus parade; ranging from issue KD (khaki drill) to lovingly-knitted weird pullovers and jackets provided by relatives in the UK or some comforts-for-the-troops fund or organisation. Basically, everything was some shade of brown — RAF blue uniform was a rarity, usually worn only by newcomers to the unit. A pair of faded

Above: Jim Currie (left) and Don Cox, the ground crew of *'Flak-Happy Harry'* of 104 Sqn, Foggia, Italy, February 1945. *S. J. Sterrett*

231

Above: 'Where's that bloody nut?' . . . engine fitter attempting to service a Wimpy's Pegasus XVIII. *IWM*

shorts, stockings and boots/shoes were normal and sufficient dress during the day, but at night it could often get cold enough to necessitate some form of greatcoat or fur-lined jacket. The sun faded everything to a neutral sand-colour, even issue black boots after a while!

'Long service in the desert inevitably produced some right characters — eccentric would be too mild a word for a few of the sand-happy blokes I met here and there. One corporal engine-fitter we had kept a trained scorpion, taking it for early morning walks on the end of a long piece of string; while one of the Wimpy air crew — a navigator from a very snooty country-gent background — used to try rounding up his private pack of pi-dogs for hunting... One lad returned from some leave in Cairo with a pet chameleon permanently tethered by a bootlace to his bush-jacket lapel, where it continually crawled around his neck and shoulders picking off flies with deadly accuracy with its long

tongue. Women, of course, were just never seen at the operational front, yet I cannot recall *any* cases of homo-sexuality among the blokes; though the immediate postwar population explosion back in the UK was hardly surprising!

'For all its apparent deprivations of body and soul, my time in the desert with the squadrons was a very happy period of my life. I met many men who showed the very best aspects of human nature (though I also met a few who demonstrated the worst sides too), but my chief memory, which even today saddens me, is of those young Wimpy air crews who went missing. Many of them were literally kids straight out of school, yet they were always cheerful, and accepted the odds against survival calmly each time they took took off. Looking at the state of Britain today, especially some of the antics of modern youth, I tend to get very bitter about the loss of those lads who gave their all for, apparently, no good purpose now.'

Tales from the Crews

Wing Commander K. H. Wallis, C Eng, FRAeS, FRSA, RAF Retd, today is internationally known, particularly for his '007'-type gyrocopter inventions, but in 1941 he was plain Pilot Officer Ken Wallis, a Wellington skipper serving with No 103 Squadron, based at Elsham Wolds, Lincolnshire. On the night of 20/21 September 1941, Ken set out in Wimpy L7886 'X' to bomb Frankfurt, but the primary target was obscured by cloud so he carried his bomb load back to the coast and released it over a secondary objective. On return to Britain the whole of southern England was covered in fog, and the added journey to his secondary target had used up precious fuel, leaving Ken with no margin to fly further north for a fog-free airfield to land on.

Using his 'Darkie' emergency radio system, he received a response from Binbrook, after following the searchlight homing set-up. These searchlights could be seen under the fog layers, and by then there was no fuel registering on Wallis's fuel gauges, though the instruments *might* have been inaccurate. Over Binbrook he requested the Chance Light to be switched on and off, noted its position, then made ten attempts to land, using timed circuits. Obviously there were many hazards to such a landing, and eventually he called up Binbrook tower requesting permission to bale out his crew before he made any further attempt at landing. Binbrook's reply was to tell him to fly to Linton-on-Ouse. Wallis pointed out that he had no fuel indicated, repeating what he'd already told the tower when he had first arrived over Binbrook.

While this unproductive conversation was going on the Wellington was steadily climbing; then, suddenly, both engines cut, came on again briefly, though screaming in fine pitch. Wallis's decision had been made for him — he told Binbrook they were

baling out. The crew started to leave, while Ken started to don his parachute; a harness/life jacket combined type, with hooks on the hips for the seat-type 'chute. The release handle from the 'chute had to be fastened by turn-buttons on the harness when required, and was usually stuffed between the 'chute and its attached cushion when not in use. Ken fastened his main 'chute hooks but was unable to extract the release handle from under the cushion. As he lifted up in his seat the parachute and cushion came up too. He therefore had to undo the main hooks, extract and fix the release, then refix the main hooks.

While all this was going on the Wellington was gliding down, with occasional tiny boost from bursts of power on the last fuel dregs. Ken left it to its own devices rather than switching off — every foot of height was crucial. When he was finally ready to leave he looked back down the cathedral-like fuselage, in which one thoughtful crew member had left an interior light on — it was empty. Ken could now leave. The altimeter read 700ft. Lifting himself down from his high, left-hand seat, he opened the front hatch, but felt unusually encumbered, even though wearing his 'chute. Looking back he saw in the faint light that his pack was still on his vacated seat, and he was firmly connected to it by yards of webbing all tangled with the seat-raising handle. If he'd jumped immediately he would have trailed under his crashing Wimpy. Gathering all the lines he could reach, Ken knelt on the lip of the hatch and let himself topple forward.

Once out Ken let go his collection of 'chute webs and pulled his rip cord. The parachute opened with a painful jerk, and at that moment the doomed Wellington passed close overhead. Ken's immediate relief at getting clear was as quickly damped by the sounds of his Wellington approaching him. It

Above left: The remains of Ken Wallis's Wellington, L7886, at Holton-Le-Moor on 21 September 1941. *via S. Finn*

Left: Sqn Ldr Jones and Sgt Dichiel of 99 Sqn at Digri (?), India in 1942. *IWM*

Above: Wellington R1013 of 40 Sqn, shot down on the night of 13 March 1941, after Sqn Ldr Hugh Lynch-Blosse and his crew had baled out. *Grp Capt H. Lynch-Blosse*

had circled and now came out of the fog, flying directly towards him — his senses were extended to the size of his parachute. The aircraft was slightly banked and as it continued its circle it narrowly missed him, then tore itself to pieces on the ground. For a moment there was a blessed silence, then Ken felt a hard blow as the unseen ground came up and hit him. He suffered concussion and some spinal injury. After being out for about half an hour he regained his senses, noticing fog dripping off a nearby hedge. Realising that he had no idea which way to go, he remembered his World War 1 Mauser pistol which he carried inside his flying suit. He fired two shots into the air, someone shouted in the distance, and he was soon discovered by a Home Guard and a local policeman. The rest of the crew had landed along the Caistor-Market Rasen road, all uninjured — the first 103 Squadron crew to bale out over Britain. Pilot Officer Ken Wallis was back on the operations list on 10 October.

Les Read was a Warrant Officer air gunner who completed a full tour of operations with 142 Squadron from Binbrook in 1941, though his ultimate survival was much in question on several of those sorties:

'On one raid over Cologne we were caught in a cone of searchlights at 14,000ft. The city below us was ablaze, and the absence of flak in our

area indicated that there were German fighters about. For what seemed hours, we dived, twisted, turned, climbed; all the while expecting to be raked with fighter cannons. Eventually our skipper, Flt Lt Dodson, yelled in frustration to our navigator, "You got me into this, now bloody well get me out!" After what must only have been about four to five minutes we dived away from the cone into the relative safety of darkness. As we came out of the limelight I saw an Me109 coming up from beneath us on the starboard side. I fired a long burst, saw the 109 shudder and then slip away to the side. I've always believed I hit him, though I couldn't claim it as a cert.

'Another particularly hairy trip was when we were briefed to bomb Wilhelmshaven. The Met boys told us weather would be favourable, but as we crossed over the island of Texel we realised visibility was going to be very bad. We were flying at 12,000ft and were met by a barrage of AA fire, and our port engine was hit. It became obvious after several attempts to restart it that it was u/s (unserviceable) and we began losing height. There was no option but to return to base so we turned. As we recrossed the North Sea visibility had been reduced to nil and it seemed highly unlikely we were going to make it on one engine. The only hope was to jettison everything loose, including our bombs. The lot went overboard, even my two heavy tanks of ammunition. By then the altimeter was reading zero, but we couldn't see any water and fully expected to crash any second. By some miracle we neared our coastline, switched on the IFF and waited. There was a sudden frantic yell from the front gunner, Holgate, and we banked swiftly to the right — narrowly missing a barrage balloon! We were over Grimsby. We made it back to base at rooftop level.

'One of our daylight raids over France was a very near thing — I still don't know how we managed to get through. The Channel was a hot-bed of dogfights and planes were going down all over the place. We were hit and had to crash-land at St Eval; where I saw another Wimpy, badly shot up. Its rear gunner had his head completely shot off, and in the turret shambles was a half-eaten orange, covered in blood. All in all, I feel we, as a crew, were lucky to come through our tour scathed. We then split up and I was sent to Yate, Bristol, at the Parnall factory for a pre-instructor's course on Boulton Paul turrets; then posted to 25 OTU, Finningley as a gunnery instructor in early 1942.

'I decided to live out with my wife here — until then I wouldn't chance it, having seen so many wives shattered by their husbands not returning — and thought that, being off ops, we could spend a few weeks together at long last. Then came the reckoning — the first 1,000-raid on Cologne. Training units were roped in to make up the magic number, and I was put into a crew with four ex-operational chaps and two pupils. I can recall the skipper's name, Pilot Officer Hughes, while the front gunner was a Sgt Greenhalgh — a pupil on his first op. We bombed Cologne and the city was alight from end to end — an awesome sight which I can never forget. On the return journey we were hit by flak over Holland, and after unsuccessful attempts to restart the shattered engine it caught fire, and in no time we were ablaze. It was about 2am with full moonlight, and we all baled out. As I neared the ground some ground gunners opened fire, but I landed unscathed in a factory in Eindhoven. The Dutch workers eagerly stripped me for souvenirs, then, as I was about to climb over the factory wall a German guard rushed up and I was clobbered. I was next taken to an underground ARP centre where I

stayed until dawn, and where I was given a bottle of pilsner and a hunk of bread. Later I was taken to the Amsterdam gaol, where I was interrogated for six days in a hot unventilated cell, before being eventually transferred to Stalag Luft III — the start of three long years behind the wire.'

Eric Barclay was trained as a navigator, passing through ITW at Brighton via No 2 OAFU in Cumbria, to 21 OTU at Enstone (satelite to Moreton-in-the-Marsh) in May 1943. Here he received his first experience in Wellingtons — mainly old Mk 1cs — and crewed up:
'In July 1943 my crew were posted to No 310 FTU, Harwell, where we received, direct from Vickers, a brand-new Wellington X, HE947, on which we carried out a 16-hours' acceptance test before flying it to Hurn, prior to taking it out to India. The trip to India went by way of Hurn-Port Lyautey-Ras El Mar-Castel Benito-Tobruk-El Agheila-El Adem-Cairo-Ismailia-Lydda-Habbaniyah-Shaibah-Kuwait-Bharein-Sharjah-Jask Island-Karachi-Allahabad; though en route we changed aircraft to Wellington X, HE957. In October 1943 the crew arrived in Jessore, north of Calcutta, where Nos 99 and 215 Squadrons were then stationed, both operating Wimpy Xs, with 16 aircraft to each squadron.

'Both squadrons were flying operations against targets in Burma, from Mandalay to Rangoon, mostly against lines of communication but including various towns and centres. One aircraft on 215 was converted to take a 4,000lb cookie and was usually a lone raider. We were posted to this squadron. On one trip, on 24 December 1943, we loaded up for a trip to Mandalay and needed to clear at least 10,000ft if we were to get over the Arakan hills. One hour after take-off the starboard engine had to be feathered and, naturally, with a full load of bombs and petrol we lost some 8,000ft rapidly — we hadn't reached those hills yet. The pilot, Flight Sergeant Nixon, managed to get the aircraft under control after unloading all bombs safely and some petrol. However, he needed help to hold full opposite rudder and some rope was tied to the starboard rudder bar, and two of the crew literally leaned on it to maintain straight and level flight. We

Above: German newspaper photo of R1013's crew after capture. From left: Sgt Caldicott (F/AG), Sgt Hammond (W/Op), Flg Off Stan Palmer (R/AG), Sgt Clay (Obs) and Sqn Ldr Hugh Lynch-Blosse.
Grp Capt H. Lynch-Blosse

had no radio (which was charged from the starboard engine) but finally landed at Chittagong at first attempt.

'Chittagong at that time was being used by fighters, and on landing there a ground wallah came tearing out to us to order us off the runway in no uncertain terms. Apparently some fighters were due to land. After our dicey trip we were decidedly edgy, and this bristling twit was informed strongly that if he could taxi a twin-engined aircraft on one engine he had better come and .... well try it!

'The 14th Army then were surrounded by the Japanese inside the Imphal valley, where Hurricane-bombers were operating from Kangla, Palel and Imphal airstrips. No 215 Squadron was given the task of supplying them with the necessary 250lb HE bombs, and daily we ferried loads of these bombs to these airstrips inside the valley. Our crew flew a total of 25 such trips during May-June 1944, returning to our base each evening, taking with us up to two soldiers on leave to Calcutta. By the end of June 1944 I was tour-expired, and 215 had begun re-equipping with Liberators. As for the Wimpy, I considered it a good all-round aircraft, a veritable workhorse for the RAF at that time, and apart from the feathering incident always found it highly reliable.'

Denys White was a pilot with No 150 Squadron in Italy in 1944:
'When I arrived on 150 Squadron in April 1944 we operated from Ammendola airfield, with a runway of wire mesh. We used this strip in con-junction with Fortresses and Lightnings of the American 15th Air Force; they bombed by day and we took the night shift. However, early in July 1944 Nos 142 and 150 Squadrons moved to Regina airfield north of Foggia and there we were on our own. Regina was just a dirt runway and caused many problems for our aircraft tyres; the stones, etc cutting the rubber. I always had to check the tyres prior to take-off of other aircraft whenever I wasn't flying ops — it was a dusty, filthy job but very necessary.

'Operating Wimpys in Italy in 1944 was something akin to Burma's "Forgotten Army". We had no navigational aids at all, and incendiaries were dropped to obtain our drifts over land, and flame floats etc by night. The most experienced crews usually got to the target area first and dropped flares, then we had to bomb visually by the light of the flares. It wasn't until about July 1944 that we received Gee and even then it was of limited range. A squadron of Halifaxes started to act as our pathfinders in late July, equipped with H2S, but their early efforts were a disastrous failure. We were supposed to drop our bombs on their target indicators (TIs), but these were usually miles from the target. Our crew became very demoralised until the Hallies finally began dropping their TIs properly on target.

'In addition to bombs we were expected to take along a load of propaganda leaflets — "Nickels" as they were termed. When dropping "Nickels" our instructions were to go

upwind of the target area to release them. As can be imagined, having dropped our bombs no one wanted to hang about the target with mere leaflets. We devised a very good system to solve this nuisance. On dispersal prior to a sortie, we'd almost close the bomb doors after bombing up, then placed the packets of "Nickels" along the inside edge of the doors, opened the packets, then fully closed the bomb doors. Thus, over the target, we dropped the whole issue in one go. This system worked remarkably well until one night when the sortie was scrubbed at the last minute. Next morning the armourers had to change the bomb load, opened the bomb doors, and the leaflets scattered from Foggia to Naples . . . at least we weren't short of bog paper for the next few weeks!

'From a pilot's point of view, the Wimpy was a very strong aircraft and would take any amount of punishment from flak. However, it had its awkward characteristics too. On take-off one always had to throttle back sharply in order to work the accelerator pump, otherwise the engines were likely to cut out when opening up to full power. The Hercules engine was very good, though it suffered from trouble with the magneto occasionally. On landing one had to engage a sort of automatic trim, which meant one had to push hard on the control column during the approach run. Then, on levelling out, one took great care otherwise the nose came well up. The automatic pilot was also a dicey affair, sometimes causing the Wimpy to dive steeply. For such emergencies a fire axe was kept handy to sever the hydraulics pipeline if the automatic pilot couldn't be disengaged smartly. One other disquieting habit was for the escape hatch over the pilot to fly off on occasion.'

Hugh Lynch-Blosse joined the RAF as a Cranwell cadet, being trained at the College from 1935-37, and by early 1941 was a Squadron Leader and flight commander with No 40 Squadron, based at Alconbury:

Date	A/C Type	Pilot	Crew	Duty
12 March	Wellington R1013	Self	Heaton Palmer Clay Hammond Caldicott	Night bombing — Berlin

Left: Crew from 150 Sqn at Ammendola airfield, Foggia, Italy on 22 June 1944. From left: Flt Sgts D. Evans (W/Op) and G. Coleman (R/AG), Flg Off D. White (Capt), Ltd G. Hunt, SAAF (Nav), Flg Off P. Wheatley (B/Aimer). *D. White*

Below left: Marseilles under attack on 14/15 August 1944, viewed from 10,300ft by a 150 Sqn Wellington. *L. Hallam*

Above: 'Madame X', Wellington 'W' of 150 Sqn at St Valentin on 20 August 1944, about to fly this crew's last op. From left: Ives (R/AG), Hindle (Nav), Walker (Capt) L. Hallam (B/Aimer), Henderson (W/op). *L. Hallam*

Left: The briefing room for 104 Sqn at Foggia, Italy, 1944. *G. Pearson*

Right: Eric Tomlin and his 104 Sqn crew, Foggia. At far right, G. Pearson. *G. Pearson*

Above: Bivvy. Eric Tomlin (Capt), Geoff Garner (R/AG) and George Pearson (Wop/AG), 104 Sqn. *G. Pearson*

Above right: Rear gunner. 'Mac' and his turret of Wellington LP303, 'T' of 104 Sqn. *G. Pearson*

'So reads my log-book for that day in 1941, similar to a thousand other entries since the very first one at Cranwell in September 1935 — but with two differences. Bertie Bowler, my deputy in A Flight, has written "Aircraft failed to return", and there was no flight time recorded (actually four hours and 45 minutes). The reason was simple — we were shot down by flak in the early hours of 13 March — on my 13th operational sortie in a Wellington . . . in R10*13*!

'The target was Berlin and three aircraft of my flight were briefed for the trip, thereby fulfilling one of my two ambitions at that time — the other being to bomb Italy. We took off at about 2100hrs along the flare-path at Alconbury. As was usually the case, the hours between briefing and take-off were accompanied — in my case at least — by tension, anxiety and some fear. Once the throttles were opened, however, all that disappeared, and the constant thrill of flying, concentration, the togetherness of the crew, and our determination to achieve our object took over.

'It was a brilliant moonlight night and I clearly remember how surprised we were, cruising contentedly over Holland and Germany, not to be attacked by nightfighters. We could see Berlin from about 10-20 miles away and braced ourselves for the inevitable ordeal to come. Then, over the suburbs, a searchlight caught us and in spite of continuous weaving we couldn't escape — eventually I could count about 40 lights, with no one but us to find (or so it seemed . . .). Then the flak started and the noise, glare, smell and necessary weaving were the worst we'd yet experienced. Dusseldorf, Cologne, Brest and the rest seemed mild compared with this.

'I realised it must be very difficult for the navigator to chart his way to the target, yet in spite of the unholy racket all was calm inside the aircraft, which by now had been hit several times. After what seemed an age Clay identified the target and we started the run-up. By that time, because of our weaving, we were down to 7,000ft, and having to fly straight and level was neither easy or pleasant. Another age passed, then Clay finally said, "Bombs gone". We didn't wait to see results and I looked round for the best route to escape the flak and searchlights. Then, just as I thought we'd made it, an engine was hit, the prop stopped, and at the same time Henry Heaton announced — quite calmly I thought — "I've been hit". I had told him to stand between the engines as the safest place — yet he was our only casualty! Flak had also hit the front turret, exploding all its ammunition, but the gunner, Caldicott, was unharmed.

'As we left the area — now without opposition — I saw Tubby Wills from

240

our squadron going in to the target at about 10,000ft and thought, "Poor bugger, hope he makes it" (he did). Some 50 miles from Berlin the good engine started to surge wildly and I now found it difficult — and later impossible — to maintain height. Soon we were down to 2,000ft and still descending and I realised we couldn't make it home, so I decided to bale out the crew. They went first, with instructions to look after the wounded Henry — which led to them being captured almost at once. I stayed behind a little in order to lay about me with the axe in the cockpit, then jumped. The Wellington circled around me in a gentle glide, and I watched it crash in a field.

'I landed, buried my parachute in the approved manner, and headed westwards, listening with a mixture of envy, fear, relief (and, I suppose, some shock) to our aircraft returning home to bacon and eggs and beer and popsies — it was infuriating. Towards dawn I started to look for a place to hide, but had obviously left it too late because I was captured soon after it became light. I was first taken to the Luftwaffe base at Salzweden and after being pushed in the cooler fell asleep. When I woke the rest of the crew were there, except Henry who was in hospital. So began four years of *gefangenschaft* . . .'

Norman Child served with 142 Squadron, both in the UK and in North Africa. Selected notes from his various experiences illustrate well some of the many hazards associated with 'Ops in a Wimpy':

'27 August 1942.
Aircraft Z1469, "A"
Target: Kassel (German Army HQ & garrison)
Bomb load: Mixed 500lb HE & incendiaries

'Airborne 2145. Routed in 10 miles south of Munster and same route out. Climbed to 9,000ft. Flak ships were active off Dutch coast. Vis good. Lot of flak ahead — somebody must have wandered off course over Munster. Good pinpoint. Approaching target and all hell let loose approx 10 miles ahead. Very heavy barrage, town ringed with guns and searchlights. Several kites have been hit and gone down. Running into target, terrific smell of cordite, searchlights are blinding, but drop bombs on schedule at 8,500ft. Weave out of target area and for a few minutes everything in chaos. Set course for home. Difficult to get a good pinpoint, and aircraft ahead running into heavy flak (shouldn't *be* any flak on this course!). Check wind again. There's been a sudden wind-change round to the North and whole force has been blown over Ruhr Valley. Searchlights and flak are forcing us lower and lower, and many aircraft are seen going down. Flak is so bad and searchlights so blinding that we decide to go right down full power to below 1,000ft. Front and rear turrets are firing at the searchlights and between them account for five. We burst our way out of the Ruhr, knowing we'd been hit many times, and climb to 8,000ft again. Make for Over Flakkee, then for base, but are forced to land at Harwell. Our aircraft looks a mess, full of holes and big chunks shot out, but except for cuts and abrasions none of crew is hurt. Next day flown back to base to discover, to our horror, that of the six aircraft of B Flight our crew are the only survivors. Duration of flight, six hours, 40 mins.

'8 September 1942
Aircraft "H"
Target: Frankfurt
Bomb load: One 4,000lb Cookie

'Airborne 2020. Set course for Over Flakkee and climbed to 10,000ft. Cloud thicker than expected over Holland

241

and we fly in cloud up to German border. Break in the cloud and we get good pinpoint on the Maas. Steered well clear of Cologne but plenty of flak to port suggests that a number of aircraft have wandered off course in cloud and are over city. Cloud now clearing, only 3/10ths cover. North of Mainz are attacked by nightfighter who score a hit on our tail fin. Rear gunner gives him a burst and we weave and dive our way to safety. Approaching target we detect a Halifax just overhead with its bomb doors open. Take quick avoiding action and prepare for our own run-in. Very heavy defences and well predicted flak. Enormous flash in sky and flaming debris falling — looks as though two aircraft have collided. Dropped our Cookie into middle of a huge circle of explosions and fires and dived away into the night. Checked damage on tail but, though it looked a ragged sight, was still functioning. Steered course for home north of Koblenz and south of Cologne. Brief encounter with flak ship off Dutch coast and a few more holes punched in us. None of crew hurt. Message from base; weather closed in, visibility very poor, divert to Waterbeach. Landed Waterbeach. Riggers inspected tail unit. Damage so severe they were amazed that the whole structure hadn't collapsed — the Wellington is a tough baby. Duration, six hours, 55mins.

'24 October 1942
Aircraft "L"
Target: Milan
Bomb load: Mixed, 500lb HE and canisters of incendiaries

'Airborne 1630. Landed Manston 1730 and took on fuel for overload tanks. Airborne again 1915 and climbed to 9,000ft over France. Clear starlit night. Fighter reported on starboard bow cruising at same speed, so we throttle back, descend 500ft and lose him. Halfway to target we start to climb to 15,500ft to clear Swiss Alps — extremely cold. Good pinpoint on Lake Geneva to port and mountain range looming ahead. Mont Blanc identified quite easily in clear night air, and set new course to target. Box barrage over target quietens down when bombing commences — unlike German targets — and we bomb through comparatively little opposition. Many fires started and large explosions seen. Bombed at 12,000ft. Turned on course for base and climbed back to 15,500ft. At course change at Haute Savoie we notice port engine is leaking oil badly and beginning to overheat. Port engine is throttled right back and we start very slow descent across France to keep up a reasonable airspeed. Everyone keyed up and anxious. We reach French coast at 3,000ft and pinpoint St Valery. Everything quiet, so we steal out to sea untouched. Port engine temperature is now so high we decide on a forced landing at West Malling. WM cleared us for emergency landing, and when we taxied to a halt the port engine died. Fitters found an oil feed line had been damaged by a shell splinter and engine was starved of oil. Across France we'd had a choice of feathering the prop and therefore probably a forced landing there, or pressing on, risking an engine fire. We had made the right choice — just. Duration, seven hours, 50mins

Below: Blida airfield, Algiers, 1944 — 'home' of Nos 142 and 150 Wellington squadrons with No 330 Wing in 1943.
W. Howarth

'7 November 1942
Aircraft "L"
Target: Brest harbour approach (Mine-laying)
Briefing: Mines to be laid at entrance to Brest harbour, three miles south of Pt. de St Mathieu. Dropping height, 700ft with 10-seconds' intervals.

Airborne 2110. Climbed to 6,000ft and set course for Portland Bill. Cloud thickening inland but clearer over sea. Set course for Ushant Island from Portland Bill. Mid-way to Ushant radio receiver reported u/s but transmitter OK. Decided to continue to target whilst fault on receiver is traced. Ushant Island indentified approx five miles to port. Dark night but vis reasonably good. No joy with receiver. Wide turn out to sea and descend to dropping height. Engines throttled right back and mines dropped on DR time track to harbour approach. Open up engines and tight turn to port to avoid the town. Halfway on turn and climbing, a terrific explosion aft and aircraft almost out of control. Groundfire continues for a few minutes but we are not hit again. Set course for base and climb to 4,000ft at reduced revs. Damage is inspected and we find an enormous hole blasted out of the underbelly and side. Freezing gale is raging through the aircraft, and .we bring the rear gunner forward of the damage. Over southern England weather has worsened, thick cloud and light rain. Descend to 2,000ft still in cloud. Call base, report damage and the u/s receiver. Checked undercarriage would lock down, then landed. Cloud ceiling at base 700ft with heavy rain. Duration, seven hours, 45mins. After-note: with our u/s receiver we didn't know that there'd been a general recall, so we were the only aircraft from No 1 Group flying that night. We should have aborted with a u/s receiver, and earned ourselves a reprimand. However, a couple of days later we heard that an enemy freighter had struck a mine and blown up in Brest harbour approach — to this day we always claim it as "Ours" . . .

'1 January 1943
Aircraft "B"
Target: Bizerte, Tunisia (aiming point Bizerte docks/oil plants)
Bomb load: One 4,000lb Cookie

'Airborne from Blida 0229. Set course for Maison Blanche beacon, then time-run to turning point 30 miles off coast. Turned on course for Bizerte, checked position with back-bearing. Climbed to 6,000ft for minimum Cookie-height, and flying in cloud. Radio nav aids very poor so rely on dead reckoning. Through small break in cloud rear gunner reports surf below and we are crossing coast and drifting inland. Winds obviously strengthened from north and we are close to Philippeville. Much turbulence. Atlas mountain range only 20 miles inland. Change course to port and climb rapidly to try to break cloud for a star shot. Reached 13,000ft and still in cloud. Aircraft beginning to ice up rapidly. Position serious, cannot climb above cloud, weight of ice too much and airspeed falling off. Target only 20 miles to starboard. Decide on shallow descent to target area. Searchlights ahead through cloud. Aircraft vibrating badly and flying speed just above stalling. Select dropping position centre of searchlight ring and release bomb. With lightened load aircraft is climbed another 1,000ft and we break cloud at 14,000ft. Ice crystallises and breaks up, great chunks being flung off the props. We get a good astro fix and set course for home maintaining height. Home on to Maison Blanche beacon, then descend rapidly through cloud, icing up again. Cloud base has descended to 1,500ft and warmer air breaks up the icing. With a sigh of relief we cross coast and fly up the valley on the Blida beacon. Duration, six hours, 15mins.'

Tom Browne completed nearly 18 months of training for air crew duties

Below: Blida, viewed from the air on 9 February 1943.
N. L. Child

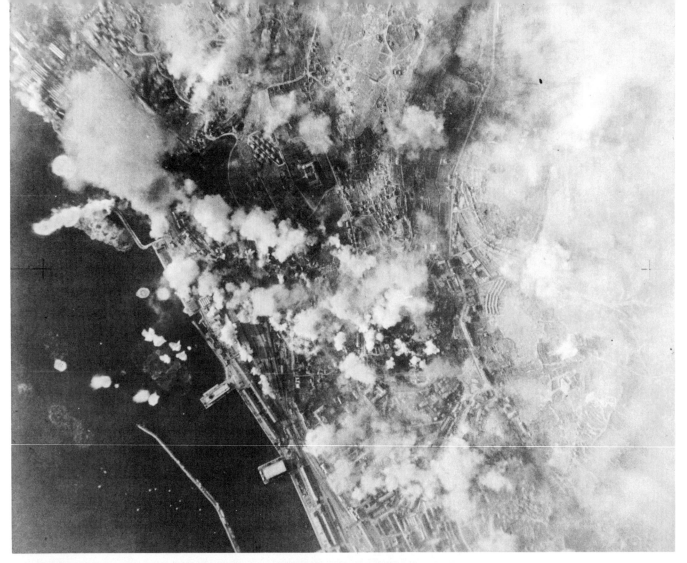

Above: Fiume 'get's it' from a 104 Sqn Wimpy on 15 February 1945, viewed from 15,000ft.

Left: Bizerta under attack by a 142 Sqn Wimpy, early 1943, seen from 10,000ft.
N. L. Child

Above right: Trieste comes under the bombsight of a 104 Sqn Wimpy on 17 February 1945, seen from 14,400ft.

as a pilot before reaching his first operational unit, to fly Wimpys against Germany. Finally having his name included in the night's battle order, he was understandably nervous, excited, yet fearful prior to the sortie:

'I was to go along for this first ride as second dickey, but it was to be my first proper operation against the enemy, and my breakfast kept threatening to bale out right from my first sight of my name on the board, right up until take-off. Veterans had reassured me that once I was airborne I'd be OK, but frankly I couldn't believe them. Came our turn to get the green from the runway controller and we started rolling — and I quickly realised that all that advice had been correct. I felt calm for the first time all day, and was really too damned busy trying to watch every item my hardbitten skipper attended to to be bothered with the butterflies doing aerobatics in my gut. Take-off was dead smooth — the skipper was a Geordie flight sergeant whose battered features suggested that he ate iron filings for dessert, but he had an oily DFM ribbon under his

wings — and we climbed away. The outward trip was uneventful (as far as I could see) and I remember being very thrilled privately when the nav announced "Enemy coast coming up, skip". Our target was Berlin — the "Big City" as the experienced crews called it — and we were just one of 14 Wimpys from our unit on this operation.

'As we approached the target area I could see fires, explosions and rising thick smoke clouds up ahead caused, presumably, by the first arrivals, while the sky seemed thick with flak bursts and writhing, twisting searchlights. To me it still seemed totally unreal, more like a Hollywood film or one of these bloody awful British moral-boosting war films they kept feeding the British public with at that time. We settled into our approach run-up for bombing and soon plunged in to the holocaust over the city suburbs. The Wimpy kept jumping about as near-miss flak bursts shoved her around in the sky, and I could hear occasional rattles and popping noises which (I realised later) were shell splinters lacing the fabric covering. We bombed OK and Geordie immediately banked hard and climbed at full boost to get out of the dangerous area. We almost made it too, but just as we were beginning to breathe a bit more freely, the rear gunner suddenly yelled, ''Fighter! Fighter! Coming in fast behind!'' Geordie swiftly flung the Wimpy into a quick dive, then banked hard to port, but not before that Jerry fighter had got one good burst into us.

'Cannon shells and bullets ripped right along the fuselage side, tearing fabric and ricochetting around off the geodetic framework. Straightening out again, we seemed to have lost the Jerry, so Geordie took stock of his crew. All reported OK, with no injuries, but the nav went up into the astro dome to check externally and told him that some shells had hit the port engine nacelle, and that it looked like some oil was trailing back over the wing. This was confirmed when the fuel gauges were checked — oil was slowly but steadily being lost. Temperature seemed reasonable for the moment, so Geordie decided to press on, keeping a watchful eye on the temperature reading for the engine. We flew fairly straight and level without attempting to gain height until we were nearing the enemy coast again, and the damaged engine then decided it had had enough and started to overheat rapidly — it was obviously starved of oil. Geordie swore colourfully, feathered the prop, and told us to stand by in case he needed to bale us all out.

'We crawled over the coastline, still hoping to reach England but losing height all the time despite everything Geordie could do to keep the old girl going. The Wimpy continued its erratic course homewards while we all chewed our fingernails down to the elbow, and Geordie and I fought like hell to keep her nose pointed in the right direction on just one good engine. Our efforts were in vain — we'd have to ditch. The Wop sent off a fix and appropriate Mayday, then clamped down his Morse key before getting himself set — as we all were — for the sea landing. Geordie flattened the Wimpy out as we reached sea level, then tried to hold her off as long as possible. The first impact sounded like a corrugated sheet tearing off my garden shed roof in a high wind — the water coolly ripped out the belly of our aircraft in one go — we rose slightly

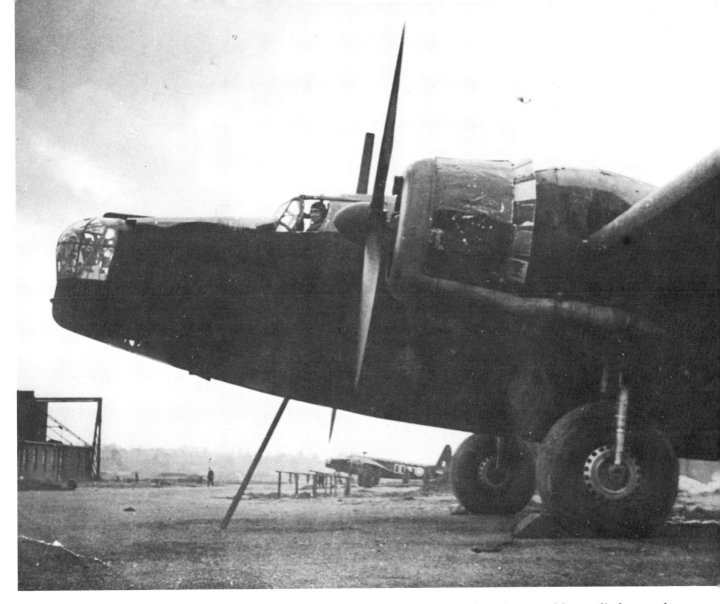

Left: W5359, QT-B of 142 Sqn at Binbrook in December 1940. *via R. Bonser*

Above: Sqn Ldr W. A. Smith in the cockpit of a 22 OTU Wellington at Wellesbourne Mountford, mid-1942. He was destined to be killed on 2 July 1943 in Short Stirling BK724 of 7 Sqn, during his second tour of operations. *R. Smith*

from the impact — then went down for good. The impact this time felt like hitting a brick wall, and I was flung forward, bashing my face on the structure hard. I passed out.

'The next thing I knew I was up to my ears in sea water with someone's arms under mine, supporting me. I couldn't see a damned thing, but after all it was still night-time. Several hands were then grabbing various parts of me or my suit and I felt myself being dragged over the rubbery side of a dinghy. My head felt as if it had been split down the middle, and I was far from fully compos mentis as yet, so I just lay where I'd been put; thankful vaguely to be out of the sea. I must have dozed off because when I next opened my eyes it was dawn, and I was no longer in a dinghy but lying on the deck of an ASR speedboat. I couldn't see anything out of my left eye, while my right eye was obviously puffed up because the lids were only just open. I put my hand to my head but only felt a wadge of cloth (it was a

field dressing roughly applied over the left eye). With some difficulty I looked around me — the rest of the crew were all there, thank God; all lying around, soaked to the skin, but very much alive. Geordie was the first to speak to me, asking how I felt. "Pretty bloody" was all I could mumble. His battered face had a couple of deep gashes now added to his laugh lines, as he had jokingly referred to his facial creases, but he seemed OK.

'I learned later that we'd been picked up fairly quickly by the ASR mercy angel, who happened to be on patrol not too far from our crash, looking for another Wimpy crew. (They never found them, by the way — poor sods). I went straight into the local civvy hospital when we landed, where I finally was told that I'd lost my left eye. Naturally, it meant no more flying for me — all that training for just one flip in anger. So now when anyone asks me "What did you do in the war?", I answer, "I bombed Berlin in a Wimpy — and I almost made it back too" . . .'

Artwork

Right: Sqn Ldr Joe McCarthy of 424 Sqn RCAF at Kairouan, Tunisia on 28 September 1943.
Public Archives of Canada

Below: Kiwi Devil. Insigne on a 75(NZ) Sqn Wellington, May 1941. *Crown copyright*

Below right: Wimpy WS-Z of 9 Sqn, 1941. 'Zola' was the girlfriend of the hero Buck Ryan in a contemporary *Daily Mirror* cartoon strip.
T. Mason

Above: Wellington III, X3794 of 9 Sqn. From left: Plt Off L. J. Brown, Sgt J. H. Harrison, 'Pam' (MT driver WAAF), Plt Off Jim Cowan (skipper of 'Barbara-Mary'), Sgt J. A. Talbot, Sgt R. W. Brown.
L. J. Brown

Above right: Crew and 'bomb-siphon' insigne of a 75(NZ) Sqn Wimpy, May 1941.
Crown copyright

Right: Wellington 'art' on a 405 Sqn RCAF aircraft, on 3 April 1942 at Topcliffe, Yorkshire. The mascot was named 'Moonshine', and the 'B' in the bomb log stood for sorties to Berlin.
Public Archives of Canada

Left: Appropriate insigne on a 214 Sqn ('Federated Malay States') Sqn.

Below left: Blues in the Nite — a 425 Sqn RCAF Wimpy, viewed with its crew at Kairouan/Zina, Tunisia on 31 August 1943.
Public Archives of Canada

Below: Flt Lt Jack MacCormack, pointing to his Wellington's dice insigne and name 'Dummy Run'. 405 Sqn RCAF, Pocklington, 14 August 1941. *Public Archives of Canada*

Right: 'Maximum Effort' was the 'title' of this 149 Sqn Wellington in 1941. The cow was usually named 'The Ozard of Whiz', and the Wimpy had completed 14 ops at the time of this photo

Far right and below right: Wellington X9684, 'Y' of 37 Sqn and its laughing donkey insigne, January 1942. *S. A. Barrett*

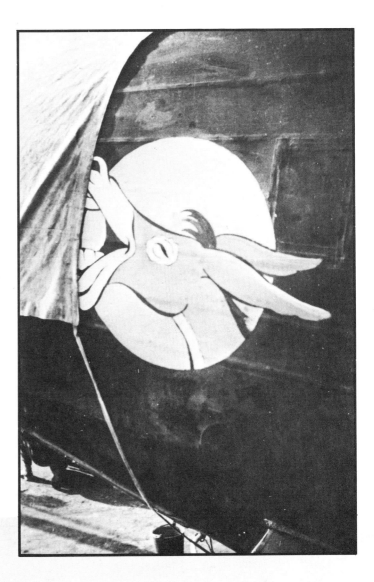

Above: The Saint, viewed at Aqir, 1943

Left: Slow but Sure, a bomb-carrying turtle, adorned this Wimpy in the Middle East, October 1943. Note DFC ribbon included in the bomb log recording 46 completed ops by day and by night. *Public Archives of Canada*

Below: A 150 Sqn Wellington, JN-A, believed to be R1016 (?), in which General Jimmy Doolittle flew on a sortie on 17/18 May 1943. The cartoon figure is 'Captain Reilly-Ffoul' of *Daily Mirror* strip-cartoon fame. *IWM*

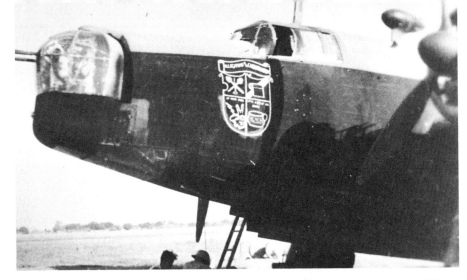

Above: Wimpy of 99 Sqn at Digri, India in 1942. The motto to the 'coat of arms' read, 'Illegitimo non carborundum. Up your pipe. Let's s-it on Jerry' . . . *W. Hooper*

Right: Flt Sgt Art Jackson, Flt Sgt B. H. Tremblay, and Flt Sgt Joe Ross with *Chat-an-ooga-Choo-Choo* of 425 Sqn RCAF at Kairouan, Tunisia on 12 August 1943.
Public Archives of Canada

Below: Wimpy with a Bengal tiger insigne in India, circa 1944 (?). *B. Philpott*

Left: V for Victory — Wellington of 12 Sqn (W5376), 1941-42. *P. Small*

Right: Popeye, Wellington 'Z-Zebra' at Marham in October 1940.

Left: Wing Cdr B. J. Roberts, OC 12 Sqn in late 1941 at Binbrook (3rd from right) and crew. The insigne on the Wimpy appears to be a stag. *P. Small*

Right: Panel from Wellington W5430 'R' of 12 Sqn, Binbrook, which crash-landed after a raid on Cologne, 30 July 1941. *P. Small*

Centre right: Flt Lt Baxter, crew, and Wellington *Toujours* of 12 Sqn, Binbrook, 1941. The cartoon behind the motto depicts a female riding a boomerang.

Below: Tail-piece. Wellington rear gunner and his personal insigne for any Luftwaffe fighter closing in from behind, 1941. *British Official*

Bibliography

Vickers aircraft since 1908; C. F. Andrews; Putnam, 1969

Vickers Wellington I & II; C. F. Andrews; Profile No 125

Book of the Wellington; Real Publications, 1943

Pilot's Notes for Wellington; Air Publications 1578C/K/L/M/N; HMSO

Famous bombers of Second World War; W. Green; Macdonald, 1959

Aircraft of the RAF from 1918; O. Thetford; Putnam, 1976

RAF Bomber Squadrons; P. J. R Moyes; Macdonald, 1964

RAF Bomber Command (2 Vols); Moyes/Goulding; Ian Allan, 1975-78

RCAF Squadrons & Aircraft; Kostenuk/Griffin; 1977

Wellington Special; A. Lumsden; Ian Allan, 1974

Coastal Command at War; C. Bowyer; Ian Allan, 1979

Aircraft versus Submarines; A. W. Price; Wm Kimber, 1973

Desert Air Force; R. Owen; Hutchinson, 1948

Middle East; HMSO, 1944

Destiny can Wait; PAF Association; Heinemann, 1949

Pictorial history of the Mediterranean Air War (3 Vols); C. F. Shores; Ian Allan, 1972-74

9 Squadron; T. Mason; Beaumont Aviation, 1965

12 Squadron; T. Mason, Private, 1960

XV Squadron; N. J. Robertson; Private, 1975

The Black Swan (103 Sqn history); S. Finn; Unpublished ms.

The Sky is our ocean (311 Sqn); B. Rijnhout/J. P. Rennison; 1980

The mystery of L7788; B. Rijnhout; De Walburg Press, 1979

We Find and Destroy (458 Sqn); P. Alexander; 458 Sqn Council, 1959

In full flight; A. Spooner; Macdonald 1965

Pathfinder Cranswick; M. Cumming; Wm Kimber, 1962

Red Sky at Night; J. Capka; A. Blond, 1958

The Restless Sky; AVM C. E. Kay; Harrap, 1964

Popeye Lucas; F. J. Lucas; Reed, 1968

Acknowledgements

The following ex-Wellington crews, air and ground, provided the virtual 'spine' of this book. I owe each a debt of gratitude for invaluable and generous help, and can only hope they approve:

M. A. Alvis; J. Armstrong; F. L. Arrowsmith; E. A. Barclay; S. A. Barrett; D. Bolesworth; J. Bowles; P. Brewster; A. K. Brown; T. A. Browne, BEM; A. Butler; L. Cawley; G. S. W. Challen; N. L. Child; R. D. Cooling; A. Cullingworth; N. Didwell; E. R. Durrant; D. A Fraser; J. R. Gardner; W. Gilroy, DFM; Group Captain J.R. Goodman, DFC, AFC; L. Hallam; R. A. Hammersley, DFM; A. Hands; A. J. B. Harding; R. Harrington, DFC; R. R. Hartley; F. Hawkins; A. Hendrie; C. Hughes, DFC; R. Humphries; A. E. Husk; Wing Commander E. G. Jones; L. H. Jordan; J. O. Lancaster, DFC; C. Lofthouse; Group Captain E. H. Lynch-Blosse, OBE; R. S. McGill; N. E. McIntyre; Group Captain N. E. Montague-Smith, DL; J. M. Morvell; J. H. F. Murphy; P. Payne; D. W. Pinches; F. N. Plum; D. Porter; P. G. Powell; J. Price; A. Ramsay; L. Read; E. A. Sanders, DFC; Group Captain M. J. A. Shaw, DSO; A. Showell; J. Skinner; R. Slater; S. J. Sterrett; W. R. Stevenson, DFM; E. M. Summers; R. G. Thackeray, DRM; W. Tidy; A. Wahlroth, BA, OD; Wing Commander K. H. Wallis, C Eng, FRAeS, FRSA; P. S. F. Walmsley, DFC; J. Ware, DFM; R. W. Watson; K. Westrope; D. M. White; W. E. Wilkinson; G. F. Wilson; R. Wratten.